The Book of the Die

Luke Rhinehart is the author of the cult classic *The Dice Man*, which was followed by the acclaimed novels *Matari*, *Long Voyage Back*, *Adventures of Wim* and *The Search for the Dice Man*. He lives in the United States.

The
Book
of the
Die

Luke Rhinehart

HarperCollins*Publishers*

HarperCollins*Publishers*
77–85 Fulham Palace Road,
Hammersmith, London W6 8JB

The HarperCollins website address is:
www.**fire**and**water**.com

Published by HarperCollins*Publishers* 2000
1 3 5 7 9 8 6 4 2

A catalogue record for this book
is available from the British Library

ISBN 0 00 226191 X

Artwork and illustrations © Josephine Sumner 2000

Set in Stone Informal by
Rowland Phototypesetting Ltd, Bury St Edmunds, Suffolk

Printed and bound in Great Britain by
Omnia Books Ltd, Glasgow

I dedicate this book to my wife Ann, who ordered me to write it – and then, miraculum mirandum, *liked it.*

And thanks too to Francis and Chris, who had nothing to do with this particular book, but who are owed thanks in general for years of support; and to Dan Mandel, who always does well no matter the paucity of potential reward; and to Susan Opie and Andrew Ashton at HarperCollins, who went way out of their way to design a book whose look mirrors its contents.

And lastly to my friends and fellow seekers who rashly let me use their words in The Book of the Die. *They must now suffer guilt by association.*

SOME SQUARE COMMENTS ON
LIVING BY THE CUBE

'The idea of a life lived to the whim of the dice is an attractive, potentially seminal notion.'   *Times Literary Supplement*

'The creator of diceliving has launched a psychiatric revolution.'   *Sunday Telegraph (London)*

'Inevitably Chance becomes a god and dice a religion. [Diceliving is] an unpleasant notion whose time has come.'   *Christian Science Monitor*

'Diceliving is an extreme kind of creative play.'   *Virginian Pilot*

'Dicepeople get from [dicing] a tolerably sharp sense of risk, impermanence and variety.'   *New York Times*

'It is all part of a conjoint project that a number of us are engaged in to render the whole fabric of bourgeois society unworkable . . . in a total and totalizing revolutionary process.'   DAVID COOPER

CONTENTS

THE TWENTY-ONE ROLLS OF THE DICE FOR THE BOOK OF CHANCES

AUTHOR'S NOTE

Back in the late sixties we wrote a novel called *The Dice Man*. It was a mild success, and it lived on through the years a sort of underground life, fed by readers fascinated by the idea of a person's being able to explode out of a typical narrow existence by letting chance and risk into one's life.

Now, almost thirty years later, interest in *The Dice Man*, as book, film and concept, is undergoing a miraculous rebirth. The book has been published or republished in more than ten countries in the last few years and is now selling more copies than at any time in history. A major television documentary about Luke, *The Dice Man*, and people influenced by the book was made by Big Table Films and shown in Great Britain in 1999 on Channel Four; it was selected for the Amsterdam and New York documentary film festivals and is presently being sold for airing throughout the world. Canadian and English production companies have jointly produced a six-part dicing TV series for Canadian and UK television. For almost three years now, a TV series called *The Diceman Travel Show* has been broadcast in Europe on the European Discovery Channel and for a year in the USA on the Travel Channel. In the series, two Englishmen travel about England, Europe and the USA by casting their green dice to determine where and how they go and what they do. Three different plays inspired by ideas in *The Dice Man* have been written for the stage in the last two years. The British publisher, HarperCollins, put out new editions of both *The Dice Man* and *Search for the Dice Man* early in 2000.

Film interest in Luke's work has also enjoyed a rebirth, with films of *The Dice Man*, of Luke's novel *Adventures of Wim* and one based on a Luke short story entitled 'Dicelady' all in various stages of development. Luke has written or co-written each of the screenplays. One of these films may actually get made.

Finally, *Loaded* magazine has for two years been running a series of stories about one of their writers, Ben Marshall, periodically living a dicelife. At their annual awards ceremonies in May of 1999 *Loaded* honoured *The Dice Man* as 'Novel of the Century'.

This new-found interest in the book has made us aware that we wrote the book to dramatize an idea, to provoke readers to reconsider their lives, perhaps change them. We saw dicing as a gimmick to make people aware of the limiting way we usually live our lives. In *The Dice Man* Luke feels that he is a kind of human guinea-pig, and that it is his duty to take the idea and practice of dice-living as far as it will go, no matter what the consequences to his own life. As a result, he does things and lives a life that he would hardly recommend to everyone. Had the book taken Luke a few years further into his life it would have permitted him to tell readers what he concluded about chance and personality and dicing and human transformation.

This *Book of the Die* is such a telling. Like *The Dice Man*, it is intended to provoke and amuse. Like *The Dice Man* it plays with ideas to force us to reconsider the ideas we usually live by. It is written by a mellower Luke and thus is a mellower book. After thirty years of dicing, we can forgive him for being a little winded.

PREFACE

Literature can be liberation or litany. It can shock us into new life or lull us in the old. *The Book of the Die* does not intend to lull. It is a collection of essays, proverbs, parables and nonsense intended to help free us from patterns which dam our lives – damming being considered undesirable. It is intended to be dipped into at random, the Ultimate Unanswer being present everywhere at any moment. Sooner or later, by Chance, the lucky reader will discover what this nonsensical book is all about.

This is a Book of Wisdom and, as is true of any book of wisdom, contains a lot of bullshit. Not to worry. The world has always been entertained by bull-shitters and we especially enjoy them when we know they are marking things up as they go along. So read this book with a pint or a beakerful or a joint in one hand and the book in the other and snicker when you feel like it, or explode a happy 'Bah, humbug!', and smile, but try to avoid frowning: it's bad for the complexion.

This book is merely trying to introduce the human race to an entirely new way of looking at life and society and so shouldn't be taken too seriously. Politicians are serious. You're not one of *them*, are you?

When we say this is a Book of Wisdom, we do not mean it is a book of philosophy. Philosophy is concerned with truth and consistency, but wisdom is concerned with moving human beings from one state to another. Truth is a fun game to play but it is often unrelated to wisdom. When a Zen master hits a disciple over the head with his staff he does it not because the blow has anything to do with truth, but because he wants to wake the disciple up. So too with our words in this book. They make only occasional pretences to truth, but they hope they are occasionally awakening you.

In the realm of science and philosophy, truth, logic and consistency are important and should be honoured. But in the realm of human living they are usually counter-productive, so a book concerned with our lives should yawn at the mention of truth. (Or puke, depending on the demands of the situation.)

Ideas are maps. When used for the appropriate terrain they are extremely useful. At other times they are burnable trash.

Rational linear books are designed to be read from page 1 to the end. Since this book occasionally suggests alternatives to linear rationality it was felt that it shouldn't be read that way. Hence, the use of dice.

The main sections or 'chapters' are defined by the twenty-one possible results of casting two identical dice. Each such section contains a variety of material – proverbs, parables, quotations, illustrations, poems, meandering essays, scenes from movies, contributions from other people who have played with the dice – and six options that a die may be cast to choose between. All are more or less related to one subject. We suggest that, rather than proceeding through the book page by page, you choose which 'chapter' to read by casting two dice and then going to the chapter chosen; for it is one of the themes of this book that Chance may have benefits beyond winning a lottery.

Although this is a Book of Wisdom it is also a work of fiction. There are four main characters in *The Book of the Die*: Luke Rhinehart, the original Diceman; the Lord Chance, the Force in the Universe that likes to stir things up; Whim, the Son of the Lord Chance, who was sent to earth to try to find Ultimate Truth (U.T.); and George Cockcroft, the man who claims to have created these three characters, but who is equally a fictional creation.

Luke originally appeared in *The Dice Man*, a book that was first published in 1971 but, for reasons that only the Lord Chance understands, has found a greater audience in the last few years than it did a generation earlier. Luke discovered that human beings can rid themselves of institutionalized misery by letting chance into their lives. The philosophy that lies behind Luke and *The Dice Man* is a major part of this book.

The Lord Chance is the Supreme Creator and thus takes full responsibility for every word you read here. Or rather, takes occasional responsibility, consistency not being one of his strengths. He (or She, depending on the time of day) is a central character in every book ever written but is rarely as acknowledged and named as He (She) is in *The Book of the Die*.

Whim is the son of the Lord Chance sent to earth to try to find U.T. Whim's adventures were once written about, but then suppressed. The true story of Whim will appear next year in a book entitled *Whim*.

Finally, there is George Cockcroft. In theory, he is the author of several books, including *The Dice Man*. For most of the last thirty years he has hidden behind the name of Luke Rhinehart, but in this book he begins to peek out around Luke's bulky presence and reveal a few things about himself. Of course, any man who has as one of his mottoes 'This Truth Above All: Fake It' can hardly be considered reliable, so the intelligent reader will take anything he says with the same pinch of salt taken when listening to any other fictional character.

You probably wouldn't be reading this book unless you know something, however vague, about the weird ideas that you fear you may find here. So, a word about dicing.

Dicing is simple: we list some options which a small part of us feels might be challenging or interesting, and then cast a die to choose what we do. At the simplest level the dice choose from among films, books, clothing, food, friends and activities open to an individual at a given time. At a more challenging level, the dice come to choose how we act, what challenges we accept, what emotions we express, what goals we pursue, which of our selves we pretend to be.

The process of dicing helps us to discover and live out the many undiscovered dreams we each have within us. It frees us from our usual bondage to control, purpose and order, into the warm realm of spontaneity and chance. Die-ing is a game to encourage game-playing; a series of acts to encourage acting; a series of selfless whims to kill the self and nourish whim.

Dicing is only one of many ideas in this book. The Taoist sage, the Zen master, the Hindu yogi, the Sufi mystic and even the Christian ascetic share one common purpose: the destruction of the self, liberation from the illusion of a separate and controlling identity. All agree with the philosophy of die-ing: man must give up his illusion that a self can control life; he must let go; he cannot live until he has died.

Since it will soon become clear that nothing in this book is particularly reliable, we suggest that you approach the reading of this book as a game. You might try the game first with the rules we suggest or create your own better rules to create a better game, or, out of rebellion against us, just read the book any way you feel like.

The simplest game is to cast two dice and read the material in the chosen section. For example, if the dice fall at a 'two' and a 'five' you open the book at page 137 and read what you find in that section.

There is a second possible way to proceed. You are in a quandary. Or perhaps in a laundry. In any case, you have a question you'd more or less like answered. Or a decision you're considering which necessitates a yes or a no.

So ask your question, then cast the dice. The material the die chooses for you to read may seem amazingly relevant to the question you ask. You may be thrilled. But the odds are equally good that the material chosen may not seem immediately relevant to your quandary (or your laundry). Read it anyway. We never know when something will awaken us.

So read this book sometimes by casting dice. Occasionally ask a question and see if the dice-chosen chapter speaks to you. Or dip into the book at random, at your own whim. Or read it straight through. Far be it from us to run your life.

PROLOGUE IN HEAVEN

What we think we know, we often come to believe is false. Having tiptoed from one error to another for half a lifetime, some of us come to feel that we are on firm ground only when we recognize that we are standing on quicksand. We do not know: of that alone are we sometimes sure.

We humans are not alone in our uncertainty. We must imagine that the Gods, yes even the Gods, suffer as we do from not knowing their origin, their powers, the extent of their freedom or fatedness. Just as we occasionally brood about whether we have created or been created by the Gods, so each God comes sooner or later to consider His own origin. Is He Himself the Supreme Creator, or is He only a creation of another God? Or, worst of all, is He merely a creation of the very human beings which He usually believes He Himself has created? We may imagine that the Gods, like us, must struggle to find their place in creation, each hoping that He Himself is the very Centre, but knowing that the evidence, unfortunately, points everywhere. It's not always easy being a God.

This note is being written because it is the ignorance of the Gods which explains to us the otherwise inexplicable adventures of Whim. Few any longer deny that Whim embodies a Force beyond that of most humans. His life has become a mystery primarily because men have assumed that their God knows the Ultimate Truth and knows what He wishes to communicate to mankind. The idea that a God could visit human beings in order to learn from them is one most humans are not willing to consider.

We, however, standing firmly on our quicksand, make no claims to having the final truth about Whim. We know that he was born, lived and (perhaps) died. We know that an incredible number of events difficult to explain – accidents, coincidences, miracles, we must each choose our own word – followed him like seagulls after a garbage ship.

Parables about his life seeking for Ultimate Truth and then trying to help others who seek for it are part of *The Book of the Die*. This *Prologue in Heaven* explains Whim's appearance in our realm.

PROLOGUE IN HEAVEN

And it came to pass that one day the Great Twin Deities Cause and Effect were called in to visit the Lord Chance and make their bi-millennial report. They arrived as usual with a huge retinue of satellite Gods and angelic hangers-on. Past and Future were there and Hypothesis, and Because – a total of several thousand in all.

The bodies of Cause and Effect were joined together, some authorities have it, by the left arm of Cause being continuous with the right arm of Effect, although some claim that it was the tip of Effect's penis which was contiguous with the buttocks of Cause. In any case, all authorities agree that the two Gods were in some way inseparable Siamese Twins. Down through the millennia this freakishness had encouraged them to develop a circus-like repertoire of acts. As a result, after offering a perfunctory greeting to the Lord Chance, who was strolling haphazardly through space and paying only sporadic attention, they began to perform.

'What happens to this apple if I let it go?' asked Cause.

'It falls,' answered Effect, and their followers applauded enthusiastically.

'What's an unpredictable causal sequence?' asked Effect.

'A real Cause playing hide and seek,' replied Cause triumphantly, and laughter cascaded through the hall.

'What happens when one looks at Chance through a microscope?' asked Cause.

'He evaporates!' laughed Effect, and cheers and applause reverberated through the universe.

Nevertheless, after three months of this sort of thing everyone was bored, including Cause and Effect, so they began presenting statistics, graphs and computer printouts to demonstrate the steady progress they had made in men's minds since the last report, giving detailed descriptions of some of their new acts: the great advances of Einstein and Gates, of nuclear bombs and missiles and spacecraft and websites, and new germs and poisons and cures – the advances of all those who had discovered new ways of joining together the separated.

The Lord Chance listened with great patience and interest. 'You certainly seem to be doing your work,' he finally said, stifling a yawn.

'Naturally,' replied Cause. 'Human beings are learning to look for Me everywhere.'

'They see an unending link of Us through all creation,' added Effect with his usual smirk.

'And seek Me as the Ultimate Truth,' continued Cause.

'Fine,' said the Lord Chance, and this time he did yawn, the yawn lasting six days, during which all stood respectfully.

But when the yawn was finished the Only Begotten Divine Son of Chance, Our Beloved Whim, He of Many Chances, who in two hundred thousand years had never before dared to speak when his Father was holding one of his sporadic formal hearings, for the first time spoke.

'Father?' He asked timidly.

'Mmmm?' said Lord Chance. He was never surprised at anything and looked down at His young Son with a vague smile.

'It seems from these reports that everyone's forgetting all about You,' Whim went on with shy determination. 'No one acknowledges your Presence. The universes are filled with unbelievers. Everyone's slobbering after Cause and Effect.'

'Really?' replied the Lord Chance indifferently.

'It's called becoming civilized,' commented Effect snidely.

'Whenever humans try to introduce You into their lives,' Whim went on, ignoring the interruption, 'by consulting yarrow stalks, cracks in a turtle's back, the stars, Tarot cards, dice, coins, random numbers, astrological predictions, or stockbrokers, Cause and Effect come up with some new act which makes humans think that, if just looked at closely enough, You aren't really important at all.'

'I know, I know,' said the Lord Chance. 'But it's just an Accident, Son.'

'You ought to break up Cause and Effect, Father. They've made your whole Creation seem a big mechanical bore.'

'I resent that,' said Effect.

'Inferiority complex,' commented Cause, 'because You always have to come after Me.' Waves of laughter spilled briefly through space.

'Break them up, huh?' said the Lord Chance. 'Could be, Son. But, remember, as a matter of principle I'm not fond of doing anything for a purpose.'

'But *I* want to do something,' exclaimed Whim.

'Oh, well, that's a different matter. I don't like to meddle with any sort of purpose into the affairs of the universe – smacks of favouritism – but if You want to do something, well, I'm sure that there'd be nothing very purposive about that.'

'Thank you, Father,' said Whim, looking up at the Lord Chance with a shy smile.

'But first it's about time I had a good God-to-God talk with you.'

The Lord Chance then made a dignified gesture with His little finger, and Cause and Effect and their numerous minor Gods bowed and began leaving the hall.

'See you next millennium, Honoured Lord,' said Cause, bowing in an exaggerated fashion.

'And in the meantime,' added Effect with a smirk, 'don't do anything We wouldn't do!' And they both exited with a little four-step and a long echoing laugh.

The Lord Chance smiled benevolently after them and then turned back to His Son.

'Where was I?' He began. 'Oh, yes. My Son, you're young. It's only been in the last hundred thousand years or so that I've really noticed you. It's time for me to let you know the facts of the Universe.'

'Yes, Father.'

The Lord Chance cleared His throat. 'As you may know, the Universe is based on the free enterprise system: every God for Himself. I work my Random Way, Cause and Effect work their Boring Way; Purpose works His; Illusion does his magic tricks; Good and Evil fight their ridiculous fights; and old Ultimate Truth sits around and feels important. In addition, of course, there are the two hundred thousand or so lesser Gods who support – '

'Oh, please, Father,' Whim said. 'I learned all this in the ten-thousandth grade.'

'There, there, be patient,' said the Lord Chance, placing His Hand gently on Our Beloved Whim's shoulder. 'What you don't know is that each of the Gods – I mean the Eight Great Gods – Each One thinks that He, and He alone, is the Lord of Creation and the Sustainer of the Universe.'

'But, Father – '

'Thus, Cause and Effect believe they control everything; Illusion feels everything is Him; Good and Evil think their petty squabbles are the ultimate events; and Purpose – '

'But, Father, just a few months ago Cause and Effect were here at your Court reporting to you. And before that I can remember Good coming here and – '

'I know, I know,' said Lord Chance, nodding his head and smiling softly. 'But every few thousand years or so *I* have to report to Their Royal Courts.'

'Oh, Father . . . '

'I know, Son. It's degrading. But I'm afraid that's the way the Universe is. And I also have to visit the courts of Purpose, Illusion and Evil. And worst of all, every two or three millennia I find myself standing for at least a year or two in front of the Court of Ultimate Truth, pretending to be respectful, even though He's the one God who has never been known to say a single word to any of us Others.'

'But you control all those Phonies!'

'Well, maybe. I think I control all those Phonies. But they seem to think, by Chance I assume, that They control Me. For Illusion I'm just another illusion; for Cause and Effect only a hidden cause; for Purpose I'm just a necessary antagonist or else an occasional servant of his boy Evolution. For some of the minor Gods like Didat, Littlebee and Jehova, I'm called miracle, and so on. I, of course, believe that each of them acts only under my own haphazard way.'

'But it's true, isn't it?' Whim asked, looking up hopefully at his Father.

'Damned if I know,' the Lord Chance replied with a puzzled frown. 'The fact is that none of Us in here is too sure of Himself these days.'

'But can't we find out for sure?'

The Lord Chance frowned again and scratched his bald head.

'Fact is, maybe there *is* a way.'

'What is it, Father? I'll do anything.'

'Well, the only thing any of us Gods knows for certain is that the only One who knows for sure is Ultimate Truth.'

Whim looked bewildered.

'But . . . but – '

'I know, Son. Most of us Big Gods think old U.T. is the biggest Phony of Us all. He never does a damn thing except sit inside that big junky Palace of His and imply that He's superior to the rest of Us. Purpose calls him old "Know-It-All" and Illusion calls him "The Big X". For Me, He's just "old U.T.", another God on the make.'

'But you think that only Ultimate Truth knows for sure which one of the Gods is actually Lord of Creation?'

'That's right. Or at least that's what all Us Gods have believed for the last few billennia. But the trouble is no God can ever get an answer out of Ultimate Truth because old U.T. seems to make Himself available only to *human beings*, and then only to a very few.'

'Human beings?' echoed Whim incredulously. 'But that's ridiculous! Why, they – '

'I know, it's casting pearls before swine, as one of Jehova's boys once said.'

'But – '

'And then the trouble is that the human beings who think they've met or seen Ultimate Truth disagree with each other about what they've seen. From in here We can't tell which one of the damned little fellows actually has seen U.T. So we can't be sure which one of Us is really the Lord of Creation.'

'It all sounds so confusing and ridiculous,' said Whim, shaking his head and looking gloomy.

'Well, that's Our Random Way, Son. Don't knock it.'

'But how can I possibly help?' asked Whim, looking up again brightly at his Father.

'You say you want to do something?'

'Oh, yes!'

'Well, Son, I think I can arrange it for you to be born into human form.'

'Oh, no.'

'And if, by Chance, you should happen to run into Ultimate Truth – '

'We'd know!' exclaimed Whim.

'At last we'd know,' sighed the Lord Chance softly, his eyes glowing.

'I'll do it,' announced Whim. 'I shall become a human being.'

'Hold it, Son, hold it,' Lord Chance said, smiling down at his Son's enthusiasm. 'You're not going anywhere until I roll the Royal Cube and see what's to be what.'

'Yes, sir,' Whim replied.

'It's one of the real glories of my Kingdom that even though I work always at random I still manage to hold my own with the other Big Gods. They can line up their every Act to try to thwart Me, while I can only shoot back sporadically, aiming randomly, and only haphazardly loading the gun.'

'It's Our Way, Father,' said Whim proudly.

'That's right,' said the Lord Chance, 'and if You want to know, sometimes it's a pain in the Royal Arse. However, we'll have to roll the Royal Cube and see what will be what.'

'And if I'm born a human being,' said Whim dreamily, 'I'll find Ultimate Truth if it's the last thing I do.'

'No need to be dramatic,' said the Lord Chance. 'If You get to see old U.T. it'll probably be by Accident.'

The two of them, Father and Son, then walked slowly to the Royal Bowling Alley, a short six billion miles away. Our Beloved Whim had often heard the awful thunder of one of the Royal Rolls but He'd never previously been invited to see one.

When at last they arrived Whim was surprised to see only a single long alley, beginning only four feet wide but widening outwards so that stare as He might Whim could see nothing but a vast sparkling horizon way off in the infinitely wide distance. It was simply a golden track expanding into infinity. Whim could see no Royal Cube at all.

'Now, you stand here, Son,' said the Lord Chance. 'And don't get edgy about what I do. Rolling the Royal Cube is tricky and a bit spectacular, but it'll come out all right in the end. Has so far, anyway, though far be it from Me to predict that it'll be the same today.'

He then moved forwards and took the bowler's crouch at the back on the lane, squinting down the infinite alley. Although His Right Hand was empty, His Aged Fingers flexed and unflexed as if He were preparing for something quite strenuous. As Our Beloved Whim watched, the Lord Chance at last strode forwards, and in an instant was Himself tumbling Head over Heels down the alley.

Whim was stunned. His aged Father was bouncing and somersaulting into the distance like an epileptic tumbler, his Form becoming more and more cube-like as He bounced until, by the time He was five miles away, He was a fairly regular Die. And the Lord Chance or the Cube, or whatever It was, was *expanding* and somehow seemed to be returning towards Whim. The further It went, and the faster It flew away, the bigger It grew, until almost all of space began to be filled with this gigantic hurtling Cube and then:

It exploded. The Cube disintegrated into a zillion fragments, each the size of a square house, scattering down the Royal Bowling Alley, the noise of the tumbling like a million earthly thunderstorms. On and on they tumbled and rumbled (they were gigantic dice, Whim realized), until million by million they disappeared into the infinite distance, and space was empty.

Whim was dismayed, it not being every day that one sees one's own father explode into a million pieces. Since nothing was reliable in the Lord Chance's most unreliable of worlds, Whim feared the worst.

'Father?' He called tentatively.

Silence.

'Father!' He called more loudly.

Silence.

'Fa . . . therrr! !!!' he yelled, and his shout tumbled through space like some last errant die, but was soon lost again in silence.

As Whim waited sadly, He began to hear something. At first it was a mere hum, then it grew into a steady noise like a herd of galloping buffalo. In the distance He spied at last something coming: an infinite number of creatures came surging over the horizon like Indians over the brow of a hill. As they came tearing towards Whim at terrific speed they slowly emerged as the returning dice zooming back.

Whim barely had time to throw himself prostrate on the ground, arms over head, when he heard a 'zzzst', the thunder ceased, and He looked up to see his Father, the Lord Chance, standing and brushing off two or three haphazard tiny dice that still stuck to Him.

'Father?' Whim said cautiously, still lying on the ground.

'It seems,' said the Lord Chance, scratching his head and speaking with dignity, 'that the weather in 11.62 per cent of the universes will be unseasonably hot. There will be 2,567 earthquakes tomorrow, an errant solar system will wipe out all life in universe 344, the Orkny Blue Sox will win fifty-three straight games in the Beta League (universe 69), and You, My Son, are going to be born on a planet called "earth".'

'Don't forget,' said Cause and Effect a few years before Whim's possible human birth, 'belief in us has produced that modern civilization you're about to be born into.'

'I wouldn't voice it around if I were you,' replied Whim, and the next thing He knew, less than a month later,

He was being born.

In actual fact the Lord Chance had more or less determined (planning in advance was not his *forte*) that Whim was to be born in November of 1932 earth time, but when He paused to scratch his right elbow the whole thing was delayed a year, and next He chanced to sneeze loudly, and then He had to blow His Royal Nose, and what with one random event and another, in the end it wasn't until April, 1968, that Our Beloved Whim was finally pushed out into the darkness of human life.

THE
Twenty-one Rolls of the Dice for the Book of Chances

WHIM AND MADMEN BUDDHAS

'I didn't become happy as a human being,' said Whim one day to his friends, 'until I suddenly realized, after years of blindness, that instead of myself being a Buddha in a world filled with madmen, instead I am a . . . I know not what, moving in a world of genuine, through-to-the-core Buddhas . . .

'Most of them,' Whim added after a pause and with a puzzled smile on his face, 'carefully and fully disguised as madmen.'

from *Adventures of Whim*

SELF

What is life but man's maddening
efforts to live a full life in
chains.
SUZUKI

Anybody can be anybody.

Luke

The self is one of mankind's ways of making life more difficult. In our effort to find and be at one with some imaginary centre, we resist our health – our variety, our flexibility, our ability to change. We seek changeless-ness in a constantly changing world, when the glory of life lies in change.

What if the development of a sense of self is normal and natural,

but is neither inevitable nor desirable? What if it represents a

psychological appendix: a useless, anachronistic pain in the side?

– or, like the mastodon's huge tusks: a heavy, useless and

ultimately self-destructive burden? What if the sense of being

someone represents an evolutionary error as disastrous to the

further development of a more complex creature as was the shell

for snails and turtles

– from THE DICE MAN

The normal personality consists of an accumulation of habits, attitudes and aspirations that lay claim to the title of character. We form these consistencies because our society rewards us for most of them and gets upset when we deviate from them too far or too often. By the age of thirty we've all become reasonably dependable machines, efficient for some operations, inefficient for others, but very limited in the tasks we can perform. It is a happy machine if it works in harmony with the other machines, but to do this the machine personality must not change. A mobile, eccentric or random machine would throw the super-machine called society out of whack. A foolish consistency is the hobgoblin of little minds but is quite basic to the development of selves and society.

Personal identification – name, beliefs, religion, family, possessions, and personal history – all are anchors thrown into the sea of life to try to control the flow. They are symptoms of fear. They represent grasping for certainty in an uncertain world; consistency in an inconsistent flow; stability within unstable societies; meaning in a meaningless universe.

Seers and mystics have often urged us to be detached, grasp nothing, be free of ego. Some imply an actual withdrawal from activity, but the best mean that we should enter into each activity with all our might, to exert our last ounce of energy to win the race, but wander away when the laurel wreath is awarded.

> *A beautiful statue*
> *Of the hardest granite*
> *looms*
> *With great dignity in the middle*
> *Of the garden.*
> *Ah . . .*
> *How the butterflies dance*
> *Around the unseeing eyes.*

We can be statues and impress people or be butterflies and dance. But we can't be both. If we choose to impress people then we are turning part of ourselves into stone – the part that we think impresses. Statues are rather weak at dancing, and anyone not capable of chance and change will no longer be able to dance.

WHIM COMMENTS: Hey, how about becoming the statue of a butterfly!? Not too cool, I guess.

Place something on a pedestal and
you turn it into stone.

The tendency of every living creature is homeostatic – it wants to stabilize its relation to its environment at the simplest level possible. The creation of the self is part of this tendency.

The tendency of chance, on the other hand, is to create instability and complexity.

Living forms evolve through chance, through mutations – scientific terminology for the play of chance. Mutations are sudden, 'unexplained' altered forms of any given species. They are accidents. All living creatures – it is hardly a surprise to us – evolve through accident. It is the purpose of dicing to let chance into our lives so that we, like the species, may evolve.

With dicing we try to let go of our attachments to attitudes and beliefs and behaviour patterns. We do this not to get at some central core of identity but rather to make room for new ones. Humans can only exist with a variety of contradictory aspirations and ideas. The error most men and most religions make is to try to force the individual into a singleness – to create One from the many. Our goal is different – to create more from the many.

Mystics who claim unity with the ALLness are in effect announcing their embrace of multiplicity, for if you are at one with everything then you are multiple. However, those who claim to have experienced a single true Self or Reality or God separate from other false entities are creating a struggle and a seriousness which is central to the human sickness. If there are authentic selves and false selves then it is clearly a valuable goal to seek the true self and kill off the false; and life is a serious business. But if all selves are illusions then we can relax: we'll never have any truer self than we have at any given moment.

I, OBOKO

In this infinity of energy I,
A single ion, slip from pole to pole
Unregistered. In this unending space I,
A speck, resume unseen my solitary way.
In this eternal toll of hours I,
A millisecond, tick my finite single tick
And disappear. In the great gasp of God I
Am swallowed up, an only atom of air
Thrust through the mighty mouth and
Rushed into the cavernous lungs and
Sucked into the hot, roaring flood
Of God's great blood, ripped
Through the arteries and hurled
Through narrow streams
To feed at last a single cell
Of bone in the great I AM.
God grins.

The healthy human being aims not for unity but for multiplicity, aims not for a stable self marching consistently through a hostile world, but an ever-expanding variety of selves wandering playfully through a world of our own creation. Although most humans are frightened at the idea of multiplicity, some of us, having opened ourselves to variety and inconsistency, eventually find ourselves emerging into a joyful fulfilment we'd rarely experienced traipsing the endless road of self and order.

The self is a dead skin which keeps new beings from being born. Shed it.

We are not ourselves; actually there is nothing we can call a 'self' anymore; we are many-fold, we have as many selves as there are groups to which we belong. The neurotic has overtly a disease from which everybody is suffering. — J. H. Van den Berg

 In internally consistent societies the narrow personality has value; men can fulfil themselves with only one self.

But today we are bombarded every moment with conflicting messages about who we should be and how we should act. Most religious traditions urge restraint or abstinence in sexual matters, but our mass media, TV sitcoms, soaps, popular fiction, popular music, MTV, the internet are urging us unendingly to be sexually attractive, and not, presumably, so we will look better in church.

Society both urges us to save money and to spend. It urges us to work hard but to vacation. It urges us to buy bigger and better and to live within our means. Our religions condemn vanity and our whole culture encourages vanity. Our religions condemn greed and our whole culture is based on the duty of every man to fight hard to climb the economic ladder and accumulate and preserve *things*. Our religions condemn lust and our whole culture stimulates lust.

As a result, each of us has hundreds of aspirations and potential selves which never let us forget that no matter how mightily we step along the narrow single path of our personality, our deepest desire is to be multiple: to explore many aspirations and play many roles. We are all husbands, wives, saints, adulterers, artists, actors, businessmen, heroes, good-for-nothings . . . In a multivalent society, the multiple personality is the only one which can fulfil. The normal person fights multiplicity; the wise man embraces it.

WHIM AND THE PSYCHIATRIST

It's not clear exactly when Whim began referring to himself as 'we' and 'us', but soon enough it led to his being forced to visit a psychiatrist.

'Why do you call yourself "we",' the psychiatrist asked.

'Because we are,' said Whim.

'I only see one of you,' said the psychiatrist.

'We only operate one at a time and use the same body.'

'Show me another of you.'

'Here I am.'

'Who are you now?'

'Whim, we of many chances.'

'But which Whim?' insisted the psychiatrist.

'Here today, gone tomorrow.'

The psychiatrist had been scribbling frantically but he now stopped.

'So you feel you have many personalities,' he commented cautiously.

'Yes, we do,' said Whim cheerfully.

'And do the voices of these other personalities sometimes speak to you?'

'We talk to each other sometimes.'

'And do some of your other selves frighten you?' asked the psychiatrist, sensing a breakthrough.

'Of course not,' said Whim. 'We're friends.'

'Which of your selves do you like the best?'

'Me.'

'Who's "me"?'

'Meherenow,' said Whim.

'What's meherenow like?'

'He's like himtherethen a few seconds ago. Now the one I like best is the new meherenow.'

'I see,' said the psychiatrist, his face twitching slightly. 'Don't you feel any continuity between your consecutive selves?'

'Oh, sure,' said Whim. 'There are family resemblances.'

'But what do you want to do with your life?'

'Whose life?'

'The lives of yourselves,' answered the psychiatrist, not believing he was having this conversation.

'Oh, we all have different plans,' said Whim.

'Well, what determines which one of you acts at any given moment?' the psychiatrist asked.

Whim smiled.

'Ignorance and chance,' he replied.

How many people have you been today?

To go from the cage of a single self to the amusement park of multiple living, we need to exercise: to play games which break down our self-imposed limitations and uncover new selves, experiences and talents.

Of course, the killing of the self is for most of us as difficult as physical suicide, although rather more rewarding. The challenge to turn over decision-making to chance rather than one's 'self' is a challenge that most people can't meet. Such a surrender of will is irrational! It's absurd! But most of the consistencies we find ourselves locked into are equally irrational and absurd – we just don't notice. But others notice. We see others, even our friends, as filled with the most absurd opinions, habits, interests, behaviour patterns, but as part of our unconscious social agreement we pretend we don't see them that way. Everyone tacitly agrees to overlook their neighbour's insanities. Unless he begins choosing his insanities by dice rather than 'free will'. Then we'll talk about him.

One dicer reported that when she first began making her decisions with dice she kept her use of chance secret. She noticed that although people thought she was behaving rather erratically they went out of their way to find rational reasons why she suddenly decided to get her hair dyed, have her nipples pierced, fly to Houston for a weekend, pick up a guy at a bar – all things inconsistent with the person her friends had previously thought her to be.

Then the dice told her to tell them that she had begun making decisions with chance. Suddenly actions that were actually consistent with her earlier self seemed to her friends to be bizarre, insane. Now if she went to a movie at random, even a movie she would have previously wanted to see, they were annoyed with her. Now if she dropped a boyfriend and announced it was a dice decision, some friends berated her, even though they had previously been urging her to drop the same guy. The moral is: we are allowed to make stupid decisions on our own but as soon as we make them by letting dice choose a few things, we are insane.

PARABLE OF THE LION

Once a lion was born in New York City's Bronx zoo. Until he was four years old he lived in cages in the zoo. When some of the older lions talked about something called 'freedom' he thought they were talking about living in the big cage – the one with rocks and a pool – rather than the small one, where he fed and slept.

Then the zoo sent him in a cage to Kenya for certain scientific experiments and there, by chance, the lion escaped and returned to the jungle. Only then did he realize how inhibited, constrained, circumscribed and caged he had been all his life. He had never realized how open and huge the world was. Now, in the jungle, he learned how he was meant to live. He realized his full, natural spontaneous life. At last he knew what the older lions in the zoo had meant by freedom.

Most of us have been brought up in a cage: the cage of the self. Until we have experienced freedom from this cage we won't know what those who have escaped are talking about. But perhaps some strange day the bars around you will melt and the world will suddenly seem immense, and yourselves immense enough to fill it. At that moment you'll laugh at those wax bars that you had remained behind for years – when all you had to do was push them aside and walk free.

Most of us live life in a daze. Every morning we retrace our footsteps, sigh the same sighs, moan the same moans and strike another day of our lives off the calendar. Habit forms a dusty crust on our daily schedule. It seems impossible to break out. But the dice are uncontrollable: Chance, not man, is their master. They will punch through to freedom, unfreeze synapses, road test fantasies. They disable the logical naysayer. They will allow us to stop shaking our heads and start nodding, stop frowning and start smiling, stop standing and start moving.

The dice are all about new possibilities. Without dice each today is like every other day. But just one die equals six different todays, two are thirty-six, and the world explodes in possibilities.

There's a part of you that's hiding under the 'you' that everybody else knows. What do you really want? Make up six options and think about them for a while. Cross out the impossible, the unobtainable and the illegal, and you'll start to see the you that you've forgotten, the you that you've neglected, the you that you've given up on. Roll the dice and let that you ride again.

If you always just do what you think you can do, you'll never do what you could do, what you dream of doing. Dice make dreams and daily life equally likely. And when that happens, the soul is changed forever.

– Matthew Davidge

It's sometimes said that it's impossible for a human to live without developing a firm and consistent sense of self, and that those dice-people who seem to be functioning happily may be doing so because they have, whether they know it or not, a firm sense of themselves as children of chance. 'The idea of being a kind of random multiple man is an idea of oneself,' said one commentator, 'and if held firmly may represent a stable self even if the actions of this stable self are multiple and inconsistent.'

Sounds reasonable. However, if we become attached to the idea of being a dice-person then we guarantee that we are not one. It is precisely against the idea of believing we are someone that our methods are aimed. A self or 'I' can certainly be said to exist at any given moment but the wise man makes no claim of permanence for any of his 'I's.

A Diemaster once said:
'All of my dieciples are good
dice-persons except Whim.
He alone is no one.'

STUDENT: But who are you?

WHIM: Here today, gone tomorrow.

STUDENT: But who *are* you?

WHIM: Me? I'm . . . oops, not any more.

Even the normal human knows he is multiple. For example, a man slaps his wife. Thirty minutes later another self bursts into his consciousness saying, 'Oh, what a horrible thing to have slapped my wife. I love my wife.' When the man returns to his wife the ensuing dialogue might go like this:

'I love you, Sweetheart.'
'You prick, an hour ago you hit me.'
'No, no, I didn't mean to. That wasn't the real me.'
'It was too you!'
'Not me. I love you. I could no more hit you than I could kill myself.'
'Then who was it using your body who belted me?'
'Beats me, but let's fuck.'

Die-ing eliminates internal conflicts by eliminating the illusion that some mes are more real, more important or morally superior to others. We assume that there is no *real* me; we are nothing but a collection of fakes, some of whom are under the illusion they are more real than others. There are layers of self-deception which wise men peel and peel until at last they stand face to face with the Ultimate: layer upon layer of further self-deception.

The sage rips off mask after mask until at last he is free of his compulsion to rip off masks. He begins instead to create mask after mask, joyfully and without guilt. He knows that no matter how many masks he ripped off he was still in self-deception; he knows that no matter how many new masks he now adds he is being utterly honest.

Scoop up water and the moon is in your hands,
Pick up dice and hold green stars.
Drop them, and watch the lightning strike.

Die-ing permits us to let go of our 'true self' and let Chance choose from among the optional aspirations we are willing to risk expressing. Soon we come to realize that our problems and conflicts are in some sense not ours to worry about: that no matter how hard we try, no 'I' can ever have any control.

In giving up trying to control life through an illusory self, one feels liberated, ecstatic, stoned. It's something like newly-born Christians giving up their souls to Christ or God, or the Zen student or Taoist surrendering to the Tao. In all these cases the ego-control game is abandoned and one surrenders to a force which is experienced as being outside oneself.

Of course, there is the danger that at first we may cast the dice to choose among our options and think: 'Now I must have the will power to do it.' But obviously the illusion that an ego controls or has 'will power' must be abandoned. We will come to see our relation to the dice first as that of a baby in a rubber raft on a flooded river: each motion of the river is pleasant; we don't need to know where we're going or when, if ever, we'll arrive. Motion is all. Later, the feeling of separation from the river will disappear. The falling die, the flow of experience, the succession of 'Is' will all blend into a single swim. The I will have died.

Of course, the death of the personality is a slow and unending process. In the early stages of die-ing only a few of the buried selves are able to offer themselves to the Die. But as we progress, more and more selves, desires, values and roles are raised into the possibility of existence; the human being grows, expands, becomes more flexible, more various. The strength of the normal dominant personality declines, disappears. We die. And, having died, at last we feel free.

DIE-ING WITH DICE, DIE-ING WITH MEDITATION, DIE-ING WITH ZEN, DIE-ING WITH THE SUFIS – IT DOESN'T MUCH MATTER HOW YOU DIE. THE IMPORTANT THING IS TO PRODUCE A CORPSE.

HOW WHIM KNOWS WHO'S WHO

One day the Zen master Oboko said to Whim: 'Have you finally discovered where your true Self is when you are driving a car?'

'Yes, Master,' said Whim, smiling happily.

'Where?' asked Oboko.

'Whenever I'm driving a car my True Self is right *there*!' and Whim pointed directly at the master's chest.

'That's very good,' said Oboko. 'But then where is *my* True Self when you are driving your car?'

'Well,' said Whim with a frown. 'I guess your True Self is right *here*,' and he pointed at his own chest.

'That's very good,' said Oboko. 'But then how can we tell who is you and who is me?'

'Simple,' said Whim, smiling happily again. 'You drive a junky station wagon and I drive a Porsche.'

When the self has been burned away,
watch the children come out and play.

LUKE PRAYS

Royal Cube and King,

Forgive me for not having communed with you more often. That fatal feeling that I am someone, and that certain actions are more important than seeking your Way has sometimes blocked my path. This week when once or twice I turned to you for guidance, I flowed free. When I tried to ignore you and guide my own life in pursuit of my quest, I often moped around like a sea-sick clown – until I heard your Laughing Men in the Sky roaring at my silliness. It is clear to me now that you are God. I know it. Your Way is my Salvation. I know it. The great freedom sought by Kierkegaard, Dostoyevski, Nietzsche and George Harrison exists, and is contained within your six walls.

I am a pebble, Lord, kick me. I am a corpse quickened only by your breath. I lie upon the sunken bed; you touch, I walk. My hate flares; you fall across the floor, extinguish it. The birds of appetites gnaw me; you speak, doves all. You but whisper and I roar; you but nudge and I fly.

But my self must first come to you, and the very selves which you create with your decisions then try to avoid you with all the cunning of dogs avoiding a bath. They fight you, my Ivory Lord, by ignoring you. In the fog that is my self, sound the horn that will lead me always to thy Cube.

Thirty years, O Die, I sold myself to self. It swallowed me. Your touch alone has vomited me free. When I hold you in my hand I share in your Divinity; when I let you fall, you raise me up.

Even now, Six-sided Seer, as I try to tell you of my progress in your way, the self steals the mind to thoughts of fame and fortune, thoughts unworthy of a twelve-year-old boy, yet mine, still mine. Liberate me, Lord, from my vanity: cleanse me of self.

I am a weakling. I have been a 238-pound weakling all my life; I see that now. You alone have given me strength.

No more sand kicked in my face, unless your foot swings.

No girl shall laugh at me, unless you provide the tickle.

I will try this coming month to place myself in your hands at every hour, to wear you near my heart that I may feel your power and use it at each turning. Those who shake my hand and pat me on the back do not know what Power lurks beneath my shirt. A tiny, spotted cube: if I let it fall it may choose to create or to kill. Not my will, Die, but Thy will be done, on earth, as it is everywhere else.

For Thine is the Kingdom, the Power, and the Glory, Forever and Ever.

– from *Luke's Journal*

Love yourselves: be a multiman.

OPTIONS

Before casting a die, read through the six options below. Throw out one or two (or, best of all, all six) and create some of your own to replace those you toss out. Then cast a die.

① Do everything differently for an hour. Preferably do everything the opposite of the way you normally do things. Walk backwards instead of forwards. Drink your coffee black instead of with milk and sugar, or vice versa. Shout at your husband or father. Stand on your head for the sheer fun of it. Walk out in the rain. Don't go to work. Spend money as if you were rich (or don't spend it as if you were poor). Do it different.

② Make a fool of yourself. Slobber coffee down your shirtfront. Fart. Talk nonsense. Tell a long story that you make up as you go along and that makes absolutely no sense. Put on the most ridiculous clothes that you can come up with. Use makeup on your face as if you were a three-year-old using it for the first time. Notice that life still goes on.

③ Tell someone why you are a great person. List for them all the ways you are proud of yourself, from the way you dress to your wonderful sense of humour. Try to list all your achievements, including those from the past that you are particularly proud of. Keep doing this for as long as you can until you burst out laughing.

④ As you are, you are dead. Anything you do differently will be a distinct improvement. Anything you do now should be aimed at breaking out of the narrow cell you have locked yourself in. This demands that you challenge yourself to *do* the things you've always wanted to do but never gotten around to doing. List from three to six important and challenging things that you might do with your life that you're not doing. Cast a die. Do it. No matter what the obstacles, and the obstacles will loom larger as soon as the die has chosen it, do it.

One dicer reported to me that the second time she did this exercise the die chose that she take a trip around the world and write articles about her adventures. She couldn't actually afford to do this but borrowed money, hustled editors and took off. Two-thirds of the way around the world, in southern India, she met the man that she eventually married and lived . . . miserably ever after – who knows what happens next – but whatever it is the odds are it beats staying where she was in Hampstead.

⑤ When someone asks you about yourself, lie. Make up things about yourself, both bad and good. Be especially sure not to tell the truth about those things you are most proud of about yourself. Instead try creating some new things you might be proud of. Make up stories about your friends, your family. Create imaginary friends. So?

⑥ Tell someone all the worst things about yourself, your weakest traits, your most horrible sins, the silliest and stupidest things you've ever done. Notice that they probably like you better after you've told them this stuff.

Why be satisfied with *just* one of YOU ?

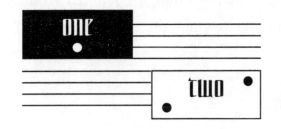

SERIOUSNESS

'I come, O Master, to seek Ultimate Truth,' announced Whim.

'Goody goody gumdrop for you,' said Grain-of-Sand.

ON BEING HUMAN

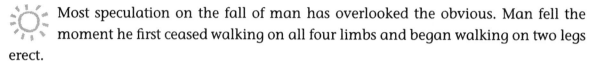 Most speculation on the fall of man has overlooked the obvious. Man fell the moment he first ceased walking on all four limbs and began walking on two legs erect.

Erections have clearly been a source of trouble for man, but historically we have overlooked this first and most formidable of erections: man going from the flexible droopiness of the usual quadraped to *homo erectus*, man erect. Why does this seeming advancement constitute a *fall*?

It is the beginning of man's tragic separation from the earth. Walking on all four limbs keeps a creature's head close to the earth; he feels, sees, smells, hears and even tastes the earth. Erect, he loses touch, putting his head, metaphorically at least, in the clouds. And in this state, man has made a consistent habit of tripping over his own feet and falling flat on his face. Or at the very least plopping his feet down on dung.

We humans have the feeling that we are suffering from some sort of low-level sickness but have never been able to be clear on either the symptoms or the cause. Any species that chooses to spend so much more time, money and energy on weapons and wars and killing than on food and housing and health cannot be entirely sane. Any species many of whose wealthy members feel they must spend part of their wealth to discover why they are so dissatisfied with being 'successful' clearly is not entirely free from sickness. What, mankind keeps asking itself, is wrong with us? What are the symptoms and problems that manifest our basic sickness?

The problem is unhappiness. Men don't like being unhappy. Frowns are bad for the complexion.

The problem is death. Death is felt to be a drag. Its silence is suspicious, a bit malevolent maybe. It is considered somewhat too permanent.

The problem is failure. It's not considered as much fun as success, but seems to arrive more frequently.

The problem is pain. Ingrown toenails, headaches, arthritis – the body always seems to stay one step ahead of Extra-Strength Tylenol.

The problem is love. It doesn't last, isn't returned, or is returned too zealously and jealously.

The problem is evil – usually other people's. Too many bad people are doing it to too few good people. God's police force is understaffed.

The problem is self. We can never quite figure out who we are or, having figured it out, find it pretty depressing.

The problem is enlightenment. We often want it, but seldom have it. We know there is some better way of life, know we're currently not living it, and want to get there from here.

And what lies behind these problems? Somehow, somewhere we seem to have built into us an unhappiness-creating mechanism. A few people seem to have escaped the mechanism, either because they never had it or they do something to eliminate it or override it or ignore it. But finding the mechanism isn't easy. Since the sickness permeates everything we do, it must be inherent – in the very way we think about ourselves and our lives, in the way we make or don't make decisions, in the way we see or ex-perience life, in the very way we try to cure ourselves. There is something fundamentally wrong with the way we usually live our lives and we'd sort of like to find out what it is.

Seriousness is the sickness that poisons human life. It kills the child in us. It teaches us to hate. It teaches us that war is necessary. It teaches us that we are right and others are wrong. It teaches us to take our beliefs seriously and therefore to be frightened of or angry at people who have different beliefs. It teaches us that our ambi-tions are important and therefore the blocking of our success is a disaster. It teaches us that 'winning is everything' and thus dooms half the population (the losers) to misery. It teaches us that death is a horror to be avoided, and thus dooms the entire population to living with the knowledge that it is headed towards an inevitable horrible end.

The sickness is being serious about right and wrong.

The sickness is in feeling that something *has* to be done and that there are permanent solutions to life's problems.

With our sickness, the more seriously we struggle to cure it, the worse it becomes.

The cure lies in a continual letting go of the temptation to fix things, to be serious, to find significance in what we do. It lies in the ability to embrace multiplicity and inconsistency – to say yes to both our yeses and nos.

The cure lies in playfulness – the intense participation in living without any expectation of result. It lies in a constant letting go of our automaton operating out of the past, a constant letting go of our ideas about our selves, and a continual playful plunging into the possibilities of the future.

A major failure of formal education is that it teaches so little about living life, or making decisions, or dealing with the illusions of oneself and others, or considering what is right and wrong and what those terms might mean. A few novels or poems or plays or even works of philosophy may deal with the problems of living, but the sciences, including most psychologies, do not.

And the worst sin of education is that it teaches taking life seriously.

There is nothing intrinsically serious about life. In fact, there is a great deal of the obviously comic about human life. But almost all cultures teach seriousness because it is a society's way of ensuring that its social glue sticks. Once someone begins to consider life as a game, or a play, or a *Dumb and Dumber* farce, then the social glue loses its adhesiveness. Laughter is the great enemy of society. Armed revolution against a society is a blessing; it lets the society clamp down harder. But laughter – how can a society deal with that? Uneasily, to say the least.

'But if we don't take life seriously, then we might as well kill each other!'

Sure. But when was the last time you read of someone killing someone else out of playfulness?

Murder, it is said, is a serious business. It certainly is. And murderers are always intensely serious. And always right.

Seriousness is sickness. A child may be intense, but is at first rarely serious. He becomes serious only after consistent lessons from the adult world. A child's natural mode is play; random, unserious, only sporadically competitive play. He loves games of pretend, whether he is the pretender or the adult. A daddy pretends to be a monster and the child shrieks and runs. He enjoys his shrieking and running; he even enjoys the fear he feels. It is a great game. In his games of cowboys and Indians or Luke and Darth Vader it is usually more fun to be the one shot and falling in a dramatic death than having the lesser role of simply pulling a trigger. You begin to know a child is in trouble when he always has to be the winner in these games and cries when he doesn't win.

If we are to make a dent in the intense seriousness with which western man takes the 'serious' things of life – death, nature, love, success, work, enlightenment – then the idea of play must be made central to the idea of the liberated human. Of course, there is nothing playful about the concept of 'liberation' so we are stuck at the very beginning of our effort with a paradox. To achieve liberation, a 'serious' undertaking, we must become playful, which, as we normally use language, sounds unserious.

But this paradox is natural. Since our language is part of our entrapment, it is unlikely we can escape from our trap without doing violence to our normal usage. Yet even our entrapping language contains hints of the truths of liberation.

Take the very term 'enlightenment'. Although the word is usually taken to mean 'seeing the light' or achieving 'illumination', it equally could mean 'lightening up', taking things lightly rather than seriously.

And even the idea of liberation implies a freeing from something, from bonds, bars, restrictions, limitations, from some sort of forced detention. It points to some sort of openness and uncertainty far more consistent with play than with order and purpose.

Eastern religions and paths have seen man's sickness as caused by his false beliefs in dualities. self and other, good and evil, man and nature, God and not-God. Yet healthy as is this attack on the illusion of these dualities, it misses the far more basic sickness of seriousness. We live in a world of illusions, and seeing through them to the unity behind the dualities, while healthy and necessary, is not in itself the final goal but rather but one step to that goal. The goal is playfulness. As long as we see death as the opposite of life (a duality), then we can't play with death. As long as good and evil are real, then life is a serious business. Once we have really destroyed the dualities there is nothing left to take seriously, but reading eastern philosophy one often wouldn't know it.

Ego and self are built on seriousness. Ego is separation from nature and God and others and thus makes death frightening, nature frightening, God frightening and others frightening. Ego and self are comparison, and comparison is good and evil, right and wrong, success and failure, life and death.

Yet all these dualities, if *played with* rather than taken seriously, are the very substances that make our game-playing possible. It is not the perception of the dualities in and of itself that is sick. It is living as if the dualities are necessary rather than arbitrary, fundamental rather than artificial, real rather than creations. It is the *seriousness* with which they are taken that causes our misery.

PARABLE ABOUT A LIGHT FAILURE

In the beginning there was a playing field, with lights, and it was called earth, and the lights were called sun and moon, and it was good.

All creatures frolicked and played and died and were killed and were born and born again, and it was good.

And different creatures developed new equipment, so that the variety and complexity of the games was increased. Some developed fast legs, others hard shells, some wings to fly, others noses to burrow, others aqualungs to swim under water. No matter what new equipment they developed, the games went on and all creatures continued to play and it was good.

And one creature developed a brain which permitted him to outsmart some of the other creatures and to win many of the games and to invent newer and more complex games, and it was still good.

But then, one by one, in isolated, divergent places, some of these brain-filled creatures began to invent the game that *there were no games*, that the rules of various games were *Divine Law* and that the referee was God, or that the rules were *scientific law* and the referee was the scientist.

And the light went out and the playing field became for ever dark.

WHIM AND THE THREE SEEKERS

One day three seekers approached Whim as he sat on a barstool with a dozen of his followers in a local hangout called JOE'S EATS AND BOOZE.

'O Wisest of Men,' said the leader of the three, 'we have searched the earth for a master who would free us from self and today we humbly place ourselves at your feet to await your instructions.'

'You're welcome here, friends,' said Whim, 'but you got the wrong guy.'

'But, Honoured Sir, we have heard of your power and wisdom from one end of – '

'I've never had a firm idea in my head in my whole life.'

'But, Noble Sage, we have heard of miracles which you and you alone – '

'Nothing but accidents, every one.'

'But, Most Great Guru, dozens of students whom we've met on the road affirm that you have led them – '

'I've never had a successful student leave me who knew his arse from a hole in the ground.'

'But, Blessed Buddha, all who have heard you say that your words always convey a spec— '

'My words never convey any more than the next fellow's. They're all lies.'

'But, Most Mighty Seer, what then are we to do?'

'Beats me, friends,' said Whim.

'You won't help us, O Sacred Sage?'

'I'm doing all I can,' said Whim.

'But, Magnificent – '

'But you guys keep sticking up your "Great Blessed Mighty Sacred Buddha Sage" crap like a shield to keep me away.'

It is one of the many catch-22s of human existence that we set out seriously to seek enlightenment, and yet seriousness itself is a prime barrier to enlightenment. Carlos Castaneda created a wonderful Yaqui Indian sage named Don Juan (or Don Juan created Carlos – it's a toss-up), and Don Juan spoke to Carlos of the sage living a life of 'controlled folly'.

'We must know first that our acts are useless,' said Don Juan, 'and yet we must proceed as if we didn't know it. That's a sorcerer's controlled folly.'

When Carlos asked Don Juan to explain exactly what controlled folly was, Don Juan answered: 'I am happy that you finally asked me about my controlled folly after so many years, and yet it wouldn't have mattered to me in the least if you had never asked. Yet I have chosen to feel happy, as if I cared . . . *That is controlled folly.*'

It might well be argued that dice-living is simply a new version of controlled folly. Don Juan is happy Carlos asked, but also knows it doesn't make any difference. And Don Juan tells Carlos that he exercises his controlled folly with everyone and does it every single time he acts. 'My acts are sincere,' he says, 'but they are only the acts of an actor.'

The idea of everything being controlled folly and the acts of an actor frightens Carlos as it does most humans, and Don Juan's further explanations frighten him even more. 'Everything I do in regard to myself and my fellow men is folly, because nothing matters . . . Once a man learns to *see* he finds himself alone in the world with nothing but controlled folly.'

If you've read all the Carlos Castaneda books then you'll see that the Carlos of these books doesn't seem to get this message of Don Juan's. Carlos began his first book as a serious young man and ended his last one equally seriously. In the books he never reaches the serenity and playfulness so vibrant in Don Juan when he speaks of nothing mattering and his life being all controlled folly. He never cackles away in life as Don Juan does. Yet in 'real life', a few people who met the author Carlos Castaneda in person (as opposed to the character he created of himself in his books) say that he was a quite playful person, perfectly happy to play games and change his personality at the drop of a hat. He apparently delegated the original staid, controlled Carlos to his books so that the liberated Carlos could live outside them. And his notorious secretiveness was consistent with escaping from the pressures of being the person people expected him to be.

And no one can list options and cast a die and turn over decision-making to chance unless he or she has made a basic hidden assumption: the decision isn't that important. Dicing is simply one of many ways to attack seriousness. If you list six options, some moral, some immoral, some ambitious and some trivial, some spiritual and some lusty, and let chance decide what you do, then you are in effect challenging the seriousness of your acts, you are saying it doesn't matter what I do. When the die chooses an action I choose to do it with all my heart – that is the dice-person's controlled folly.

Dice-living works because it forces one to let go of importance, of self-importance, of seriousness. Other paths to enlightenment present the danger that the path itself is solemn and serious and the seeker never achieves the insight that the path itself may be part of the sickness and that he must let go of it too. Dicing is controlled folly, and because it is folly the danger of taking it too seriously is minimal.

CARRYING THE WORLD ON YOUR SHOULDERS IS TOUGH.

THE WISE MAN LEARNS TO SHRUG.

'The price of freedom is eternal vigilance.' — Someone
'The price of eternal vigilance,' commented Whim, 'is freedom.'

Education is, at one and the same time, a great liberator and a great narrower. On the one hand, education gives us greater options, skills and experiences, but on the other it inculcates certain illusions about life and reason that inhibit our taking advantage of the knowledge and skills being given to us. It is in inculcating consistency and seriousness as virtues that education most fails us.

'Billy just loves to read all the time . . . '

But wouldn't he sometimes much prefer to be outside hanging out with the gang?

'Isn't Joannie sweet? She always lets the other person win.'

Imagine how miserable Joannie's going to be in later years if she's been trained always to let the other person win.

'Sylvia's so pretty and grown up; she just loves to dress up all the time.'

Sure. So what do you do when she climbs a tree or splashes in a mud puddle with those clothes? You call her a bad girl. And a whole set of wonderful options are banned from her life.

'My Brad can't stand to lose. The kid's a fighter. He'll battle you to the last ounce of his strength and if you win, watch out: he'll probably try to steal the trophy.'

Sure. And if you keep saying that, imagine what a fun guy Brad's going to be when he grows up.

Parents mouth a thousand oversimplifications a year that betray the truth in the child's heart: Billy ached to be out splashing in the mud with the other boys, but . . . ; Joannie wanted to chew the penis off her brother every time he won, but . . . ; and Sylvia daydreamed of a world in which she wouldn't have to worry about how she looked.

Patterns are prostitution to the patter of parents. Adults rule and they reward patterns. Patterns it is. And eventual boredom.

What if we were to bring up our children differently? Reward them for being inconsistent, for varying their habits, tastes, interests, roles? Reward them for hacking around instead of seriousness? We could discipline them to be reliably various, to be conscientiously inconsistent, determinedly habit-free – even of 'good' habits.

'Oh, my Johnny, he's so wonderful. Last year he got all "A"s on his report card and this year he's getting mostly "C"s and "D"s. We're so proud.'

'Marie! Don't you dare brush your teeth again tonight! It's getting to be a regular *habit*!'

'What, my boy, haven't told a lie yet, today? Well, go to your room and stay there until you can think one up.'

'What should I wear, Mother?' 'Oh, I don't know, Sylvia. Why don't you try the cardigan that makes you look flat-chested and that ugly skirt your grandmother picked up at the thrift store and always twists?' 'Sounds cool.'

'Goddamn son of mine. Hasn't goofed off in a week. If I don't find the lawn unmowed or his room a mess one of these days, I'm going to blow my top at him.'

'Oh, Barbara, your drawings all tend to look like the thing you're drawing. You seem unable to let yourself go.'

'This essay is too logical and well-organized. If you expect to develop as a writer you must learn to digress and be irrelevant at all times.'

Of course, we're exaggerating here. Consistency and reason and even seriousness are absolutely necessary in many educational games and should in such cases be used to the hilt. But though logic and consistency are necessary in maths and science and clear thinking, they are not always useful in living, where lightness and looseness are perhaps better virtues.

The child, we are informed, needs to see order and consistency in the world or he becomes insecure and afraid. But *what* order and consistency? Perhaps he might grow equally well with consistent, dependable inconsistency. Life is in fact that way. If parents would only admit and praise inconsistency, children wouldn't be so frightened of their parents' hypocrisy and ignorance.

'Sometimes I'll spank you for spilling your milk and sometimes I won't give a damn.'

'Occasionally I like you when you rebel against me, son, and at other times I feel like kicking the shit out of you.'

'I'm usually pleased with your good grades in school, but sometimes I think you're an awful grind.'

Such is the way adults feel; such is the way children know they feel.

Why not bring up our children to value humour and playfulness and condemn seriousness? We certainly don't do so now. The 'class clown' is always somewhat looked down upon; he might better be honoured as valedictorian. Children who are mischievous are called 'imps' or 'little devils'. We know what sort of a person a 'little angel' is. Laughter in a library is outlawed. If the kids were reading the right books, laughter would be mandatory – although, of course, making it mandatory would effectively kill it.

And of course that is the problem: there is a natural war on between rules and humour, rules and playfulness. Education and society, to exist, must make rules. But you can't legislate humour. Humour and playfulness need rules to play with and mock.

THE SQUARE BLACK HAT

The graduate wears black
At his graduation.
            Why?
The graduate's hat is flat
And black
And keeps the sun away.
            Why?
The graduate sits and listens
To other men in black
Tell him truths he knows
Aren't true, but he listens
In black, under his flat hat.
            Why?

THE GRADUATE WEARS BLACK BECAUSE HE'S IN MOURNING.

WHIM ADMITS HE'S A MESS

'You're a walking, talking disease, Whim,' said an ambitious disciple.

'I am?' asked Whim.

'You don't take yourself seriously. People coming from all over the world to hear your words of wisdom and all you do is make fun of everything.'

'I know. I'm a mess.'

'How do you expect other people to take themselves seriously if you don't take yourself seriously?'

'Exactly,' replied Whim.

After Whim had discovered old U.T. (Ultimate Truth) some of his disciples reproached him for too much frivolity and others for too much seriousness. But Whim saw that it's impossible for us to live fully without both. When Whim once spent two years working to create a new society with more flexible rules and more openness to inconsistency and variety, some of his followers claimed that he had fallen victim to Purpose, to grasping at the future. At that time Whim devoted himself to creating an alternative way of life for others. So focused was he that at times the whimsical Whim seemed to have disappeared. He was challenged about his seriousness dozens of times. Although most of his answers were in his normal style – brief, paradoxical and amusing – once he answered seriously:

'To create a game you must have a goal, rules for reaching it and players. When I have seemed frivolous and goal-less, it's because I have been refusing to play some of the games which you or society try to thrust upon me. My frivolity is simply a ploy in the game I play to break down the boring limitations of my culture. In such cases my frivolity is playing my own game hard and seriously to win against the dominant society.

'To have any game you have to have players who are trying as best they can to reach a goal. As soon as a player stops trying hard to reach the goal, for him the game has ceased to exist.

'It is a paradox that when I am a lion trying to destroy old games I often play the role of child or fool or clown. Now that I am trying to create new values I have to play the role of master, leader, hero. Since the role of master or leader has been polluted by a thousand serious adults playing at them, you see my new roles as a regression, a falling from the path. But both when I appear frivolous and when I appear to be a serious leader I am playing, playing hard but not expecting to win anything, able to take up a new game at any moment.'

Whim abandoned his game of trying to 'change the world' exactly two years after he began. His comment at the time was: 'The world got lucky: I failed to change it. I got lucky: I failed to change it.'

*The shortest path between
two points is the long way through life.*

You can't force humour. Nothing kills it faster than saying: be funny.

Humour is a letting go of something that one takes seriously and is often personal. One woman takes her cooking seriously, another is always making fun of her own cooking. One man is proud of his job and can't joke about it, another is proud of it but mocks it publicly. One might argue that anything you can't joke about is a personal hang-up, something you are taking too seriously and thus is, whether you know it or not, causing you unhappiness. Can you make fun of your own children? Of your spouse? Of your parents? Of your religion? Of your presidential candidate? Of your country? Of capitalism? Of socialism? Of love? Of your figure? Of the way you dress? Of your athletic ability?

Whenever you make fun of something you are detaching yourself from that thing. To laugh at a man slipping on a banana peel and taking a pratfall is nothing; we have no attachment to that man's dignity. But to laugh at our own falling flat on our arse is a sign of our detachment from our own dignity.

I was once with two other young teenage boys at a small dinner party hosted by Governor Thomas E. Dewey, famous a few years later for losing the American presidency when the *Chigaco Tribune* declared him a winner. The governor was telling an anecdote about being at a carnival and evaluating how strongmen were able to swing the hammer just right to ring the bell at the top of the pole. He brought his fist down to illustrate the swing and sent a fork spiralling back over his shoulder and on to the floor.

No one said a word. A cadaverous waiter appeared, stooped to pick up the fork and soon replaced it with another. No one commented. Governor Dewey at one level maintained his dignity. But on another level he was missing life.

How much nicer if he had immediately turned to his two sons and me and said with a smile: 'Now let's see if you can do that.' And he then might take the fork from his adult neighbour and try to send it flying as he had accidentally sent the first. What joy it would have been for us boys and the adults if all were soon banging away on the formal tablecloth to send silverware flying every which way.

WHIM TRIES TO BE SERIOUS

'Come on, Whim, you can do it. Say something positive and definitive which isn't mocking either me or itself or yourself or anything.'

'Do I have to?' Whim said grimly.

'Yes, just this once you have to say something positive and unmocking.'

Whim thought for a moment.

'OK,' he said, 'I got it: I love myselves.'

'Hmmm.'

'I would have said "I love God" but you might have thought I was being religious.'

'I see.'

' "God loves Whim" says it too, but I didn't want to give God a bad reputation.'

DICE HOUSE, A PLAY IN TWO ACTS, BY PAUL LUCAS

Act One

Scene 1. Dr Drabble's Practice

[Drabble pacing about, swigging from a half-empty whiskey bottle. Mathew listening politely.]

DRABBLE: The anti-depressants seemed to work at first but soon I found I was taking more and more of them and feeling worse and worse . . .

MATHEW: What do you mean when you say you started feeling worse?

DRABBLE: Well, no sleep, haven't slept in days, and these sudden sweats, sudden panic attacks, my heart'll just go bo-bo-bo-boom like it's going to pop out of my mouth on to the floor and get covered in all the hairs and the vile things that are down there, the dust.

MATHEW: And does anything seem to trigger these attacks?

DRABBLE: Nothing, they just come out of the blue. And I've started to hear voices now. Little voices, my God, I really think I'm going to ond up doing something stupid and . . .

[He looks around to check no one's listening.]

DRABBLE: . . . the walls in this place are very badly behaved.

MATHEW: The walls?

DRABBLE: Yes. They keep closing in. Naughty.

[The phone rings.]

MATHEW: I'm afraid that'll be Tina telling us that the hour is up.

DRABBLE: Yes. Excuse me a minute.

[Drabble answers the phone.]

DRABBLE: Doctor Drabble speaking. (*Listens*) Yes I know the hour's up, Tina, but I'm at a crucial point with Mr Day. Can you cancel my next two patients, please? Thank you.

[Puts phone down. Sits, exhausted.]

DRABBLE: So that's me, and how have *you* been, Mathew? Long time no see.

MATHEW: I feel fine, it's over a year since I last did anything I shouldn't do with ribbons. After our final session together I went and lived in a hut by the sea and these days I mostly just take myself off for walks along the beach, collecting mussels sometimes and I find the walking takes my mind off ribbons, even the pretty yellow ones.

DRABBLE: Good.

MATHEW: The pale, lovely, yellow ones.

DRABBLE: That's just what I wanted to hear. You've made remarkable progress, Mathew, and I think the time has come for us to close your file and let you put your past indiscretions behind you.

MATHEW: It's all thanks to you, Doctor Drabble.

DRABBLE: Yes, it is, yes. Solid technique I use, tried and trusted methods from the wise minds of Freud and Jung and co. And it works, you're living proof of that. But just before I sign all the necessary paperwork, there is one last thing I'd like you to do.

MATHEW: What's that?

DRABBLE: I'd like you to kidnap my wife.

[Silence.]

MATHEW: (*quietly*) . . . I sell the mussels I collect to a man in a toupee . . .
DRABBLE: Won't take long, couple of hours at most.
MATHEW: I don't think I want to.
DRABBLE: No, I can understand that, and I wouldn't normally ask, but – I'm a desperate man, Mathew. Look at me.

[Mathew does look at him.]

DRABBLE: No, don't! Don't, actually, I'm too horrible to behold. And all because . . . all of this because . . . Dice! I mean, dice!
MATHEW: Dice?
DRABBLE: Dice! (*Shakes head*) Dice.
MATHEW: Why do you keep saying 'dice'?
DRABBLE: Why? *Why?* (*Laughs bitterly*) Why.
MATHEW: Now you keep saying –
DRABBLE: Do you enjoy sex, Mathew?
MATHEW: I think I left the door of my hut open, I'd better –
DRABBLE: I enjoy sex. God, I enjoy it. So when my wife suddenly wanted it at all times of the day and night and in all sorts of exotic locations I wasn't the kind of man to complain. I was happy to oblige. Barely able to stand with fatigue, but happy too.
MATHEW: My hour's up, I think, so –
DRABBLE: When she made me sleep in the spare room a week later I put it down to the enigma of womanhood. Even when she cleaned out our joint savings account to purchase a silver Harley Davidson I remained I think fairly stoical and understanding. No, it was the evening I got home to find her sharing the marital bed with two tramps from the local park that things came to a head. My wife explained she was undergoing something called Dice Therapy, that all her behaviour was deliberately

	patternless, random. I can't describe my horror. For it was I who delivered her into the hands of The Diceman.
MATHEW:	The Diceman?
DRABBLE:	Charles E. Ratner, my former colleague and a leading expert in the treatment of phobias. I referred Polly to him to try and cure her fear of flying. Little did I know he was about to throw away every tenet of his training and cook up this . . . Dice Therapy. God knows, in this game you meet your share of freaks and lunatics but Ratner's odd even for a psychiatrist. There are some people saying behind closed doors that he should be taken out into a lonely field and clanged on the head with a shovel.
MATHEW:	Those sorts of ideas upset me.

[Drabble mimes swinging a shovel.]

DRABBLE:	Wham, like that, bust his cranium open, he's asking for it. Some people are saying. B-behind closed doors. Ratner's solution to the human condition is that we should all throw dice to decide what to do. List a set of options on a piece of paper and then let chance determine which path to take. The idea being that we are all trapped within the narrow parameters of our personalities which he contends are artificial constructs that do not reflect the essence of our selves – a view I have some sympathy with. But Ratner's therapy involves ignoring every social, legal and moral boundary there is. Did I mention that some people think he should be clobbered senseless with a big knotty log?
MATHEW:	Clanged with a shovel, you said.
DRABBLE:	Well there's some debate about the . . . details . . .
MATHEW:	Why are you saying all these things?
DRABBLE:	My wife's actions while playing the dice resulted in a variety of lawsuits and financial ruin. When finally we had to sell the house I gave her an ultimatum: give up playing the dice or she would not be welcome at the

bedsit I'd rented. After rolling a seven she packed a bag and moved into Doctor Ratner's newly opened Centre for Research into Randomized Living – referred to by the tabloids as the Dice House. You've probably read about it.

[Mathew looks blankly, shakes his head.]

DRABBLE: Delapidated gothic mansion in the middle of a lake, it's been in all the papers.

[Takes a newspaper from his desk and taps front page.]

MATHEW: I live in a hut.

DRABBLE: Oh, yes. Yes, you said. Well, Ratner's patients all live there together to practise 'pure dicing' in a mutually supportive environment. The police are powerless to help me since Polly is there of her own free will. Desperate measures are called for.

MATHEW: I don't want to kidnap your wife, Doctor Drabble.

DRABBLE: Call me Anthony.

MATHEW: No, I think I'll call you Doctor Drabble. Doctor Drabble Who's Always Helped Me So Much.

DRABBLE: Come on now, Mathew, show me how good you are at abduction.

MATHEW: Er, no.

DRABBLE: You'll be my favourite abductor.

MATHEW: I'd like to go now please, my hour's up.

DRABBLE: I'm prepared to offer you a hundred pounds in cash for your trouble.

[He produces a wad of notes from his pocket.]

MATHEW: I make enough money selling mussels, thank you, Doctor. Goodbye.

[Mathew stands.]

DRABBLE: Mathew, now – now, Mathew. I am a psychiatrist. We both know that. I only ever have your best interests at heart. And in my professional opinion what is in your best interests at this moment is to rescue my little sweet pea of a spouse.

MATHEW: I don't really see how that can be true, though.

DRABBLE: Because if you don't I'll have you sectioned.

[Silence.]

MATHEW: Par-pardon, Doctor Drabble Who's Always Been So Kind?

DRABBLE: Damn my black heart to hell, I'll have you sectioned, Mathew. I'll sign a few forms and they'll lock you up in some anachronistic institution with dark high towers up on top of a spooky hill. Full of noisy misfits who jabber and throw poo at each other. I'll toss you down one of the many cracks in our fragile society to fester out of sight of all but the rats and the unblinking schizoids. I really am most terribly sorry.

MATHEW: That's in some ways blackmail.

[Drabble goes and places his hand on Mathew's shoulder.]

DRABBLE: I will never be able to truly look myself in the mirror again after doing this to you. But there we are.

[Takes his hand off Mathew's shoulder.]

DRABBLE: The fact is a psychiatrist has the power to abuse his position of trust and I find that idea just too tempting. I'll render you a right old cabbage-job with drugs better suited to the placation of elephants. Mathew, forgive me.

MATHEW: I think then, I think –

DRABBLE: I've helped you in the past, haven't I? With the ribbons problem? Is it too much to expect a bit of help in return?

MATHEW: I think, Doctor Drabble, that you must love your wife very much to do this, to degrade yourself like this. How much you must love her.

DRABBLE: God help us both, I'm the last of the romantics.

MATHEW: There must be an ombudsman I can report you to.

DRABBLE: My behaviour's too outrageous for anyone to believe you. I'm a respected psychiatrist and you're mentally ill. Capable of anything, and a clear danger to children.

MATHEW: I'm not a danger to children.

DRABBLE: It's not for you to decide who you're a danger to, Mathew. It's for me to decide, that's what makes this world of ours so unfair.

MATHEW: Then I'm a helpless pawn with a touch of the puppet in me?

DRABBLE: I have you by the balls, God it's dreadful. Only a madman would rather spend his life in an asylum than abduct a psychiatrist's wife. I might allow myself an ironic smile at that when this tragic aberration is over.

MATHEW: It's over a year since I last did that silly thing with the ribbons.

DRABBLE: I know. You're cured. That's why I know I can trust you with my wife's well-being. The rest of my patients are no less insane than when I first saw them. In fact, the majority are a good deal worse. You're a sensitive, intelligent man over whom I have complete control. Take the money, Mathew, and abduct my little lamb gently.

[Mathew reaches for the cash.]

DRABBLE: I can promise you at least that the job is quite straightforward: I'll get you referred to Ratner as a patient I can do nothing for. It's a common enough scenario. I'll bring you to his Dice House where you'll secretly be carrying this . . . banana.

[Drabble produces a banana from his desk.]

DRABBLE: Polly can't resist bananas, I try and avoid contemplating the Freudian implications of that. This particular banana will knock her out for three or four hours.

MATHEW: (*pause*) So . . . what, I just hit her on the head with it?

DRABBLE: No. No, I've injected the banana with sedatives, Mathew. You just get her to eat the banana. Then once she's gone droopy, you'll wrap her in a blanket and ring me with this mobile phone.

[Hands Mathew a mobile phone.]

DRABBLE: We'll rendezvous at my car. Then I'll take her to a traditional mental hospital where a quiet room with a one-foot-thick steel door has been reserved for her. With time and support she'll soon see sense, and we'll both be able to return to our normal lives. I will once more be a rising star of the world of psychiatry, and you can go back to your idyllic life of collecting bi-valves from the beach. Albeit with an understandable mistrust of therapists.

OPTIONS

Before casting a die, read through the six options below. Throw out one or two (or, better still, all six) and create some of your own to replace those you toss out. Then cast a die.

① Burp or fart during your boss's next talk. Look at him or her with intense seriousness, as if the burp or fart never existed.

② At your next group meeting – at work, at church, at a bar with buddies, at a coffee klatch, in the locker room – consider some far-out and seemingly irrational idea that has some some of appeal; for example, that the whole group repair to a new meeting ground: a bar, lake, nightclub, etc. Or that the group dispense with its usual bullshit and talk today only about 'X', something you sense people might like to talk about but never do. Or suggest that whoever is leading the meeting be replaced by someone else. Present your suggestion seriously (but don't you yourself *take* it seriously). Note the results.

③ Enter the next group meeting you attend – at work, church, bar, kitchen, living room, bowling alley, wherever – with the assumption that you are attending not a meeting but a party, and that the purpose of a party is to have fun. Have fun. We'd advise you try to encourage others to have fun, but fear that then you'd become a party pooper.

④ Lecture someone about how seriousness is sickness and ruins people's lives.
   Notice immediately how your serious lecture dulls both your life and that of the person who has to listen to you.

⑤ With children, play. Encourage them to be inconsistent. Encourage them to pretend. Encourage them to make up stories (to lie). Encourage them to pretend to be someone different from their normal selves. Encourage yourself to join them in their games. Unless you become as a little child you shall not see God.

⑥ The next time you pay a bill, send at least 10 per cent more than the total amount of the bill. Tell the recipient that they are doing such great work (no matter what you really think of them) you wanted to send them extra.
   Note if their computer system faints.

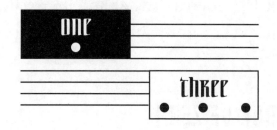

LIFE AND DEATH

When life comes, it cannot be declined;
when death greets you, his handshake is for ever.

THE COMPLETE BOOK OF ZEN I

The raindrop races with hesitation down the windowpane, stops, merges with the other victors in the race and, in an hour or two, ascends once more to the sky.

It is a full life.

'The trouble with Death,'
said Whim one day, 'is that
it takes up a lot of time.'

Life without death would be, paradoxically, life without life.

For living is change, is growth and decay, is birth and death. Death is another form of change. We tend to see it as an end, as changeless-ness, and fear it, but only because we believe our consciousness ends with the decay of our body. But if consciousness lives at all then it, like all other forms of life we know of, must go on, changing, decaying, being reborn.

Death is also changeless-ness. It is a paradox that humans, who seem to organize their lives to control and limit change, should fear the ultimate security of death. Once dead we have nothing more to fear. Perhaps that is the reason why most people who have a near-death experience find life much lighter afterwards. It's as if they have taken the best punch the enemy has to offer and realize it isn't so bad after all.

ON DEATH

A leaf, quite thick-veined, brittle, dry,
Weakened by the chill of winter's breath,
Loses its grip on the trembling limb so high
And falls to the frozen earth, and death.
I step on it.
Do you hear it cry?

The fear of death is healthy on the one hand and an illness on the other. When a train is bearing down on you, it is usually wise to step off the tracks. Death is the end of the play, the end of playing, the end of games. It's lights out on the playing fields of the Lord. If we enjoy playing, then we want to keep the game going.

We grieve when a loved one leaves us at the height of his or her powers. But when a loved one leaves us who has long declined and is now capable of only the most repetitious of games, should we grieve? Or should we celebrate the passing by remembering and celebrating the life that went before?

Life can be seen as a continual expanding of options beginning at birth and expanding into and through adulthood and then beginning to diminish as we age. Aging is a narrowing of life, a narrowing of the things we can do, a narrowing of our ability to see things freshly. Illness is a further narrowing. Finally, with death, we narrow our existence to one simple option: rest. Eternal rest. Not bad.

But not as much fun as change.

TWO PARABLES ABOUT WHIM AND DEATH

One day a disciple asked Whim: 'If a man suddenly appeared here with a gun and pointed it right at you and threatened to shoot, what would you do?'

'I'd run,' replied Whim promptly.

'But then what would all your disciples think?'

'I don't know,' said Whim. 'But I'm interested in surviving to find out.'

* * *

The next day Our Beloved Whim was talking with a group of disciples in a large tent when a man suddenly appeared in their midst and, aiming a shotgun at Whim, announced loudly: 'You claim that death isn't something to be feared. Convince me you're not afraid and I won't shoot.'

Whim leapt up and ran out of the tent, leaving the man and the disciples open-mouthed in astonishment. Before anyone could say a word, Whim walked back into the tent and sat down.

The man with the shotgun, baffled, let his gun fall to the floor and waited uncertainly. The disciples, after a respectful silence, burst into long applause.

After another long silence the foremost disciple asked: 'Teach us, O Most Beloved Whim. Why did you run away?'

'I was afraid,' said Whim.

'But then why, O Master, did you return?'

'To see if any of you guys got hurt.'

Disability is limitation. Illness is limitation. Aging is limitation. And death is the ultimate limitation. One is capable only of stinking.

So we properly seek to avoid it.

Yet about nothing are most societies more hypocritical and filled with damaging illusions than about death. All societies create rituals and expected behaviour patterns around someone's death and expect everyone involved to follow them. In most ways we are expected to treat the death of an eighty-year-old loved one the same as that of a twenty-year-old. We are expected to treat the death of a mean alcoholic the same as that of a kindly grandmother. Society insists on the same rituals and grieving for each.

There are some people's deaths we feel like celebrating, we're so happy finally to be rid of them. There are other deaths that make us want to honour and celebrate the deceased for their full life and graceful death. On both those occasions any service or gathering held would be a happy occasion, but such is not what societies make easy. We are asked to go through the motions of a grief that we may not naturally feel. It is one of society's cheap tricks always to try to get us to express and feel emotions that we may not in fact feel. Then, when we become dimly aware that we're not feeling the appropriate emotion, society urges us to feel guilty about it.

It is at least conceivable that societies might exist that react to human death in entirely different ways than those we are mostly familiar with. Most other mammals, for example, are not particularly upset by the death of a mate or sibling; a few sniffs at the corpse and then off to look into getting some dinner. In wartime or in times of mass plagues, societies have been forced to treat the deaths of its citizens like the deaths of animals: the bodies must be dealt with quickly and that is about it. I think we can conceive of a society treating the death of an individual like the falling of a leaf: a natural event neither to be grieved nor celebrated.

Every man is a load
of firewood; the question is
not whether we are going to be destroyed
but with what kind of fire and light we will burn.

A PARABLE OF ONE MAN'S DYING

Two men were visiting an old friend, almost seventy years old, at his home where the man was seriously ill with what the doctors diagnosed as cancer. After exchanging a few polite remarks with the old man the first friend leaned towards the bed and asked sombrely: 'So how's it going these days, old friend?'

'I'm dying, Jack, that's how it's going,' the old man replied pleasantly.

'Oh, no,' said the second friend. 'Don't be silly. You'll be out swimming again in a couple of weeks.'

'Could be,' said the old man. 'But right now I'm dying.'

'Nonsense,' said the first friend. 'You look great.'

'Could be,' said the old man cheerfully. 'But right now I'm dying.'

'Oh, come on,' said the second friend. 'You look as happy as if you'd just won the lottery.'

'Well, that's natural enough,' said the old man. 'I feel pretty good.'

'Feeling pretty good!? I thought you said you're dying?'

'Oh, I'm dying all right,' replied the old man, 'and I feel pretty good.'

'But – ' began the first friend.

'I find I'm enjoying dying just as much as everything else that comes along.'

'But – ' began the second friend.

'Bit better, matter of fact,' concluded the old man, smiling. 'Every day the doctor lets me have ice cream.'

Naked came I out of my mother's womb and naked shall I return
thither: the Lord Chance giveth and the Lord Chance taketh away:
blessed by the name of the Lord.

– from OLD TESTAMENT (REVISED VERSION)

That I am writing *The Book of the Die* today is an accident. Or rather a series of accidents. That I am alive today has taken a million tiny decisions and tiny events that have permitted me to escape the hundred opportunities Death has had to remove me. Most of the times Death almost gets us, we are unaware of. We hesitate before leaving the house to finish a cup of coffee. Had we not hesitated eleven point two seconds we would have been involved in a fatal car accident.

Our evading Death, or rendezvousing with Death, begins with what might be called the First Accident: our conception. My own father was ravaged by cancer in his mid-thirties and was dead by forty. When I was conceived – how many little coincidences went into his even making love to my mother that particular night – thousands of his sperm swam up the great vaginal river and one of them arrived a millisecond before hundreds of others. Whammo! I was conceived. But did the genes in that sperm contain the tendency to cancer that was to kill my father in another nine years? Or was it one of the only 4 per cent of his sperm that was free of the gene that predisposes a human to cancer? By accident, now almost thirty years older than the age at which my father was afflicted with cancer, I still remain free.

And then there are some times when we become frighteningly aware that Death had us in his grip but for some reason let go. Thirty years ago Death had me and my entire family so firmly in his clutches that I apologized to my wife for killing her and our sons, since it was I that had led us to our obvious doom. But Accident spared us.

It began just after I'd finished writing *The Dice Man* and mailed it off to the English publisher who had spurred me on, after four years of dawdling, to finish it. At that time I was a poverty-stricken college professor, living on the island of Mallorca, where a colleague and I had created a study abroad programme for college students interested in art and literature. Having finished my first book, I then gaily took my lifetime savings (ten thousand dollars) and bought a sailboat to live aboard that summer and cruise the Mediterranean. The decision to buy a boat was mine, but the dice had said 'no' to my buying a sailboat I really liked the look of in Greece. But then it didn't veto the catamaran I bought on the south coast of France. Had the dice said 'yes' to the boat in Greece . . . I would have lived another life, or died another death.

So my wife and my three young sons – twelve, eight and six – and I went off to Antibes, climbed aboard our squat thirty-foot cruising catamaran and prepared to sail around the Med a bit and meet my English publisher on Mallorca in late July to discuss the manuscript of *The Dice Man*. We sailed east along the French Riviera to Nice and Genoa and then south down the coast of Italy and then west to Corsica and west again to Sardinia and then prepared to sail across three hundred miles of open sea to Mallorca.

The weather forecast was for fair weather, our pudgy catamaran had given us no trouble, it was only a two- or three-day sail, and my wife had a premonition of disaster so strong that she went to the tiny chapel on the hillside beside the sea to pray. Even after prayers, so convinced was she that something horrible awaited us out on that calm sea that she wanted to fly herself and the boys to Mallorca, to let me alone pay the price of my folly. There were no flights to Mallorca from Sardinia. And my wife thought: What if it is my being on the boat that saves us? She and the boys came.

And so off we sailed. Or rather motored. The Mediterranean was flat and calm. For twelve hours we motored, ploughing serenely through the motionless sea, the boys bored, I disappointed in the lack of wind, and my wife in fear. Porpoises swam along on each side of us for hours, the boys joying in their play, my wife seeing it as another warning. The sea was calm, calm, the sky a strange red.

Then the first obvious accident occurred. The 40 horsepower outboard engine, which had run flawlessly for six weeks while we brought the boat to this point, began to sputter and stutter and hiccough and generally begin to act like it wanted to quit working. Which it soon did. I then applied all my considerable lack of mechanical skills to trying to resuscitate the engine, but to no effect. But the Gods compensated us for the loss of our engine fifty miles out by bringing up a bit of a breeze. Yes! Wind!

The sailor in me rejoiced, fool that I am, as the wind, first a zephyr, then a light wind, then a breeze, then a stiff breeze, and then . . . It didn't take more than four or five hours for the wind to go from nothing to full gale. The weather, as predicted, was fair. This was a *mistral*, the wind that barrels out of the Alps and sweeps across the Mediterranean for no particular reason except the fun of it. A fair-weather wind, of gale force, indeed, of hurricane force.

The seas began to build. I reduced sail. I reefed. I further reduced sail. I further reefed. I dropped all sails.

As a sailor in those days, I was a good reader. I loved reading about great sailing adventures, but had myself done little sailing. So being a hundred miles from the nearest land in steep twenty-foot seas with winds approaching or exceeding hurricane force was not an experience I'd had too often. In fact, I'd never been in winds even half this strong or in seas one-tenth as high. In the books I'd read, I knew that the disadvantage of a catamaran is that if a wave capsizes the boat, the boat doesn't right itself as a mono-hull would. A capsized catamaran floats nicely upside down. The people inside the capsized catamaran fare less nicely. I knew that experienced sailors would throw out a sea anchor to keep the boat's head into the seas to reduce the possibility of a capsize. Naturally I had no sea anchor, but I could improvise.

As each of my sons took turns pointing at oncoming waves and claiming that he saw a bigger one than his brothers, and the wind shrieked through the rigging, I jury-rigged a sea anchor by tying line around my deflated dinghy and letting it drift out to windward. The effort was a marginal success: the boat pointed at a forty-five-degree angle to the waves.

That second night at sea, after a full day of the gale, and the wind and seas seeming still to build, I reached the conclusion that sooner or later a big wave was going to capsize us and we were going to die. This conclusion was made less painful by the fact that for the first time in my life I was seasick – totally and fully and actively seasick. The fact that my 'sea anchor' dinghy had disappeared and the catamaran was lying beam to the seas, and that the crest of the seas were now hissing and breaking as if rolling over a shoal made this conclusion seem reasonable.

That night my wife and I lay huddled in the windward hull of the catamaran as tense and fearful as it is ever the lot of humans to be, listening to the roar of the wind above us, feeling our pudgy little boat begin to rise and heel to the next wave, hearing the hiss of an oncoming breaker and, with the boat at a thirty-degree angle, feeling the shock impact of the surf crashing against the side of our boat, sending drawers sliding out, toppling books and dishes from supposedly safe niches, and scaring us even more shitless.

We were going to die. Simple as that. So I thoughtfully apologized to my wife for dragging her and our boys to certain doom.

My wife is made of sterner stuff. While I, encouraged by seasickness, was resigned to death, she, fierce mother that she was (is), insisted that we all wear life-jackets so that if we capsized we would be as prepared as possible. While I managed to sleep, she stayed awake for three straight days.

The storm continued that long. The next day we awoke to find that one of the boat's two rudders had broken off and our dingy–liferaft–sea anchor was gone. On the third day, a freighter appeared in the distance and we fired up a flare.

The freighter actually noticed us. He came up to us and shot us a line and eventually pulled us alongside. With our boat bobbing first twenty feet down and then twenty feet up beside the huge freighter my wife and boys clambered up the side to safety.

I, a victim of too much reading to the very end, remained aboard, determined to stay and jury-rig a new rudder and sail on to Mallorca single-handed, completing an epic journey.

My wife is made of sterner stuff. She immediately told the crew: 'Tell the captain to get my husband off that boat!! Cut it loose! Sink it!'

Eventually a crew member shouted down to me: 'The Captain wants to speak to you on the bridge.'

So I grabbed a bottle of scotch as a thank you present and climbed up aboard the freighter and proceeded to the bridge. The freighter was British and the captain a Scot, but I think the sight of the owner of a disabled sailboat climbing up to safety carrying only a bottle of scotch may have given me an image problem. In any case, the Scottish captain knew a jerk when he saw one, or in any case a not particularly competent sailor. He told me the storm had swept us almost two hundred miles south and we were then only fifty miles from a deserted, rockbound Algerian coast. His freighter was a hundred and fifty miles south of its usual route because of the storm, and the winds were forecast to continue. Don't get back on the boat, he suggested.

To ease, perhaps, my romantic vision of a captain never deserting his ship, he added that he would make an effort to salvage the catamaran by towing it behind the freighter. He didn't think it would work but he would try. I stayed aboard the freighter.

I lived.

The catamaran and my lifetime savings capsized and the boat cut loose within the first twenty minutes of the tow, but I and my family lived.

But how many tiny, unpredictable, unfathomable events had to occur first to put us into such danger and then to permit us to survive it? Had our outboard broken down at any time in the first five weeks of our cruising we would have had it repaired and been delayed. We would have had to wait for the *mistral* to blow itself out or, if we'd left at the same time as we actually did, we'd have had a working engine that would have permitted us to make progress despite the storm.

Or that's one theory. For Chance is never simple. If our engine hadn't broken down we would have tried to motor into the waves rather than rig a sea anchor; we would have tried to motor on towards Mallorca. And with my infinite capacity for making mistakes it's quite possible that if the engine hadn't broken down I'd have manoeuvred our boats so that it *did* get capsized. If our motor had broken down along the coast of Italy earlier, I might have been struck and killed by a car rushing to a marine repair shop.

We lived. While our friends and my English publisher awaited us on Mallorca baffled by what had happened to us (the publisher wondering if having a posthumous author would help or hurt soles), the freighter carried us to O Porto, Portugal, and we lived.

And yet I'm sure over those three days of the storm there were dozens of rogue waves, 20 per cent bigger than its neighbours, that could have capsized us, but we were in the wrong place at the wrong time. They missed us. And that freighter. How many decisions that Scottish captain must have made that led to his ship being a hundred and fifty miles south of his normal intended route. Had he not been close enough to us, and in daylight, and had we not had flares aboard (from the previous owner; I would never have bought any), and had he not been a decent man reluctant to ignore a distress signal, then . . .

Life, it might be said, is all 'if's. But not the ifs of cliché. The person who says if only '*w*' had happened then I would have been '*x*', is spouting nonsense, for '*x*' is for ever and always an unknown. I can never say, 'If only my engine hadn't broken down . . .' since I know full well that I might have gotten us into even worse trouble with a working engine.

Life is all ifs. And 99.44 per cent of these ifs are invisible.

Life is accident, and the wise man learns to love what is because he knows that what he thinks might be better is probably an illusion or a shortcut to hell.

Life is accident and, as they say in Hollywood, nobody knows nothing about anything. Chance will save us one day and kill us the next. Blessed be the name of Chance.

from *My Life at Sea* by George Cockcroft

```
Death is lurking outside your front
door. Go to the front door, open it,
look Death right in the eyes. Give
Death the middle finger.
```

DEATH AND A LIFE INSURANCE SALESMAN

One day a student asked Whim whether Death was something to fear.

'Well, not fear exactly,' said Whim.

'Well, what then?' persisted the student.

Whim frowned for a long moment and then suddenly broke into a big smile.

'You should treat Death like a life insurance salesman: He's not something something to fear, just something to be avoided.'

A journalist once asked Luke what he would like to see as his epitaph.

Epitaph? That implies death, doesn't it?

But an epitaph; we like that literary form, it's short.

On the other hand, it's permanent. It's chiselled in stone, and we're not too comfortable with anything that can't be changed.

So on our tombstone, which we won't have, there will be a six-sided die and on each face, instead of a number of dots, will be an epitaph.

1. We were afraid this would happen some time.
2. Here Lieth George Luke Rhinecock: He Always Did Lieth.
3. When we were living, we were die-ing.
4. The Lord Chance giveth, the Lord Chance taketh away.
5. Wow! A new experience!
6. Here lieth Luke George Cockhart: May He Rest in Pieces.

OPTIONS

Cast a die.

① You are dying. That's right. You're dying.

Of course, you're in good company. Everyone and everything else is dying too. The graveyards of the universe are always full and always expanding. And not a single creature has ever existed who hasn't decided to make the graveyard his permanent home.

You're dying.

Big deal.

② You are alive. That's right. You're alive.

Of course, you're in good company. Everyone and everything else is alive too. The nurseries of the world are always full and always expanding. And nothing has ever existed that hasn't made it to the nursery.

You're alive.

Big deal.

③ You are going to die. Write a few epitaphs for your tombstone, something you'd like to see there after you're gone. Try to create six but, in any case, then cast a die to determine which one will make it.

How do you feel about it?

④ You are dying. Prepare a new will. Thank everyone you can think of for all the nice things life has given you. Forgive all your enemies all of their worst sins. Write the IRS or Inland Revenue a thank-you note; apologize for the times you cheated. Tell all your children or grandchildren or siblings or parents or spouses, how proud of them you are, how wonderful they are. Include all of this in your will (except the letter to the Inland Revenue). Apologize to each of the legatees for not leaving them more. Insist on the cheapest possible funeral and burial service.

There. You did it.

Isn't life wonderful?

⑤ Let a die choose some important individual (mother, spouse, son, yourself, etc.) and then spend ten minutes eulogizing this individual as if he or she had just died. Do this sincerely and with feeling.

⑥ You are dying. What is the one thing that you have wanted to do over the years that you've not yet got around to doing?

Do it. Do it immediately, no matter how much it costs or how long it takes or how silly or impractical it may appear to others. Do it.

WHIM MEETS DEATH

'I met Death once,' Whim said casually.

'You did!' exclaimed several of the disciples. 'Tell us about it.'

'It was during a hurricane in the Caribbean. I was alone aboard a thirty-foot sailboat whose lifeboat had been swept away, rudder broken, engine flooded, mast toppled, sails ripped away, bottom leaking about a bathtub full a minute, the pumps not functioning and the wind and waves were pushing us towards an uninhabited reef two miles away. To top it all I was seasick.'

'What happened?'

'All of a sudden, Death appeared in the cockpit beside me. He was a big guy about six foot two, a hundred and ninety pounds with curly red hair and a tattoo on his right arm. I recognized him immediately. "It's about time you got here," I said. "What the hell took you so long?"

'For a while he looked at the wrecked boat and the huge seas and my vomit washing back and forth in the cockpit and finally, looking directly at exhausted, miserable me, he said: "With your luck you didn't expect me to get here when you wanted, did you?"

'"Good point," I said, vomiting neatly into a wave that rolled past under my nose. "But now that you're here, for Christ's sake hurry up and get to work."

'"Shit, no," he replied. "I was just sent here to get a small flying fish that died from water pollution here in the cockpit of your boat."

'"But – " I began.

'"When I come for a person," Death went on, "he can't see me." And He began climbing on to the almost submerged cabin top.

'"Hey!" I shouted, feeling worse than ever. "Don't leave me!"

'"Sorry. I got a million things to do today." And as Death began fading off, fish in hand, into the roaring storm, He added: "See you later."'

After Whim had ceased his narration all of the disciples sat quietly in respectful silence. Only after several minutes was it broken.

'Did you live?' asked the youngest disciple.

from *Adventures of Whim*

Death is the tap on the shoulder which makes you wish you'd eaten that ice-cream cone when you had the chance.

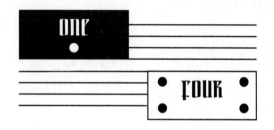

PURPOSE AND SUCCESS

The king glows on his throne.
Lovers lick
At his limbs. Slaves roll bowls
Of red wine across marble halls
Where worshippers pour forth gold
From old hoards.
All is well. Even for the insects
Who banquet even now
On the legs of the chair.

The race is not to the swift, or the battle to the strong, neither yet bread to the wise nor yet riches to men of understanding, nor yet favour to men of skills, but time and Chance rolls them all.

– from ECCLESIASTES (REVISED VERSION)

We sit in front of TV sets, we read the sacred tables of the baseball statistics, stock quotations, bank balances; we check the grades of children, loved ones, self; we measure salaries, complexions, grades, cars, penises, bosoms, square footage, frontage, savings, neighbourhoods, nations – everything but vitality, which can't be measured and so is ignored. We measure and triumph or measure and fear; in either case we lose, for both are on a scale which is recognized as valid by only a few. Our triumphs and our tragedies are both mountains of the moment, to be turned at the toll of another hour to ant-hills in the dust.

WHIM AND SUCCESS

'Why are you always cheerful, Whim?'

'Always cheerful!!?' Whim replied. 'I should hope not. Whatever gave you that idea?"

'When something goes wrong, you alone of all of us seem undisturbed and gay.'

'Oh, well,' replied Whim. 'That's nothing. It's easy for me to be cheerful when I fail, but you should see me when I'm successful – then I'm terrible.'

'How?'

'I'm anxious, ambitious, grasping: a real human.'

'But with success you should be happy!'

'Nope. Success feeds the old ego in me. Whenever I need cheering up, just slip me a good failure.'

'Well, you must be enjoying an unusual string of failures. To me you always seem cheerful.'

'Yeah,' replied Whim. 'Things are going pretty badly, thank God, but with my luck I'll win a lottery and soon be miserable.'

We are brought up to believe that it is important to have purpose in our life. Goals. It is purpose that permits man to rise above the other beasts. Because of purpose, men create great civilizations, advance knowledge, become better and better and smarter and smarter. Or so the story goes.

And we are equally brought up to achieve success and avoid failure. It is the twin values of purpose of success, and the resulting fear of failure, that keep us huddled in the cave of self: a group of behaviour patterns we are successful at and have no intention of risking failure by abandoning.

But there are two quite different meanings of failure. When a child tries to solve a maze he knows when he fails and when he succeeds: no adult need tell him. A child building a house of blocks knows when the collapse of the house means failure (he wanted to build it higher) and when it means success (he wanted it to fall). Success and failure here mean simply the satisfaction and frustration of desire. It is real and important; the child doesn't have to be rewarded or punished by society in order to prefer success to failure.

But there is a second, much more important meaning of failure in the eyes of a child: failure is failure to please an adult; success is success in pleasing an adult. If the mother chastizes the child for the collapse of the house he has built, even if it was his intention to make it collapse, then the mother is calling what he at first experienced as a success – the knocking down of the house – as a failure: mum says I was bad.

A growing child enjoys the success of learning, but he has to be taught that getting stars and 'A's is a also a success. A child running against another child enjoys winning, and the loser enjoys the running too. But after the adults work on them for a few years it is not the race that is fun but receiving the trophy, and the loser suffers a large failure that was, as a child, a minor failure. Competition is enjoyable. Succeeding in competition (success) is enjoyable. But there is nothing intrinsically enjoyable about receiving a trophy. This is an adult version of success unrelated to the competition itself.

Children, it has been written: 'Rarely trouble to keep scores, little significance is attached to who wins or loses, they do not require the stimulus of prizes, it does not seem to worry them if the game is not finished. Indeed, children like games in which there is a sizeable element of luck, so that individual abilities cannot be directly compared. They like games which restart automatically, so that everybody is given a new chance.' How unlike the adult world of competition we have created.

But what if before every game the dice were thrown to determine whether the winner or loser 'wins' the trophy, with fifty–fifty the odds for each? Thus half the time the 'loser' of the game would end up being congratulated for having been lucky enough to have 'lost' the contest and thus won the trophy. The one who won would be consoled for playing so well.

'But!!!' shout our American (and western) souls. As adults we feel the loser of the game would still feel badly and the winner still exalt. Children, though, would understand: they want luck to be a factor; they attach 'little significance' to who wins or loses, until we poison them with our notions of success.

'Don't knock success,' Whim said firmly. 'Some of my best friends are successes.'

'But it's *you*, Whim, who keep warning us about the hollowness and misery of success.'

'I didn't know you knew my friends.'

The fool says in his heart, There is no Chance. They are corrupt, they do reasonable abominable deeds, there is none that does random good.

Chance looks down from heaven upon the children of men, to see if there are any that act randomly, that seek after Chance.

They have all gone astray, they are all alike corrupted by purpose, there is none that does everything randomly, no, not one. FROM **Book of Psalms (Revised Version)**

✳ Success in the sense of achieving what we are trying to achieve is basic to human happiness. Success in the sense of pleasing others is basic to human unhappiness.

A failure to achieve something we have attempted is disappointing, no more. We move on to something else. But failure to achieve something in the eyes of others represents a permanent black mark on our 'self' – we are forced to carry it with us as a stigma as long as we are attached to how people view us.

So too with competition. Children race each other to see who will be first in the water. 'Last one in's a rotten egg.' Someone wins, someone is last. But ten minutes later not a single child remembers who was first and who was last.

Adults race fifteen hundred metres. The winner noses out the second-place finisher by three one-hundredths of a second. He is awarded a gold medal. The second-place finisher, bitterly disappointed, accepts his silver medal with a hangdog look. Madness. Utter madness.

Two soccer teams, the two best in the world, battle it out for two halves and end up tied. They play two sudden-death overtimes, but still are tied. They have a five-shot shootout. One goalie guesses right once, and the other doesn't, and one team is proclaimed the winner and the other the loser. One team returns to its home country heroes; the 'losing' team returns home in shame. Madness. Both teams won in every meaningful sense of the word and both should have been carried off the field on the shoulders of fans. Both should have been treated as heroes.

Rarely in any sport these days do the winners and losers congratulate and honour each other as if they genuinely appreciated how the skill and effort of the other contributed to their own skill and effort. The two runners who ran the fifteen-hundred-metre race and ended up only a millisecond apart should have embraced and enthused to each other about how well they had both run, how wonderful it was that they forced each other to put even more effort into the last twenty metres to the finish line.

Yet, the winner undoubtedly raised his arms in triumph and the one who finished second slunk off abjectly as if he had bad acne and body odour.

Competition could be experienced as a form of lovemaking. Each competitor-partner needs the other for his physical and emotional pleasure and triumph. Together they play and the result is marvellous for both.

Imagine if we treated lovemaking as we do athletic competition: first one to climax wins and gets the trophy. So the lover who climaxes second, or worse, doesn't finish, is supposed to feel inferior, a loser. Imagine what that would do to the quality of lovemaking.

From children to men we come to cage ourselves in patterns and selves to avoid facing new problems and possible failure. After a while we become bored because there are no new problems, no new challenges that might involve failure. Such is life under the fear of failure.

Fail! Lose! Be bad! Play, risk, dare.

We humans need purposes. Dice-living should not be seen as anti-purpose but as a device for expanding our purposes out of the narrow range most of us end up being limited to. And dicing is also a device to take the focus away from some ultimate goal and on to the process of doing. Man's joy in life is doing things, not in anticipating his successes. We list six fresh options or purposes, and the die chooses one. The focus should immediately shift to *doing* what the die has chosen and not on some ultimate goal that may result from doing. In fact, the very way we list options may determine whether or not we successfully begin to change. If we list the option as 'I will lose twenty pounds within two months', then we are focusing on goal rather than on process. If we list instead 'I will exercise at least thirty minutes a day and conscientiously eat less at each meal for two months', then we are focusing on the present and not on any ultimate goal. It may be we will lose twenty pounds. Perhaps only six. In either case we will have enjoyed the two months (or suffered less from them) than we would have if our focus was only on the ultimate goal.

Man who make waves most likely to sink boat

WHO'S UP, WHO'S DOWN

Whim once saw two boys rocking up and down on a seesaw. First one boy went zooming upwards and then the other.

'Which one of you is higher?' yelled Whim, smiling.

'I am!' cried one boy.

'I am!' cried the other, a moment later.

'That's the way it goes,' said Whim to himself.

'And which one is lower?' he yelled to the boys.

'He is,' cried the first boy.

'He is!' cried the second, a moment later.

'That's the way it goes,' thought Whim.

AN ADVANTAGE OF FAILURE

One autumn, several members of Whim's school left for one reason or another and many more began discussing leaving. One of the oldest disciples came to Whim distressed by these developments.

'In four years,' he explained to Whim, 'we've never had so many members leave, never had so many talking of leaving. If you don't act decisively there will be fewer people here in a month than there were a year ago.'

'I see,' said Whim, slowly shaking his head and frowning. 'But then,' he went on, suddenly brightening, 'if a lot of people leave, each of us remaining will get a larger portion of brownies on Fridays.'

WHIM REACTS TO SUCCESS

'What's the matter, Whim? I've never seen you look so depressed.'

'I'm depressed.'

'But why? Never has your following been greater. Thousands are coming each week from all over the world to be near us. Everyone is writing about us. How can you be depressed?'

'It's easy, believe me.'

'But why?'

'Never has my following been greater. Thousands come each week to be near us. Everyone writes about us.'

'That's what I said.'

'That's why I'm depressed.'

'But – '

'If I had something that I could say just once that would summarize my message or my methods, I'd say it and shut up, but I can help a person change only by seeing where he is, and then placing a verbal or behavioural firecracker under his chair so he'll wake up and move. But thousands! Most of them hear only a lot of noise a long ways off and settle more contentedly into their chairs, convinced that the distant noise is somehow helping them towards Enlightenment.

'And to be written about! Better a millennium or two of obscurity than to be written about by the mass media.'

'But then what are you going to do about it?'

'I'm already doing it, and with all my might too.'

'What are you doing?'

'Feeling depressed.'

'But it's against your principles to be depressed.'

'No,' said Whim. 'It's against my principles to have principles.'

'But it's *wrong* to be depressed.'

'No, it's depressed to be depressed.'

Chief Little Pebble had a son who grew up to be chief too. We named him Chief Medium Size Pebble because he not as great a chief as Little Pebble.

Who was your greatest leader?

Greatest leader is Grain-of-Sand. Him we barely notice.

Whim was once asked why he so often laughed when he lost a game.

'Simple,' said Whim. 'At that point I've got nothing to lose.'

OPTIONS

First consider some action that you hope and believe will lead to success in some area of your life – business, school, relationships, whatever. Then cast a die to see below what comment Chance makes.

① Yes. Absolutely yes. This will work. At least for a while. An hour say. Or a year. So go with it. Success. Just remember that one man's success is another man's snare.
   And they're both you.

② Nope. No go. You've chosen the wrong path. What you should do is list a few other ways you might tackle the problem, write them out as options and let a die choose the one to try. Whatever the die chooses can't be any worse than the one you were just now thinking about.

③ You are crossing the Great Water and it is the crossing that is the triumph. The arrival itself will only mark a new beginning. With luck you may never arrive.

④ Have you chosen a goal or a process? Is the act you've chosen one that is good for its own sake or is it only good depending on the result? Are you running this particular race for a winner's trophy or for the joy of it? We speak of a means to an end but if the means isn't fulfilling in itself then it's doubtful the end will ever be reached.

⑤ Ooops! Everything is going to go wrong. Your plan will not work out as you expect. However, look at any setback as the Gods' way of showing you new opportunities.

⑥ The Gods have blown it: you've just won the jackpot. Advance to Go. You have inherited four hotels on Park Lane. Everything you do works out. Anything you do works out. You can do no wrong, even when you do wrong.

WHIM'S PARABLE OF THE THREE WISE MEN

Three wise men lived in a tree.

The first guy, who lived at the very top, watched other people walking on the earth below and said: 'See the lowly people below us; they will never achieve the heights I've achieved.'

The second guy, who lived about halfway up the tree, said: 'Yes, we are certainly fortunate in being above the herd.'

The third wise man, who lived on the branch closest to the ground, frowned and said: 'I'm sick of eating leaves, bark, and insects; the smell of the fruit trees and flowers is good.'

'From where I am I can see the stars,' went on the guy highest up, 'and watch the highest-flying birds. The air is always clean and I of all men am closest to the sun and light.'

The second guy said: 'That's true, and we're lucky we're above the herd.'

But the lowest wise man only said: 'I'm hungry.'

'I have computed the exact position that all stars will have for a trillion years into the future,' said the first guy. 'I know the exact date when each species of bird will move south or return north. I can predict the weather days in advance.'

'Right,' said the second guy. 'The ignorant down below know nothing of the stars, the birds, the weather. They only sleep, eat and reproduce. They are herd. How lucky we are to be above the herd.'

The guy on the lowest branch only said: 'I'm hungry and I want to get laid.'

The first wise man, observing a distant star, fell out of the tree and split his skull; the second guy, while predicting that the storm would pass by in just three days, died of pneumonia. The third guy climbed down out of the tree and ate and got laid and lived happily ever after.

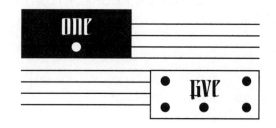

DISASTER

Your sailboat has lost its mast, its rudder
Gone, motor broken, a hole
In the hull, the pumps clogged, liferaft
Smashed, the captain
Drunk. A rocky reef
Lies a few miles to leeward. A hurricane
Approaches.

It furthers one to consider travelling
By land.

Disaster. All things tumble together to create
Total and complete failure
In all you aspire to do.
Nothing can be achieved. Perseverance
Brings more failure.

It furthers one not to cross the Great Water
Unless
One is willing to sink.

Disaster is a symptom. It implies you may have made a few mistakes. The Gods often use disaster as a Nudge. A Nudge from the Gods is a hint that maybe you ought to begin doing things differently.

Disaster is only opportunity wearing a mask. For the Man of Chance disaster is not something to be feared but rather something to be welcomed like a new friend. Failure to reach what one grasps for may be seen as success in not being snared by the desired goal. A great sage once said: 'When I fail, I remain empty. When I succeed, I'm stuck with another ego hang-up.'

WHIM COMMENTS: Still, a little success now and then might be worth a hang-up or two.

There are two kinds of disasters: the one that all men see and the one that only you see.

A flood sweeps away your house. You're in a car crash and have six broken bones. Your mother dies. You're fired from the job you've held for six years.

A birthday cake didn't rise. A child scraped a knee. You have a cold. Your team lost. The stock market fell five hundred points.

One man's disaster may be another's yawn. Even the flood sweeping away the ancestral home. Imagine Socrates and the Yaqui sorcerer Don Juan and Saint Francis of Assisi standing side by side as a flood sweeps away each of their homes. I distinctly see three yawns.

> WHEN THE EARTHQUAKE SWALLOWS UP HIS HOUSE, HIS BUSINESS, AND HIS LIFETIME SAVINGS, THE WISE MAN USES HIS LOT ON THE EDGE OF THE ABYSS TO SELL TICKETS TO TOURISTS.

'What do you think of storms?' Whim asked the old sailor.

'They scare the shit out of me,' the old sailor replied.

'Then why do you always go out on new voyages?' asked Whim.

'To be free of shit,' the old sailor replied.

Disaster kills the past. Home destroyed, loved-one lost, savings wiped away, long-time job erased. You are suddenly free from a part of your past. Disaster? So we usually experience it.

But we are fools. Disaster is the Gods' way of waking us up to the present and freeing us from the past. Disaster is the Gods' way of trying to free us from our attachments. Can't live without your wonderful home? Boom! A gas explosion. Behold, you are living without your wonderful home.

Can't live without your job? You're fired!!! Behold, the universe still exists. Moonlight still reflects off puddles.

Can't live without your son or daughter or spouse? Bang! Life goes on. Grieve, cry, tear your hair, eat sand, destroy furniture, mope. The sun keeps rising, the moon still sets.

If we think of the wisest humans who have existed we will be thinking of people who are left untouched by disaster. A Zen student when enlightened suddenly found everything 'Empty and Marvellous'. In this context the two words are almost synonymous. It is because a person when enlightened is empty that life is marvellous. There is nothing to fear, nothing to lose, nowhere to go, no one to be. So how can there be disaster?

Disasters, unless they attack something we are personally attached to, are fun. We love hurricanes. They provide us with skies and winds and waves we've never experienced before. Seeing a house smashed into kindling by a surge of surf is a wonderful thing – unless it's our house. A raging fire, the zzzzt of lightning and roar of thunder, the mighty elephantine flow of a flooded river, the black dance of a tornado, two speeding vehicles crashing together head on – what wonderful creations the Gods come up with! Seen in themselves they may be things of exceptional beauty. It is only when our fulness gets in the way – our attachments, our egos, our fears – that the beauty goes unseen.

One man's disaster may be another man's miracle. The fire that 'destroys' one family may 'liberate' another.

There is a saying that there are two happy moments in a sailor's life: the day he buys his boat and the day he sells it.

So we have this paradox, if the sailor's boat sinks on the very first day of his ownership it is a disaster. If it sinks in exactly the same way five years later and is insured, it is a gift of the Gods. Same boat, same event: one a cause of lamentation, the other a cause of jubilation. The difference: at first he is attached to his boat; when he has ceased to be attached, then no disaster is possible.

So too with all things.

'The boat is sinking, Whim! The boat is sinking!'

'The boat is always sinking,' replied Whim.

'But what should we do?! What should we do!?'

'Sail it around the world.'

True disasters are rarely recognized when they arrive. You win ten million dollars in the lottery. The man you love has just proposed to you. Your daughter has just won a beauty contest. You have just got a promotion. Some beautiful woman is climbing into bed with you.

Years later you may look back and say to yourself, *that's* when all the trouble began, with that apparent triumph.

Of course, in fact there are no disasters, true or false, unless you create them by your attitude. You got the promotion and that led you into conflict with your boss and that led to your later being transferred to Siberia which led to your wife leaving you for a man who lived in a warmer climate and . . . etc.

But neither Siberia nor a leaving wife are necessarily disasters. After all, didn't you notice that knockout Russian translator?

WHEN THE SKY FALLS AND SOMEHOW
MANAGES TO STRIKE ONLY YOU, IT'S TIME
TO RECONSIDER YOUR POSITION.

Our reaction to a disaster is dictated by what society expects of us. If we can imagine a crowd of people standing on high ground watching a rampaging river sweeping their homes away, we can only see grief and sadness and fear. And if Socrates and Don Juan and Saint Francis were standing among them, each would stand out like a sore thumb. Their serenity in the face of the disaster would be a royal pain in the arse to the others. Wailing is expected to be universal in such a situation and those who don't wail may well get themselves stoned.

And yet if we do not escape from the overwhelming force of society's pressures then we can only suffer from a disaster. Society expects us to suffer; ergo we suffer. The first step we might take to escape from the expected into the possible is to sit down and see what options are actually available to us. If our house has been lost then do we want to rebuild? Do we want to buy another house in the same town? Do we want to use this opportunity (disaster) to move somewhere else in the world? Do we want to use this opportunity (disaster) to look for a new job? It is likely that just the act of listing the possibilities will break through the depression and despair that is 'natural' to the situation.

'Shit,' says the man. 'Looks like we'll have to move to Hawaii' – something he's dreamed of doing for years.

When the Deluge has covered everything
he owns, the wise man learns to fish.

LUKE AND DISASTER

One day when Luke was being chased by two FBI men with .45s, he came to a cliff and leapt off, just catching the root of a wild vine twenty yards below the ridge and dangling there. Looking down, he saw fifty feet below him six policemen with shotguns, mace and tear-gas canisters, and two armoured cars. Just above him he saw two mice beginning to gnaw away the vine to which he clung. Then he noticed just in front of him a cluster of luscious ripe strawberries.

'Ah,' he said. 'A new option.'

from The Dice Man

WHIM, THE PRIEST, AND THE PILOT

One day Whim was flying in an airplane between the East and West when the Pilot announced that due to 'special circumstances' they would land first in Rome before proceeding on to their original destination.

The Priest sitting next to Whim said pleasantly: 'We are all in the hands of God.'

'That's very good, Father,' said Whim. 'I wonder if He'll drop us.'

A little later one of the four jet engines burst into white flame, relaxed into heavy black smoke and finally became silent. The Pilot then announced that due to 'technical difficulties' he had decided to cease employing the outside starboard engine. After the few isolated screams had died away the Priest turned again to Whim.

'Being in the hands of God,' he said, 'we have nothing to fear. He watches over all that happens here on earth. Not a sparrow can fall that He does not notice.'

'That's very good, Father,' said Whim, again smiling enthusiastically. 'And with us being so big, when we fall He'll be especially sure to see us.'

'Er . . . yes,' said the Priest, as Whim returned to his comic book.

A little later the other outside engine burst into flame, subsided into black smoke and slid into silence. The Pilot then announced that 'to get a better balance' he had decided not to 'employ' the outside port engine any longer, and that to 'facilitate the taking of photographs' he would initiate the plane's descent towards Rome two hours earlier than planned.

After the few hysterical people clambering for parachutes had been silenced, the Priest turned a third time to Whim.

'Because God sees even the smallest sparrow,' he said, 'and because He has a Divine Plan and Purpose for all that happens, I rest assured in my heart that whatever happens, happens for the best.'

'That's very good,' said Whim, smiling happily. 'So whether we stop over in Rome or our plane does some tobogganing in the Alps, God's Master-book has the page already written.'

'That's correct,' said the Priest.

'Ever tempted to peek?' asked Whim.

At that moment a third of the four engines flamed, smoked, and silenced. The Pilot announced that 'to conserve fuel' he had ceased to 'employ' engine number three, and that he would 'probably' soon be landing the huge 747 in a small abandoned tennis court in the Austrian Alps.

When the screams had subsided and the noise had become the cacophony of prayers in a dozen languages, the Priest turned yet again to Whim, who was still reading his comic book.

'I am calm,' said the Priest, 'because I know I am but a pawn in the Divine Game-plan and that He works everything for the best, for me and for all of us. But you, why are you not more . . . concerned?'

'Ah,' replied Whim, 'I've noticed that when a plane crashes it crashes, and when it doesn't it doesn't. I figure trying to steer the plane from here doesn't work too well.'

'But what do you think will happen?'

'I don't have the slightest idea what's going to happen next: all is accidental in the most accidental of worlds.'

'But that's horrible!' cried the Priest. 'You have no hope.'

'None at all,' replied Whim, smiling. 'No hope, and no fear. You're calm because you see the future predetermined for the best, I'm calm because I don't see the future at all, and the Pilot's calm because he's crazy. As far as I can see these are the three paths to happiness.'

At this point the last of the four engines burst into flame, spat smoke and subsided, and the Pilot reminded everyone of the 'no smoking regulations in Sections thirty-one to fifty'.

As the plane glided serenely towards some unknown and possibly violent fate in the Alps, the Priest shouted loudly above the sound of muttered prayers: 'We are all in the hands of God!'

And Our Beloved Whim shouted even Louder: 'Look, Ma, no Hands!'

– from *Adventures of Whim*

The Die is our refuge and strength,
A very present help in trouble.
Therefore will we not fear, though the earth be removed,
And though the mountains be carried into the midst of the sea;
Though the waters thereof roar and be troubled,
Though the mountains shake with the swelling thereof,

I had rather be a doorkeeper in the house of my Die
Than to dwell in the tents of consistency.
For the Lord Chance is a sun and shield:
Chance will give grace and glory and folly and shame:
Nothing will be withheld from them that walk randomly.
O Lord of Chance, My Die,
Blessed is the man that trusteth in Thee.
                        – *from* Book of Psalms (Revised Version)

OPTIONS

Cast a die. Do it.

① Consider something that you feel would be a personal disaster. Consider the consequences of this disaster. Consider especially all the good things that might follow
from the 'disaster'. Consider all the ways your life might improve if only this disaster would occur. There is not a single event in the history of the universe that does
not bring with it blessings as well as griefs.

② Look back at your young life. Think of some event which, at the time it occurred,
you thought was a disaster – some destroyed relationship, a death, some accident,
some failure. Try to imagine what your life might have been like without that disaster. Can you imagine scenarios in which your life might have been *worse* if you
had not suffered your 'disaster'? Be fair. Isn't it just possible that the disaster was a
blessing in disguise?

③ Look back at your life. Think of one of your greatest 'successes' – some personal triumph that at the time or even now you consider to be one of your greatest successes
– an athletic achievement, a financial coup, a business triumph, a personal relationship win. Can you imagine scenarios in which your life may actually have been
made *worse* by this triumph, of ways in which the triumph may have led your life
down a path that might not have been right for you?

④ Give two hundred dollars to some undeserving beggar on the street, one you are convinced will use the money only to continue personal disintegration. Tell the person you hope he will use the money unwisely.

A total waste? A small disaster? Experience it.

⑤ Tell off your boss, or a parent, or a spouse: someone you've wanted to tell off for some time but never dared do so. If you really let it all hang out you may achieve a small disaster.

But is it a disaster?

⑥ Next time a fire, flood, hurricane, tornado, blizzard or some other large-scale disaster hits your area, go to it, get near it, help the victims if you can, and observe how the people are responding to the disaster. Observe your own feelings too.

THE ADVANTAGE OF BEING SMALL AND SLOW

One day the smallest and youngest of the boys at Whim's school came up to him and complained: 'Why am I so small and so young? All the other kids are able to push me around whenever they want. What can I do?'

'Practise your running,' suggested Whim cheerfully. 'That's what I did when I was a kid like you.'

After a few days the little boy came up to Whim a second time.

'But I'm slow too. No matter how hard I practise I'm slow.'

Whim asked him to run across the room, and when the boy had returned Whim said: 'You're right, you're slower than a paraplegic turtle. Aren't you glad you're so lucky?'

'Lucky! How am I lucky?'

'Now you'll have to develop brains.'

A life without disaster is a life without life.

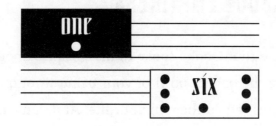

E M P T I N E S S

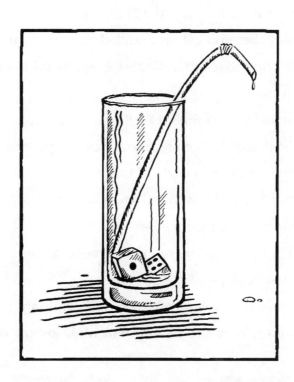

OBOKO SPEAKS ABOUT EMPTINESS

And it came to pass that Oboko spoke to his disciples about emptiness.

'You must prepare the golden bowl of your being through emptying it of all the sludge that has settled there in your life. And you can't separate the sludge of hate from that of moral striving, the sludge of lust from that of religious longing. To cleanse the bowl, all must be removed: then and only then will the original bowl be able to receive things purely for what they are.'

'But what, Master Oboko, do we gain by emptiness?'

'Only in your present filled state can you ask such a question. Being filled and wanting to be yet more filled, you wish to know what you can gain, with what more desirable filling you will be filled.

'Let me answer only that you will be emptied of tension, anxiety, irrational fears, emptied of compulsive, unfulfillable desires. What will exist in the emptiness no man can say.'

'Does an empty man climb a mountain?' asked a disciple.

'Yes. And when he descends, the mountain has disappeared.'

'Does an empty man write a book?'

'Yes, and when it is finished it is found there is no author.'

'Can an empty man love someone else?'

'Oh, yes, and when he is filled with another, behold, the other is empty.'

'Does the empty man compete?'

'Yes. The empty man runs the race to win and, winning, returns empty-handed. The empty man runs the race to win and, losing, returns complete. The empty man runs the race to run, and, running, always wins. The empty man never fails because there is no one there to lose or win.

'You must become as a circle. Each point on the circle is always perfect. A circle begins where it ends and ends where it begins. And whenever it begins it is already at the end, and when you have travelled a certain distance you are still at a beginning. And even as a circle is complete, it remains . . . empty.'

'So if we study hard with you . . .' began a disciple hopefully.

'If you study hard and faithfully with me then when you're finished I guarantee you'll have absolutely nothing.'

For a long moment everyone was silent. Then the most serious disciple piped up.

'Oh, how empty you are, Beloved Oboko,' he said.

'Drop that nonsense,' Oboko snapped back. 'I'm half-filled just listening to you.'

The mind is a wonderful instrument, but the trouble is it wants to hog the whole show. It always wants to butt in. It always wants us to remember the past or worry about the future. We can't take a walk beside a mountain stream without the mind trying to remind us of appointments, of problems past and future, of what people will think. The mind is the cellular phone that keeps ringing when we are in the middle of life. The mind is often so noisy we can't even hear the gurgle of the mountain stream, and it keeps throwing at us so many images of the past or future that we can't see the ferns or mossy stones. It's a wonder we don't fall in.

Zen masters encourage their disciples to empty their minds.

'I did it, Master! I did it! I emptied my mind!'

'Good,' comments the Master. 'Now throw it out.'

Unfortunately, a human being has as much chance of emptying his mind as New York City or London has of getting rid of all its garbage. But at least in the city most people recognize the garbage when they see it. In our lives, our minds are spilling out garbage into our consciousness at almost every moment and we don't even recognize it.

It is the great paradox of our existence that our greatest evolutionary develop-ment is our brain, our mind. And almost all of a human being's happiest moments involve the mind going on vacation.

We are making love to our beloved. The more magnificent the lovemaking the fewer thoughts manage to stagger into our minds. If anyone is thinking anything dur-ing an orgasm he or she isn't having an orgasm.

An athlete is performing at the height of his powers. Is he thinking should I cut left now, or cut right? If he does think that, he just got tackled. An athlete performing at the height of his powers is thoughtless, is on automatic, and the greater he plays, the more marvellous he feels, the less he is thinking.

A writer who is thinking and planning isn't writing. When a writer is writing her best stuff she doesn't have a thought in her head: the words pour out without thought. Thinking comes in only when the flow stops.

All ecstasy is thoughtless. All ecstasy involves an empty mind. A single thought kills ecstasy.

The mind is a wonderful instrument and we're happy we have one. But we're even happier on those few occasions when we don't have one.

To act from Whim or whim is to act *ex nihilo*, to create from nothing. God clearly created the universe from Whim since to have created it from purpose would imply that God *lacked* something, needed something that would be partly fulfilled by his act of creation. God needed nothing. God needs nothing. God acts always at whim.

We, being humans, seldom act at whim. We, being unfulfilled, are ever purpose-ful, act always out of the fulness of our past and the fulness of our future. Never empty, we can never act *ex nihilo*, never act out of whim, never act as God.

An empty man doesn't care if he's seen as empty or filled, since to consider one-self empty is to be instantly filled with emptiness.

As soon as one has any sense of being always one certain self – even being always empty or random – one is stuck with an ideal image which one will feel forced to live up to. 'There's no reason at all to use the dice in one's life; it's just a game one may play like any other.' As Luke himself once said: 'Dice-living is a lot of useless crap.' We make such statements in order to kill the tendency to think that die-ing is important, that being a child of chance is something superior to being a normal person. As soon as the idea of the importance of becoming a random multiple man possesses someone, exactly then is he possessed with a confining and destructive illusion. Above all else, a child of chance must be free to be a normal, serious, consistent, stuck, single-selfed human; otherwise he is not free to be not such a person.

> *The wild goose has no intention of leaving traces*
> *The water no thought of engulfing reflections,*
> *The dice make no dent in the table.*
> *Why do you press against the world?*

If you think you are important, then most of the world and hence most of life will seem unimportant. If you let go of your self-importance, and see yourself as no more than a flea on the backside of a flea, then, paradoxically, everything is more important than you and thus everything in life is important. A cat is suddenly a miracle, a weed a giant tree. Once you cease to evaluate importance, the universe is filled with friends and miracles instead of filled with trivialities.

Emptiness is the ideal. Thoreau was horrified at seeing how human beings carried around with them so many things. Simplify, simplify, simplify, he urged, and then began to clutter up his mind with an endless collection of facts.

To empty the mind is difficult because it is personal. One man's garbage might be another's treasure.

Emptying the mind is like trying to empty our house of unnecessary material possessions. As soon as we look at an object to consider throwing it out, it suddenly takes on added value. Not *that* vase, we think. Not *that* book.

There is probably not an object in our house nor an idea in our head that we wouldn't be better for by throwing it out.

'But', you begin, but we say the more valuable to you an idea or an object, the freer you would be to find new gems – whether ideas or valuables – once the old one you worship is gone. If you lived day after day with the greatest painting in the world, it would soon fade from your view and become dead. Throw it out. Clear the space for a work of art that you can *see*.

So too with a great idea. When the idea is fresh it can transform your life. When it grows old it deadens your life. Throw it out.

So too with the ideas in this book. If they enliven your life, good. Use them a bit. Then throw them out. Nothing is deader than an idea that has outlived its usefulness.

There are live Christians and there are dead Christians. Live Christians are those who have discovered truths in the New Testament as if they were hot off the press. Dead Christians are the rest of mankind. They have put on old ideas because it is the clothing the society encourages them to wear. They could probably throw out every 'Christian' belief they have and not notice it.

Ideas are like experiences: the new ones are the best. The ones we discover for ourselves are the best. Take a new idea and run with it as far and as long as you can, and when it grows stale, throw it out. Make space for the next one.

Our physical lives are filled with one kind of trash and out mental lives another. When in doubt, throw it out.

Most of the world's paths to 'enlightenment' develop methods or tactics to empty the seeker's mind of everything: purpose, fear, morality, everything. At first, the guru may permit the seekers to retain the single goal of achieving liberation or enlightenment, but ultimately that too must be emptied out.

Meditation is the almost universal tradition of spiritual paths to empty or cleanse the mind. By counting breaths, or focusing on a burning candle, or chanting over and over a single mantra or *wazifa*, the seeker is forced to stop thinking, stop judging, stop desiring. If we sit down to meditate and vow to count our breaths until we've reached one hundred, unless we are experienced in meditation, we can't do it. By the time we have counted six breaths, our mind is evaluating our performance, or our body is shouting for attention to pain in the knees or the behind, or we are remembering what we really want to be doing instead of this stupid counting of breaths. Most of us lose the count before we reach the teens. We think that sitting and counting our breaths until we've reached one hundred would be simple, but I doubt that one in a hundred can do it. We are too full – of judgements, memories, sense impressions, desires. Yet, if and when one of us achieves this minor miracle – counting a hundred consecutive breaths – that one will know a serenity or joy he or she has never enjoyed in fulness. Meditation is the most reliable of methods to emptiness, but, like all of them, is hard, hard, hard.

Gurdjieff used to force his followers, almost all intellectuals, to do hard physical work, often of a rigorous and repetitive nature: digging ditches, sawing and hauling wood, hoeing endless rows of vegetables. He would urge them to concentrate on their task and, if they did, their minds became necessarily empty of all their usual thought processes. Gurdjieff also had his people create and perform complicated movements or dances – again forcing his cerebral students to live in their bodies and give up their thinking, thinking, thinking. Just as many people are bored or annoyed with meditation, so too his followers often deeply resented the meaningless tasks he gave them. Then one day they awoke to find that they were enjoying doing their senseless tasks, indeed were feeling a bliss they had rarely experienced in pursuing their purposeful and rational tasks.

The meaningless tasks Gurdjieff gave his followers closely resemble some forms of dicing. One idea that lies behind dicing is that we train ourselves to do the option the die choose no matter how purposeless, undesirable or boring it may seem. Just do it, *without thought*. This letting go of our usual way of being and doing things is a form of emptying. One dicer formed the habit of each day listing six non-essential or even somewhat silly tasks – emptying half-empty waste baskets, writing to a distant relative out of the blue, tidying up the attic, sweeping the cellar, buying and reading a different newspaper, digging a hole in the ground, burying something, and then filling it up again, watching a randomly chosen channel of television for thirty minutes, lying down on the ground and staring at the sky for ten minutes, wrestling with the dog, or chasing a cat – in essence giving himself a

Gurdjieffian task and just doing it and focusing on doing it. Of course, by doing such non-rational, non-purposeful things, he was opening up his life to new things.

The problem of being a 'reasonable' dice-person is that one only lists reasonable and purposeful options and thus makes sure that one remains filled with purpose. It is always wise when listing options to list one stupid option, one option that makes no sense at all. One time out of every six or so the die will choose the 'stupid' option. After a while the dicer may sense that his 'stupid' options have a wisdom he didn't realize.

Without being aware of it, I think many of us find hobbies or jobs or physical activities that in effect empty us of reason and purpose and morality. For the lawyer or professor it may be some sport he plays regularly: tennis, handball, pickup basketball, golf, fishing. All of these are essentially meaningless activities – all games are meaningless, are ends in themselves. In becoming absorbed in such games we let go of the purposes and desires that run our lives most of the week. We in effect take a temporary vacation.

For me, for many years, it was sailing. Since I was a man driven by reason and purpose, sailing, an activity that involves doing a lot of trivial things to propel a boat very slowly to no particular destination, was an ideal 'vacation' from my usual self. And since I often sailed alone, I had no time for thoughts; the wind and the waves and the sails demanded constant attention; a single wandering thought and the boat jibes, luffs, or spits a bowwave of water into your face to wake you up. And sailing at night forced me to see the stars,the moon, entities that I had managed to overlook most of my life. And then in the morning, lo and behold, there was a sunrise. On land I am rarely awake for a sunrise.

Sailing was my personal Gurdjieffian task: an irrational, non-productive physical task that took me out of my mind, made me mindless,made me empty. For others, it is gardening, bowling, hiking, mountain-climbing, spelunking, scuba-diving.

Of course, all of the sports and hobbies listed above are usually used by most of us in 'rational', 'purposeful' ways. We play golf to make important business contracts, we play tennis to stay in shape, we garden to create beauty (or vegetables), we climb a mountain in order to impress somebody. We use our sailboat to win races or impress clients. The human mind has an infinite capacity to poison the good things life has to offer.

OBOKO'S FIRST SERMON ON ZEN

Bare-toed in the chill turned-earth, look seaward,
Listen for whispers in the wind, watch
Waters wet-lapping rock and dock, boats
Bobbing toy-like in the swollen sea, and ask:
Are we king? Or are we tiny ants who hasten crumb to crumb,
Climbing millimetre mountains to divinity on dirt?
Don't know.
Kingship, ant-hood: both betray.
The toy-like rise and fall of boats, the bowl of night
Sieved with stars, the hiss and whir of winds
Which bully leaves. Questions create; solutions
Solidify to stone. Seek
But do not find. See
But do not say. Race
But do not win. Life is impulse
Unresolved, is swallows
Sliding down the sky, bluebells blinking in the sun, frogs
Plopping leaf to leaf. And death
Is words
Chiselled into stone, pressed to wood, stuffed
In minds like rags in bags. Death is swallows
Charted height and speed, bluebells
Melted into chlorophyll, frogs
Chopped into wires, rubber bands and blood.
While minds machine-like clatter, let senses
Sing. Let worlds flow through. Be
A sieve to the Universe. Be
The wind-world into others blowing.

Think of some of the happiest things you do, the things you enjoy most – running, painting, dancing, singing, cooking, exercising, lovemaking, whatever. Think about them. How much thinking is going on during any of them?

Emptiness is the ideal. Henry James once said of someone: 'He had a mind so fine no idea could violate it.' When we were young we thought that was a horrible thought: ideas are marvellous. But now we understand it: 'Have a mind so fine that no idea colours everything you look at, for then you have closed off 99 per cent of the universe.' Ideas are fine, but they are toys that should be played with and then, as we grow older, abandoned for new toys.

MASKS

masks over masks I plaster
and peel plaster and
peel, until one day asked:
what
is beneath the faces you wear?
the faces you wear so gaily each day?
what
is beneath the masks over masks
over masks
you wear: My mask
replies and peels itself
and peels itself replying twice
rips off again the rubber face
revealing smiling a
rubber face (masks over masks
I plaster and peel
plaster and
peel) until I'm asked
to peel the last

to peel the last
to peel the
and I do
I do
I
peel the last when asked and
RIP
from my rubber face
my rubber mask,
and stand at last
revealed
revealed at last
revealed at
revea
rev
re
r

.

> **Liberation is saying 'yes'**
> **to your Emptiness and 'no'**
> **to everything that tries to fill you.**

OBOKO'S SERMON ON THE COOSEKETOE RIVER

A disciple once came to Oboko and asked: 'Master, how can one identify the truly random man? In what manner speaks and acts an illumined man of Chance?'

And the Master Oboko did reply, saying: Know then that while the normal man
wants to be sure, the man of Chance embraces uncertainty. The normal
man is always intent in going from 'a' to 'b', while the sage rejoices in 'a'
even as he moves on to 'x'.

The normal man lives by a chart; the sage knows you rarely discover new land
with old charts.

The normal man knows most of the answers and is always right, while the sage,
always confused, always uncertain, is usually wrong, or, when right, only by
Accident.

The normal man walks within narrow walls, always seeing the light at the end of
the tunnel. The sage is blind, can't see the light, thinks walls are for climbing, and over he goes, no pattern to follow, no end in sight.

The normal man seeks to master his ship always with fingers lashed to the wheel,
always afraid of accidents. The sage is always sailing free, letting water and
wind enforce their will, using the wheel for playing roulette, fingers for
touching the sun and sea. He knows that the greatest accidents of all are
nothing more than the wind, the wheel and the 'me'. He leaps again to
wonder and whim.

The normal man knows what is success and what is failure. The sage is stupid: he
is lucky and does not rejoice, he is unlucky and does not weep. Chance casts
him into the darkness and he may smile; Chance raises him to the light and
he may glower. Him I call illumined.

The enlightened, calm-hearted, Chance-abiding man is not elated by the good
nor saddened by the bad, but sits serene in the tumbling torrent, rides with
unmussed hair the whirlwind. His mind is dead to the touch of purpose,

alive to the flow of Chance, serenely absorbed in the random flow. Unweighted by will, knowing no worry in heat or cold, in pain or pleasure, in win or loss, but always leaping from wonder to whim.

Tickle the toes of the purposeful mighty and watch him topple, felled by feathers; but try crushing with mountains the man of Chance and see him rise untouched – a cork amidst the tidal wave, a flea beneath a boulder, a speck of dust indifferent to the mountain's fall. The sage slips by untouched because always empty, always all. Him I call illumined.

Water flows eternally into the ocean but the flow of the sea is never disturbed. Thus desire flows into the sage, whose tides still rise and fall with the moon of whim. Being an ocean he contains all; containing all, there is nothing left for him to desire. Being full, he is empty. Him I call a sage. Him I call illumined.

As the tortoise can draw in his legs so the sage can draw in his desires. The ascetic hides from what he desires, but carries them hidden within him. The sage is at one with what he desires and goes always empty-handed.

The normal man feels for the fruits of his acts as a mother feels for her child. As his acts fall from the sage, whether they grow or not the sage does not care. Turning his face from the falling fruit he acts again.

The sage wanders and wonders without having hope and without despair, die-ing to all his desires, to all his ideas, mind attuned to ubiquitous Chance. When lured into idea or purpose or will, he leaps again to wonder and whim, utterly quiet, cleansed of clutching, leaping again to wonder and whim.

The professor grows by hoarding knowledge, the businessman by hoarding gold. The sage grows by daily loss; loss upon loss until he is empty, leaping again to wonder and whim.

What Change gives, the sage takes and is contented. Pain follows pleasure and he is not troubled; gain follows loss, he yawns. Of whom should he be jealous, he who is everyone and nobody? He acts, but why he acts or who he is who acts, even Chance may not know. He neither longs for one thing nor loathes its opposite. As the lotus leaf rests unwetted on water, so acting rests the sage, untouched by action. As the lotus leaf flowing on the wet film of stream to the sea seeks not to return to the root or soar to the sky, so too the sage: unattached to old growths, unaspiring of the distant sky, free from fear and longing, he floats along unresisting to the irresistible, not hurried by the thought of dams, nor hesitant in the rapids nor fearful of the distant sea. He is a glint of light off a single ripple.

Him I call illumined, he a man of Chance.

WHIM COMMENTS: This man of Chance seems to do a lot of leaping. I hope he's in good shape. As for floating along unresisting to the irresistible, anyone can do that. It's not resisting the resistible that's tough. And as for this lotus leaf business, I don't know. I think I'd rather be a catfish living in the mud at the bottom of the pond. Fire, earthquake, flood, tornado, hurricane; hey, a catfish just yawns. On the other hand, the catfish never goes anywhere, never does anything. At least the lotus leaf gets a free ride to the sea.

OPTIONS

Before casting a die, read through the six options below. Throw out one or two (or all six) and create some of your own to replace those you toss out. Then cast a die.

① Take all your awards, all your trophies, all your high marks, all your symbols of success and throw them out. How you feel after you have done this, or, more likely, after you have failed to do this, will tell you a lot about yourself. Do you exist if the trophies and awards don't exist? Apparently, for most of us, no.

② Sit down. Make yourself comfortable. Breathe. Feel your breathing. Begin to count each time you exhale. See if you can actually reach twenty before you lose count because your mind wanders. Start again, breathing, counting each breath. For a few moments at least your mind will be empty.

③ Each day for a week list six objects that you acknowledge you can do without. Cast a die. Give it away or throw it out.

You will notice at the end of the week you feel richer.

④ You are at a dinner party. Listen. Try to say as little as possible. Speak only when asked a question. Answer as briefly as possible. And as you sit there listening, say to yourself over and over 'empty umpty dumpty empty' or 'abcdefg' or 'Engelbert Humperdinck'. Say something over and over that means nothing and thus lets you listen to the talk around you. Try it.

You'll like it.

⑤ List six things you can empty out: an attic, a bookcase, a wardrobe, a bureau, a filing cabinet, a cellar, a computer folder, an 'inbox', a kitchen cabinet. Cast a die. Empty it out. If you throw out or give away everything, you get an 'A-plus'; you may advance to 'Go' and collect two hundred pounds. If you are able to give or throw away nothing, you may stop reading this book. You are hopelessly lost. If you are able to throw away or give away half of what you found there, then ask yourself: what was it doing there in the first place?

⑥ List six amounts of money or certain valuables that you might be willing to give away. Cast a die. List six people. Cast a die. Give what the die chose to the person chosen. Don't tell them why.

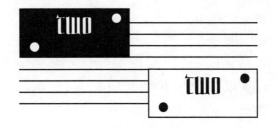

CONFLICT

A man with two heads
Looking to right and to left
Walking this way and that,
Getting nowhere, slowly,
Each head shouting of the 'one true way',
The legs churning,
In place.
Where is the sword to help this man?
Even one head may be too many.

A man with two heads
Has a problem.
But if you tell them both to shut up, look!
You have a third head.
Best to fall asleep and pretend it's all a dream.

Conflict cannot be permanently resolved by the victory of one head out-shouting the other. If you are divided into two warring selves, neither will ever rule happily. Selves always want eternal power. The only solution lies in the withering away of both heads. A headless man has no fear: how, after all, can anyone hang him? A headless man may seem strange at first, but at least when his legs start moving they move in harmony.

As for the advice of falling asleep and pretending it's all a dream: where's the pretense?

WHIM COMMENTS: My mom always said that two heads were better than one, but this guy seems to think that none is best. What bothers me though is, where do I wear my hat?

ON THE IMPORTANCE OF DECISIONS

There was born on the moon Rombie on the planet Giox of the star Rella X2913
of the galaxi Orion in the year 13,657,256,890,358,682,555 of the birth of
the galaxi, the creature Morpo, a humanoid (a creature physically and psychologically related to what we call humans), the 15,899,008,345,298,446th
humanoid on that moon which was only one of 378,100,678,566,000
spheres containing humanoid life.

One day, at the age of seventeen, Morpo said to himself: 'Should I ask Lulu for a
date or shouldn't I?'

And he despaired that such an important decision should be thrust upon him.
What he chose to do seemed of the greatest importance to himself and to the
universe. He chose to date Lulu.

Both he and Lulu and the universe survived.

Conflict is the essence of drama, of play, of games and of life. However, conflict that
leads to two evenly balanced forces each going nowhere is like World War I – trench
warfare where nothing happens except dead bodies.

Our lives are an eternal series of decisions. When we are immersed in society, we
make decisions by habit, by our society's 'reason', by compulsion, by inhibition, by fear,
by our image of who society says we are. But because society is continually giving us
conflicting messages, we are often caught in indecision.

Indecision is one symptom of our sickness. It results from our trying desperately to
be consistent in a world that is continually urging us to be multiple and inconsistent. It
comes when we are aware that we can play many roles and think it is important we
choose the right one. Indecision is the most obvious symptom of seriousness. If life is

real and life is earnest, if God is watching our every move and, worse yet, keeping score, then every decision is monumental and we feel we must act in a rational and informed manner.

Nothing kills living faster than trying to act in a rational and fully-informed manner. In science such behaviour is fine. In life it is deadly. Although we don't know it, we can never act in a rational and fully-informed manner. Our minds are wonderful creations but weren't designed to give us accurate information. They are made for creating our personal illusions, illusions which are in fact the very bedrock of our particular human existence, but which can never be described as rational or informed.

Know that should you wait 'til hell freezes over you can never have enough information and rationality to make an informed decision. So, armed only with your vague recognition that your mind will always try to fool you, act, not out of reason, or with much hope that what you intend will actually ever come to pass, but out of . . . dare we say it, whim.

For children it is easy to decide. Impulse rules and a healthy child knows wholly that he wants to go to the movie and knows wholly after he gets there when he is bored. Being uninterested in consistency, he may reverse his decision within a short period of time, but both his decision and his contradictory redecision are both executed without delay or conflict.

We adults are less fortunate. Many decisions are accompanied by doubt and conflict. Once we make a decision and begin to act on it we find it very embarrassing to change our mind. Consistency is one of our unnamed gods. But in a world of multiple values the forces tugging at us in different directions around every decision are many. 'Dad expects me to . . .; 'My girlfriends expect me to . . .'; 'A real man would . . .', 'As a woman I ought to . . .'; 'What I actually feel like doing is . . .'

It is to avoid what would otherwise become a problem of recurring conflict and indecision that we adopt religions, moral systems, stereotypes, habits, beliefs – our personalities: the solidification of arbitrary decision into habit and religion. With a firm image of ourselves, decisions can come more automatically. 'I'm a gin-and-tonic man';

'I never read *TIME*'; 'I'm just not an early riser'; 'I always date tall men.' A million such sentences stabilize life, make us dependable, predictable, patterned, rigid, bored.

So long as someone exists who feels he has to make decisions, so long will there be indecision. The trick is to cut the string to the illusory puppet-master self and roll (role) free. Act. But don't try to justify your action as well-informed or rational. Acknowledge that you're uninformed and that your mind is feeding you a basketful of lies, but that's what life is all about. If you can't beat 'em, join 'em.

The man who fights himself always
carries around a lot of sore losers.

WHIM AND THE BEE

One day Whim got carried away speaking to his friends on the theme of rising above the dualities, of becoming detached from success and failure, life and death, pleasure and pain. Surrounded by a dozen worshipful disciples he was preaching with unaccustomed eloquence on flowing above all the dualities when a bee stung him on the nose. Whim leapt up screaming and ran in a circle twice around the room.

When he finally reseated himself and assumed a position of dignity there was an embarrassed silence. Finally the youngest disciple dared to speak.

'O Beloved Whim,' he asked. 'What is the lesson to be learned from this event?'

'It's simple,' said Whim, looking stern. 'To rise above pleasure and pain one must be very detached and very careful about bees.'

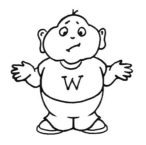

Indecision is like an arrow fired straight from the bow that suddenly begins to wobble and then turns back for the archer, wobbling. It is a rather a laughable matter.

It is naturally only an accident that the world's oldest book is a book of chance: the *Y Ching* or *Book of Changes*. Through various methods of random selection one of sixty-four hexagrams is chosen and from it the seeker is able to interpret an answer to the problem he posed. It is mankind's first effort to deal with the problem of decision and indecision.

Originally the *Y Ching* was solely a book of chance. Only as civilization developed and most sages became supporters of the status quo instead of its natural enemy did the *Y Ching* begin to be filled with such typically human folly-filled gems as 'Supreme success', 'perseverance furthers', and 'it furthers one to see the Great Man'. By talking about the future in terms of success and misfortune and perseverance and furthering, the *Y Ching* came to invite worrying about the future, grasping after it. In fact any book or method which pretends to divine the future is a source of grasping and misery.

So gradually the *Y Ching* became an unfortunate mixture of insights urging us to live in the present and not grasp after effects, and the more conventional moral advice which urged men to act in ways that would lead to success. People consulting the book are thus put in a nice double bind: on the one hand don't think about the future, but, on the other, if you want success in the future then you must act in a certain way.

Whim discovered the weakness of the *Y Ching* when he noticed that every time he consulted it and it predicted 'Supreme good fortune' he was either indifferent or vaguely anxious. When it predicted 'misfortune' or 'the abyss' he was, on the other hand, exhilarated. The reason, he concluded, was that when the book predicted supreme success his interest hooked on to the future and away from the present, made him want success, made him anxious. In predicting failure and misfortune the *Y Ching* very effectively eliminates a person's interest in the future. Nothing like an abyss up ahead to make one quite happy in the desert one finds oneself in.

And Whim noticed that the people he knew who consulted the *Y Ching* rarely came away from it happy. If it predicted success they only partly believed it; when it predicted misfortune they wondered what it had in mind.

> Two paths diverged within a wood, and I,
> I took the one less travelled by, and that
> led to other paths diverging in a wood, and I,
> I took the one selected by the the die, and that
> Has made all the difference.

Of course, some people have the same reaction to dice decisions. As soon as the die chooses an option, the dicer begins to question the wisdom of the choice. And as soon as one questions the wisdom of the die, the usefulness of dicing is ended. Someone once wrote a book about Zen with the title *WALK ON*. Daring is risky, No daring is fatal.

There are crucial differences between consulting the dice and consulting the *Y Ching*. When one consults the *Y Ching* one is permitted, even encouraged to read in one's own interpretations of what one is being advised to do; the book is purposely vague. And the seeker is encouraged to believe he can overcome the course of events that is naturally unfolding, and thus to see himself as an active, responsible agent, a 'self' in fact, encouraged to perpetuate that self.

The wise dice-student goes to the die humbly, knowing that both he and it are totally fallible. He knows that he can never be sure which dice decisions are going to turn out to seem brilliant and which disastrous. His only faith is that in following the die, however many options he wishes the dice hadn't chosen, dicing will nevertheless introduce a variety and originality into his life that acting without chance would not.

In a way, the most basic use of dice-living is to end conflict, to make a choice where the usual rational methods have momentarily broken down. But before one dares to turn one's 'fate' over to chance, a hidden decision must be made – that the decision isn't very important.

One of the most effective games developed for dice centres or dice groups is the 'Master–Slave' game. A die chooses whether a player is master or slave. A partner is then the opposite, or, if there are more than two playing the game, all the others may be slaves of the one master. The master is encouraged to be a creative master, one who stretches the realm of the possible for every slave. The slave is encouraged to surrender totally to the master, no matter how irrational, unfair or cruel he or she may be.

It is strange that most people find it easier to play the Master–Slave game than they do to follow the whim of a falling die. If a human master in the context of the game says, 'Take off all your clothes', the slave may be able to do so without thinking. If the die chose the same thing as a one in six decision the task is strangely more difficult.

But slavery to a master in the Master–Slave game is the same as slavery to chance in dice-living. In both cases the 'slave' is learning to surrender his or her self to an apparently outside force. Of course, in both cases the individual has made the choice to obey the master or the die.

The Master–Slave game works best in two different areas. The first is when masters order slaves to do non-rational physical things like crawl on the floor, do twenty situps, run in circles, wrestle with another slave, kiss someone's foot. The process works best when the slave is commanded to do one such act after another in pointless succession. The slave soon becomes mindless and egoless.

But another area occasionally has more dramatic consequences. The master orders the slave to fly to a distant place, express love to a certain person, write an auto-biographical story, submit an artwork to a gallery, look for a new job. When masters order slaves to move into new areas in life the results can sometimes be stunning. One woman was ordered to leave her husband for two days and go to visit an uncle in New York. She ended up never returning to her husband. A man was ordered to apply for three new jobs. Although he had thought he was happy in the job he had, when one of the three made him a job offer, he suddenly realized how excited he was about the prospect of change. It turned out he didn't take the job offer but several months later he developed a different job offer and happily accepted it. To escape from the traps that some of our lives have become, we must find someone new to make decisions for us – whether a human or a plastic cube.

The turtle
Stretches his stiff neck
Through his hard shell,
Looks around.
Yikes!!
Withdraws back into his shell.

The turtle always carries an umbrella
Is always ready for a rainy day,
Always lives alone
In the same mud.

WHIM COMMENTS: Any leap is better than a wobble.
Actually, Lao-Tse said it better: 'He who sits on fence, gets it up the arse.'
Or something like that.

ON FOLLOWING THE FALL OF A DIE

In ancient times a long, long time ago, two Japanese dicers met near the River Lau travelling in opposite directions. After exchanging the traditional greetings they entered into a spirited and competitive discussion about dice-living, which both enjoyed immensely. Both agreed that the fundamental key to die-ing lay in always obeying the fall of a die no matter how stupid or impractical the dice decision came to seem.

Before they knew it the sun was setting behind the hills and they decided to spend the night together under a little shelter built on a rock on a small hill next to the river.

In the morning they shared some bread and wine, each packed his small bundle of possessions and they prepared to depart on their separate ways.

'It's been very pleasant,' said the older of the dicers, a man close to seventy years old. 'I may be returning this way in the spring. Will I see you here then?'

The younger man, only in his forties, replied smiling: 'To have my head battered by the staff of your empty mind has been refreshing. By spring my dice-living will be stale again. Die willing, let's meet then.'

'A two, three or four I will be at this spot at the spring equinox,' said the old dicer. He dropped his large wooden die and it was a 'two'.

'That's fine,' said the younger man. 'And if my die falls an odd number I will meet you here.' His die fell a 'three'.

'At the setting of the sun then,' said the younger man, 'at the equinox, the die says we are to meet here at the little shelter on this rock.'

'Very good,' said the older man. 'And the first one here can have the tea water boiling.'

'Don't be late, old man. I don't like drinking with only one Buddha.'

'Keep your wisdom in your sake bottle,' said the old monk. 'I always follow the will of the die. But I'll probably have to hike to Kyoto and carry you on my back to get you here on time.'

And the two men parted.

Six months later, after a long cold winter, the spring floods of the River Lau were exceptionally high. When at noon on the afternoon of the spring equinox the younger of the monks arrived near the meeting spot, he saw that the shelter on the rock on the little rise was now surrounded by rushing water. The hill was mostly submerged and the rock was now a tiny island sixty feet from the new shoreline of the river.

The monk, humming quietly to himself, set about examining the pine trees growing along the bank and soon took out a small hatchet from his bundle and begin hacking at a thick trunk. Three hours later the tree fell into the river, its topmost branches lodging on the upriver side of the rock with the shelter on it. Carefully repacking his hatchet in his bundle, he quickly scrambled along the trunk of the tree to the rock and up under the shelter. Half an hour later, however, the force of the raging river swept the pine tree away from the rock downriver.

The monk watched it swirl away and, humming again, began to prepare a small fire to boil water for the tea.

An hour before sundown the old diceman arrived on the river bank sixty feet away from the shelter. The two men looked at each other across the torrent but neither man said a word.

The old man looked at the pine trees near the river bank, at the stump of the toppled pine, at the sun hovering over the western ridge of hills. He knew that to arrive by sunset he didn't have time to chop down another tree.

He walked rapidly upriver. When he was a hundred yards above the island he tied his bundle tightly to his belly and waded into the river. Twenty feet out from the shore he was swept away downstream at incredible speed. With choppy strokes he tried to swim further out into the river in order to be washed up on the island where his friend awaited him, but so powerful was the current that within a few seconds he was alongside the island and then, as he and the younger monk watched each other, swept past.

It took the old man ten minutes to struggle through the current to get back to the bank. His body was badly battered and he had to drag one leg behind him, but he began again to trudge back up the river bank to try to reach again a position upstream from the island he had promised to get to.

On the hill that was now an island the young monk noticed that the sun was now setting and the water for tea was boiling. He had noticed no sign of the old man since he had been swept past the island more than forty or fifty minutes before. Gently he placed a metal cup on the earthern floor of the shelter opposite himself and another cup right in front of him. He removed the pot from the flame, put in the tea, and left it to steep. He hummed to himself. After fifteen minutes he noticed that it had grown quite dark; he could no longer see the shore from the island. The only sound was that of the river rushing by and crashing against the rocks on the upriver side.

He finally reached forward, picked up the small teapot and poured tea into the cup in front of him. Then he reached out and poured tea into the cup opposite him. Still sitting, he hummed quietly. After another few minutes he began to sip his hot tea.

After ten minutes he was pouring a little more hot water into his mostly empty tea cup when he heard a groan behind him at the upriver side of the hill, then silence except for the steady roar of the river. Then he heard another noise and, turning, saw the old man clawing his way up the rocks towards the shelter. He was moving painfully slowly, and took three minutes to crawl up the rock and across the few feet of pounded earth to his place beside the fire opposite the younger monk.

When he had finally arrived he pulled himself painfully into the half-lotus position. For many minutes the two monks sat opposite each other without speaking, the fire casting tiny speckles of light over their faces.

'I'm sorry I'm so late,' finally said the ancient diceman.

'Your tea is cold,' said the other.

OPTIONS

Consider some important area of your life where you are in conflict. You can see two seemingly opposite directions or decisions involving this problem area. Write down two clear options, one a 'Yes', the other in some sense a 'No'. Cast a die.

① Yes. In your present state, the answer is always yes. Do it. Get off your arse. Move. Leap. Anything beats wobbling. Better disaster than indecision.

② Do both things. Or first one and then the other. The best way to see the folly of either choice is to try to do both. Marry. Divorce. Go. Stay. Lie. Tell the truth. Do one. Then the other. That would be ridiculous, you say? Good. Now we're getting somewhere.
   Laugh.

③ Do neither. Stop fighting. Surrender. Retreat. Pretend to be dead. Retire from life. Resign for a few days from the human race.
   Notice the universe doesn't collapse.

④ Go for it. Play to win. Fight for every inch of ground. Never let up. When your opponent surrenders, give him the winner's trophy.

⑤ You are in conflict with someone. Change sides. Back the person or side you were fighting. Show tremendous enthusiasm for your enemy's cause – your new cause. Notice how good you feel.

⑥ You are in conflict with someone. Pretend the opponent is not Joe Blow but rather Buddha in disguise – a Divine Incarnation slumming in a human body. Continue the conflict with the Buddha. Notice how the game changes.

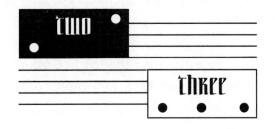

THE PAST

The past, the glorious, heritage-proud, history-rich, memory-filled past! What would we do without it?!

Be a lot better off.

Just ask the Jews and Palestinians, the Irish Catholics and Protestants, the Pakastinis and the Indians, the Serbs and the Albanian Kosovars.

The past is what divides us.

But doesn't the past also unite us?

No, we are united by the present. We all live in the present and, in dealing with the same environment, struggling with the same weather, catastrophes, victories and defeats, we are united. Our pasts divide us.

What if the native Americans were to remember their past as ardently as did the Serbs, who tried to kick out the Albanian Kosovars because nine hundred years earlier the Serbs had controlled Kosovo? What if African Americans were every moment to remember their treatment at the hands of white Americans during the last three hundred years? What if the Irish or Italians or any other European emigrants were to dwell on their experiences as despised newcomers a hundred years ago?

It is because Americans are partly urged to forget the past that we can live together with what harmony we do.

Our pasts divide us.

Societies, however, need to dwell on the past in order to add to the mixture that makes the social glue. So societies dwell on Independence Day, Memorial Day, President's Day, Martin Luther King Day, in an effort to remind people of what unites them. But of course what unites one society divides it from every other.

Within a society, smaller ethnic units also dwell on their past. So we have St Patrick's Day, or Yom Kippur, or Easter, or other celebrations of a common past. And such celebrations divide the celebrator from all who do not belong to his ethnic group.

Our pasts divide us.

That is why accidents and catastrophes unite us. During a hurricane, earthquake or flood, the past is irrelevant and we are all brothers fighting a common enemy for survival. We wonder how often during a Mississippi flood a white racist has worked side by side with a black American and felt vaguely uneasy: he's not quite sure whether according to his racial beliefs things are supposed to work this way.

The past divides us. Not just the past of brooding injustices but the past of our triumphs.

SHADOW

A shadow trails behind you like
    Seaweed, pulling you
        Backwards,
    An anchor to your flow.
The shadow is your past.
    It can cloud everything
You do.
    All men have a shadow, you say.
Yes,
        Except
When they are surrounded
    By Light.

STEP TWICE ON THE SAME EARTH AND YOU WALK IN MUD.

Worst of all, the past divides us from our present. Past injustices and past triumphs are irrelevant to our present. We may have received an A-plus in third-grade mathematics but no one cares. Michael Jordan may have been the greatest basketball player ever to play the game but it was irrelevant when he went up to bat in a baseball game. His jump shot was irrelevant to a curve ball. His leaping ability is irrelevant to his golf game.

Our past triumphs are memories which we can cherish or ignore, but if we choose to cherish them, know that we do so at the expense of the present. You can't feel the wind on your face when you're daydreaming of the time you scored a goal in extra-time or won a flower-arranging contest in 1986.

If you know someone who often dwells on the past then you know someone who is often dead. The aged often dwell on the past and it is a symptom of their losing interest in the present; in effect, losing interest in life, since life can be lived only in the present. When you see an old-timer who never talks about the past and seems always involved in doing something in the present, then he will seem younger than his age. Life is involvement in the present. When we die, then we can live entirely in the past: it will be all we have.

'I don't have any personal history,' once said the Yaqui sage Don Juan. 'One day I found out that personal history was no longer necessary for me and, like drinking, I dropped it.'

It's interesting that Don Juan should compare his dropping of his past to his giving up drinking; he sees them both as addictions: something that he was compulsively attached to that was bad for his health.

The past is bad for our health. Health is living life fully in the present, and thinking of past triumphs or failures blots out the present. Imagine Michael Jordan standing on the foul-line with two seconds left in the game and his team a point behind. He thinks of the wonderful jump shot he made to win a championship the year before. 'Clunk' goes the foul shot in the present.

Memories can be pleasant, even memories of past triumphs, although it is probable that most of our pleasant memories are not of triumphs but of living. We have pleasant memories of shagging fly balls, catching passes, getting the feel of a basketball in our hands or a soccer ball on our foot, but memories of final scores are generally dull.

We can choose to live in the past, the future, or the present. Those who live in the past are dead. Those who choose to live in the future aren't yet alive. Those who choose to live in the present, live.

> *Hope is the rope we wrap*
> *Around our neck to choke*
> *Ourselves from flowing free, and make us gasp*
> *And grasp and clutch*
> *For 'me'.*
> *Caged in the smallest cave,*
> *Tied tight against the tallest tree,*
> *Manacles made fast to all your limbs,*
> *But loose the rope of hope*
> *And you are free.*

'I'm desperate, Whim. I can't overcome my past and I can't stop worrying about the future. Worse yet, I don't understand how I can ever overcome my past or stop thinking about the future.'

'I had the same problem myself,' said Whim.

'How'd you solve it?'

'Never did.'

'You didn't?'

'It just disappeared the day I saw a potato.'

'Really?'

'The potato was a little on the fat and lumpy side. Somehow I sensed that the potato wasn't sitting there brooding about its figure. Or thinking about its past.'

'Yeah, I know, but – '

'And whether it became French fries or mashed wasn't a big deal either. The potato simply was. It was sitting there being a potato and it wanted nothing more and nothing less.'

'But a potato – '

'When I saw that I myself was running around in circles trying to be anything except myself, I realized how much more intelligent the potato was. From that moment on, past and future haven't been much of a problem.'

The student was silent.

'So if you want help,' said Whim, 'the best I can do is suggest you look closely at a potato . . . Or look closely at anything else for that matter.'

Whim sighed and then grinned.

'Except humans.'

The past operates in two forms: in the minds of those who know us when they see us in the present, and in our our mind as memories and attitudes. We might eliminate the first form of the past by eliminating from our lives all those who have known us, or, less drastically, by developing an indifference to their views about us. The first might be more immediately effective but sooner or later we must learn to become indifferent to the views of others.

After we have conquered the influence of our past in others' minds, we have the far more difficult job of killing off the past in our own minds. Here the secret is simple, but almost impossible: we must learn to act without thought, on instinct, on whim. Thinking is always powerfully invaded by the past; whim escapes the past as much as we are ever able to.

WHIM GIVES *DARSHAN*

Whim's disciples decided they wanted him to give them individual *darshan*, a session where Whim was supposed to attune himself to the individual, listen to what he or she had to say, and then say something profound that would deal with the person's particular problem and help him along the path.

Whim agreed to 'play the game', and over a period of two days all forty of the students in the ashram spent up to an hour sitting with Whim and sharing their problems with him.

Incredibly, each one exited from his *darshan* amazed that what Whim had said to him or her touched precisely on the particular problem area and cleared it up, whether the disciple had actually told Whim about the problem or not.

So a few days later, an enthusiastic disciple, convinced that Whim had extraordinary psychic powers, went into Whim and asked him how he was so able to attune himself to each separate individual who came to him for *darshan*.

Whim smiled craftily and asked the disciple to come closer.

'To each one who came to me,' he whispered, 'I said only three words.'

The disciple's eyes widened.

'To most,' Whim went on, 'I said simply "What is, is".'

Whim leaned in closer, a mischievous light in his eyes.

'And in especially tough cases,' he went on, 'I'd say, "What ain't, ain't".'

To begin to free ourselves from the past, new modes of making decisions must be developed.

The one we are playing with is, of course, die-ing: making decisions by casting a die. This simple device guarantees that we stop the habitual flow our society has immersed us in, and for that moment at least, we step free.

'The first principle of die-ing,' Whim once said, 'is never step today on yesterday's turd.'

'Do it different' is the simplification of this idea. But the difficulty lies in determining what is really different from our habitual way. A man may go from one woman to another day after day but be, in effect, stepping always on the same – this metaphor isn't coming out right – turd. If he acts always out of compulsive promiscuity he is no more free than the person who is compulsively monogamous.

The first principle is 'Do it different', but our ignorance of our own habitual patterns is so great that even when we create six options we are usually only listing six alternative habits.

How can we discover the new?

The difference is always either difficult or divine. If we experience neither difficulty nor joy when acting, then it is part of our habitual life. When we flow out of and with our past, all is easy and a bore. When we have freed ourselves into our own games, then we may experience long periods which involve neither difficulty nor joy but rather the intense pleasant concentration of any good game. But when trying to break our bondage to our past and our attachments we will experience difficulty and, as the attachment is beaten, joy.

There is no strength without exercise, no victory without effort, no escape without the work of breaking down the walls that confine us. Liberation is lightness, but the way to lightness involves moving a lot of stones. Unlike Sisyphus, however, when we have removed all the boulders and reached the top of the mountain there is no need to descend and begin pushing them up again. The mountain has disappeared.

OPTIONS

① Take your most important trophy, your most important triumph. Bury it. Pretend it never existed. Pretend that instead of triumphing that day, you came in last.

Do you still exist? Does the sun still shine? Does a baby still smile, a dog still wag its tail? Take your most important trophy, your most important triumph. Bury it.

② Take your heritage, whatever it may be. If you are proud of it, then imagine that your grandmother secretly slept with . . . a member of an ethnic group that you think is inferior. As a result you are the grandson or granddaughter of that inferior ethnic group. Are you different? Are you less? Are you more?

③ Look at memories of some of your happiest moments; vivid memories of happy moments. How many of them have anything to do with success or failure?

④ Go through an entire day without once mentioning anything that happened in the past. If you begin thinking about the past, spank yourself ten times on your behind. People will stare at you, and your embarrassment will effectively end your thinking about the past.

⑤ Imagine that the Lord Chance, in one of his more spectacular Accidents, accidentally transferred you to a new universe. You are suddenly living in a brand-new universe in which everyone looks human and speaks your language, but absolutely no one knows a thing about you or your past. Each of these humans has his own history, his own triumphs and tragedies. Worst of all, no one in this universe has ever heard of soccer or football or tennis or even money, and what's cool in clothing for these people seems totally absurd. So what counts in this universe? Your past wins? How much money you once had? Your car? How smashing you looked that day?

If you think you might enjoy being in such a world then you're probably in pretty good shape. But if the thought makes you shrivel up, then you're probably totally ensnared by the past, hooked to it so badly you can't shake it loose.

⑥ Next time you're with a group of people go out of your way to start telling people about your past, telling people about your heritage, your childhood, your youth, your school, your college, whatever. Can you get a feel for which things mean a lot to you and which are of no more interest than someone else's past? When you notice you are losing your audience, it's probably in the middle of something that means a lot to you, but is of no interest to the rest of the universe.

Every act is new, no matter how many times we repeat it.

Every act is old, no matter when we first discover it.

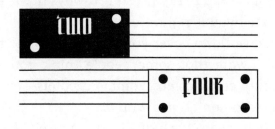

BELIEFS

You're right. Of course you're right. You're always right. So go ahead. Do exactly what your beliefs tell you is right.

But don't expect the world to cover you with kisses. One man's belief is another man's absurdity. You're aware that some people think you're mistaken, but those people are obviously wrong: nerds, creeps, zombies, zealots – or any other word we love to use to describe people who don't agree with us.

And always being right doesn't actually work very well, does it? Being right means that others are wrong. That separates you from them. Notice that if you feel you are wrong or that you don't know what's right, you'll suddenly find yourself no longer separated from people because of your beliefs. In fact, you'll find yourself separated only from those others who are convinced *they*'re right. Unfortunately, that represents most of the human race.

There are no truths but little truths; the large ones,
like dinosaurs, are extinct.

THE MIND IS LIKE THE PROVERBIAL MONKEY

AT THE TYPEWRITER: ONCE A DECADE IT

PRODUCES A THOUGHT WORTH CONSIDERING.

Socrates once won first prize in an Athenian quiz game by answering that he knew nothing, but his answer has won few prizes since. Men continue to be ignorant of their ignorance, enamoured of their illusions. Play-living begins with the assumption that men are fools and the wisest man is he who plays the role to the hilt. Men's lives are based 90 per cent on lies; about the other 10 per cent we don't yet know enough to be sure.

Fortunately, the theory that men are constantly fooling themselves necessitates the corollary that our theory that men live in illusion is itself false and an illusion.

Having so few premises in which we can believe, we are unable to muster up a squad of them that might pass as an argument. Men are fools; with us it must be taken as an article of faith.

In living life freely, any insight held longer than the moment appropriate to it becomes an illusion and a snare. For every name, idea, insight applied over any period of time deadens that part of the universe it touches. To name is to experience. To name a part of the flow always the same way is to experience it always the same way. To live freshly entails continually re-creating experience, continually unlearning, continually destroying the old names, the old beliefs, and creating a new world and fresh experience by giving to the flow new names.

God names. We can live divinely only when we are continually naming.

By letting chance determine who we are at a given moment we are trying to give not only ourselves but our experience new names and a new flavour.

Some new students came to Whim where he was staying with some followers near the sea and their leader said to him: 'We've come to follow you, O Honoured Whim, wherever you lead, for we understand the first principle of all Paths is that one must surrender one's will to the sage.'

'You're welcome to hang out with us, friends,' said Whim, motioning them to sit in the sand nearby, 'but you'll certainly be making a mistake to surrender your will to me because you think I'm some sort of sage.'

'But we've heard that you – '

' I know, that's the problem,' interrupted Whim. 'You come here stuffed with a certain image of me which even on my best days I can't live up to. You may surrender to me successfully for a while, but sooner or later you're going to start asking, "Is this guy really a True Blue Guru?", and part of you will yell in reply: "No way, José." That's trouble. So if you want to follow me, don't do it out of respect, but out of your own whim. Decide to follow me as a lark, a sophomoric escapade, not to gain enlightenment, but to see what will happen.'

Beliefs are just plain silly. They are usually so arbitrary, so little based on either experience or knowledge that it is a wonder that anyone can take his beliefs seriously.

But we all do. One man will love Bill Clinton or Tony Blair and another will detest him. Are they both right? Of course not.

Are they both wrong? Of course.

Every belief is an illusion and if we take it seriously we are wrong.

Any passionately held belief is continually having to duck away from reality. Reality is the great belief buster, but we all develop hard turtle shells so that the blows of reality usually just bounce off, leaving our beliefs nicely intact. The more passionately we hold the belief, the thicker must be our turtle shell. Never argue with someone who has a passionately held belief. If you do, you will soon realize that somehow your words are not penetrating his . . . turtle shell.

On the other hand, if you want a friend, go out of your way to agree enthusiastically with his passionately held belief. Soon he will barely be able to restrain himself from embracing you. It is such a treat for him to have reality patting him on the back instead of rattling his shell. The fact that you are faking it never enters into his mind. Since his belief is Truth, it is only natural that you should agree with him.

The more passionately we believe something, the bigger fool we are. Simple as that. Read it and weep.

We must simply accept the fact that our morals, religions and philosophy are as much a matter of personal taste as our shirts or jeans – and of about as much ultimate importance. If we could realize this, the great tension which makes our choices in these areas so often in disastrous taste is removed. We can browse and finger and experiment as we might with sportswear. We can have a variety of philosophical clothing for various occasions: Christianity for a funeral, paganism for an orgy. The bleak black of a permanent religion can be replaced by modish variety, colour and cut. People might become interesting again. When we begin to pay as much attention to trying new values as we do to trying new foods and fashions, life will become more lively.

Unfortunately, most of us find our values as hard to shed as our skins.

'There is only one belief which is really worth having,' Whim announced to a group of friends one day, and then he smiled. 'Fortunately, I've forgotten it.'

A stone tablet carried down from the mountain.
On it are written in ancient hieroglyphics
Ten Magnificent Rules of Conduct.
The Universe gathers around:
All strain to hear as You
And You Alone, read out the Divine Words
Of the Lord of the Universe.

You speak. The Awaiting Populace hears –
A shopping list: Don't forget pickles,
Need toilet paper, Pick up toothpaste.

You wonder why the Universe doesn't listen.

The Universe never listens.

The more passionately you believe
The less it will listen.

The Universe is right.

ONE MAN'S RELIGION IS ANOTHER MAN'S NONSENSE.

WHIM ON GOD'S SPECIAL GIFT TO MEN

'Every man's mind moves continually from wisdom to madness and then back again in endless oscillation,' said Whim.

'What do you mean?' asked his youngest disciple.

'It's simple,' Whim replied with a big smile. 'A man's mind moves in wisdom whenever it is aware of its madness, and moves back into its madness whenever it comes under the illusion of having wisdom.'

'But . . . but that seems to mean that the mind is always mad.'

'Mmmmm,' said Whim.

'Then the very words you're now saying must be mad!'

'Obviously my belief that all my beliefs are madness must itself be madness,' agreed Whim.

'But – '

'Of course, there's another way of looking at it,' said Whim, brightening. 'Every belief is a unique, specially-wrapped personal gift of the Supreme Creator of the Universe.'

'But – '

'We ought, therefore, to treat each one with reverence.'

'Then, they're not madness!?'

'Oh, they're madness all right. Each and every belief is a unique, specially-wrapped gift of insanity from the Supreme Creator.'

A man's belief, given sufficient tender,
loving care, soon becomes his illusion.

'If all beliefs are illusions, Whim, then your statement that all fixed beliefs are illusions is itself an illusion.'

'Absolutely.'

'Then what is one to believe?'

'Exactly.'

PUT JUST TWO PEOPLE INTO THE ENTIRE UNIVERSE, EACH WITH BELIEF, AND BEFORE THEY DIE THEY'LL SOMEHOW MANAGE TO FIND EACH OTHER AND HAVE A WAR.

ON RELIGIONS

Within every great religion there is a subterranean tradition at war with the Church that the religion has created. The Church is the religion's social establishment: it helps hold society together and helps hold the people faithful to the religion. The subterranean tradition at war with the church is usually called mysticism because the 'anti-church' tradition embraces all, sees the Divine in all, and thus rejects the dualities which are the essence of any Church. The Church believes in the reality and seriousness of right and wrong. The Church believes in a System of Moral Laws. The Church believes in a System of Beliefs which form the core of the religion.

The mystic tradition denies the reality of right and wrong, the usefulness of moral laws, and the benefit of having a system of beliefs. The mystic tradition talks about the heart and love and unity.

One cannot afford to look too closely at a religion's moral and belief system. The idea that the Almighty Creator of the entire Universe of a billion billion galaxies is concerned with when and where and with whom a guy uses his pecker on the planet earth is a bit much. The idea that the Almighty Creator is concerned with what a man eats on Friday, and how his food is cooked, or whether it's pork or lamb, stretches our credulity a bit too.

But come to think of it, does it really ring true that the Lord God Almighty, Supreme Creator of a billion billion galaxies and probably a billion billion other universes, really gives the slightest fuck about *anything* we pathetic earthlings do? As Woody Allen might say: any God that has nothing better to do than to care what I'm up to, is such a pathetic God that I refuse to have anything to do with Him.

All beliefs are absurd, but religious beliefs make a mighty run for first place on the absurdity hit parade. However, because a belief is absurd doesn't mean it might not be useful. Dice-living is clearly an absurd idea, but it may be useful. The belief that Christ died for our sins may be absurd, but it has probably been helpful in millions of human lives. If Christ died for our sins, then we don't have to worry about our past or even worry much about right and wrong; good ol' Jesus has taken the sins of the world on his back. And I'm saved because I believe he died for my sins. Nothing to worry about.

So we should judge beliefs, whether religious or other, not by whether they are true or false – they are all more or less some form of bullshit – but by how useful and life-enhancing they are. 'Day by day I'm growing better and better' may be absurd but it may well be a helpful absurdity.

Look at any self-help book – including this one, if that's what this is – and you'll find them filled with the most obvious oversimplifications and vague prescriptions that would fail every logic and truth test we can imagine. But do they help people live more fulfilled lives? Sometimes, sometimes.

So don't knock a belief simply because you happen to notice it is wrong. That would be like a supra-rational doctor refusing to give a patient a placebo that the patient believes has helped him and the doctor knows has helped him, because the doctor knows that the placebo is chemically irrelevant to the patient's condition. The fact that the placebo works – improves the patient's condition because of the psychological belief of the patient – mostly annoys the doctor. Sometimes we may at first be annoyed to see some human being supremely happy because of some absurd belief they have.

They are living in illusion, you say to yourself, feeling superior in your misery. But don't knock it: was happiness ever based on anything but illusion?

It is very easy to notice how wrong other people's beliefs are; the real challenge is to see the absurdity of our own. Most of us can see the arbitrariness of, say, the sports team we root for, or the pop singers that we respond to, but we don't see that our political, religious, and moral tastes are usually just as arbitrary. Happy people find happy philosophies; depressed people find gloomy philosophies. We, being absurd people, have found an absurd philosophy. But they're all arbitrary, all with only the most tenuous links to basic reality.

All beliefs are placebos: content-less nothings that nevertheless can have an effect on us because of our belief.

WHIM ADMITS IT

'If we all live under illusions no matter how hard we try to escape,' asked Whim's brightest disciple, 'then what's the sense of preferring one set of ideas – yours, for example – over someone else's?'

'None whatsoever,' Whim replied.

'Then why should I be looking for enlightenment with you?'

'Shhhh,' whispered Whim, glancing nervously over his shoulder. 'Don't let the others hear.'

Everything you believe, you kill. The moment you have a belief in God, bang! you got Him.

It is a strange business that in life certainty is often a disability. If two people are walking through a terrain and one, having been there before, thinks he has seen all there is to see, he will move through the scenery blind. If the other knows nothing about the land and vegetation he's walking through he will see, freshly, whatever he is able to see.

You see (Don Juan went on) we only have two alternatives;

we either take everything for sure and real, or we don't. If we

follow the first, we end up bored to death with ourselves and

with the world. If we follow the second and erase personal

history, we create a fog around us, a very exciting and mysterious

state in which nobody knows where the rabbit will pop out, not

even ourselves . . . When nothing is for sure we remain alert,

perennially on our toes. It is more exciting not to know which

bush the rabbit is hiding behind than to behave as though

we know everything.

– from JOURNEY TO IXTLAN by Carlos Casteneda

As a sailor cruising up and down the Atlantic coast of the US I was quite happy not to know where I was. The idea of having radar or a computer readout that would permit me to know my precise position at any moment was depressing. I wasn't out on the ocean because I wanted to be certain of my position and what was going to happen next; I was out there in order to be in the midst of uncertainty. When I look at the lush sailing magazines and see the fabulous equipment advertised to make sailing safer and more reliable and to assure the sailor he will always know where he is, I shudder. We have created a society that is determined to eliminate risk – when risk is what most enlivens us. Risk means uncertainty. Certainty means relaxation, boredom, death.

OPTIONS

① It is time to create some new (if only temporary) beliefs. Take a good chunk of time and create your own proverbs, adages or moral principles. Your task is to write out some ideas that strike you as pertinent or important or witty. Don't worry if they're not brilliant or even original, get as many out there as you can. When you're worn out and can create no more, go through and see if you haven't actually come up with some very fresh thoughts that you had never expressed before. Be proud of yourself. Then tear them up. You can create even better ones next week.

② Take the one important belief about yourself that you are most convinced is true but that you know some people doubt. Consider this belief about yourself for a moment. What if others are right and your belief about yourself is wrong? Is that necessarily a disaster? If you aren't as you see yourself but rather as a few others see you, does the universe crumble? Interesting question.

③ List six of your beliefs about life that you think are important. Cast a die. Look at the belief chosen. Now cast a second die to see whether you renounce this belief for a week, or spend a week preaching this belief to as many people as you can. Then do it.

④ If you are an atheist or agnostic, try for a day to believe that there is a God over-looking and permeating the Universe or whatever. For a day create your own God. Give Him or Her whatever characteristics you find most easy to believe in. Live the God you have created for one day.

  If you do this, really do this, the world will be transformed, not because the God you have created is 'True' and your atheism was 'false', but because you have created a new world and are in touch with the power of belief.

  Of, if you are a believer in a God, try for a day to believe that that God has died, or retired, or zoomed off to another Universe – in any case, no longer exists. The world is now, for a day, devoid of God and whatever your belief in that God entailed.

  Live without your God for a day.

  Well?

⑤ Take one of your strong political beliefs. Consider its opposite. The next time you're in a political discussion, present as your view this view that is opposite to the one you normally express. Put all your passion into it.

⑥ The next time you are in an argument, argue your position for from two to five minutes and then begin to agree completely with the opposite side. Begin to express new arguments in favour of your 'opponent's' position. Become enthusiastic about this new position. Thank the person you were arguing with for helping you to see the light.

Isn't life amazing?

The inkpot, filled, holds all the world's books.
The inkpot, empty, holds all there is to know.
The inkpot, broken, in fragments, still says it all.
Says it all.

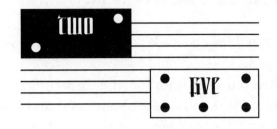

GOOD AND EVIL

Ahh, good. Ahh, evil. What would the world be without you?

A lot different.

Actually, good and evil are like order and purpose and success and failure: lines for creating interesting games.

If none of us created our own rules (good and bad) for ourselves and others, we couldn't play. This book is filled with ideas about good and bad. For us, good is flexibility and variety and playfulness and joy. And bad is rigidity and narrowness and seriousness.

So we all have our goods and our bads. Things get messy only when we feel we have to impose our goods and bads on others. We can *recommend* our goods and bads, but the moment we try to impose them we have entered the realm of trouble-making.

```
It is better to marry than to burn in
hellfire forever.
```
St Paul

There are occasionally other options.
Whim

Nothing reveals the human sickness more than moral righteousness. The Lord save us from 'good' people. No one is more likely to be marching off in the wrong direction than someone marching off on a crusade. The more powerfully someone is convinced of his moral rightness, the more damage he is likely to do.

If seriousness is the core of the human sickness, the core of seriousness is the need to be right. Show me a human being who has to be right and I'll show you a miserable human being, in every sense of the word.

When two people argue, the only winner is the one who doesn't mind losing.

There was a famous man who once said, 'I'd rather be right than be president.' Of course, he ended up being neither.

Most humans would rather be right than happy. When the Lord Chance was creating the universe and came up with the idea of giving human beings the impulse to be in the right, he doomed billions to unhappiness.

Now there are two kinds of 'right'. A man may be 'right' in arguing that if you accept such and such a premise then it logically follows that *x* is true. Now if someone out of ignorance and an untrained mind disputes this logic, the man may feel that he *knows* he is right, in the same sense that a man *knows* that two plus two is four. But we say unto thee, if you find someone who is arguing that two and two is not four, do not spend your energy disputing him. After you have heard what he has to say and are convinced it is utter nonsense, say to him, 'Hey, thanks, Buddy. I always thought two plus two equals four but now, listening to you, I realize that two plus two equals a hippopotamus.'

The more important sense in which someone feels he is right is about moral opinions. 'It is *wrong* to do that.' Well, maybe so, maybe not. And if we disagree we can advance our opinion and we may enjoy an exchange of arguments with a worthy thinker, but there usually comes a point where logic has run its course, and the wise man gracefully withdraws, nodding and bowing, leaving the other man to hold the field of battle and to be 'right'.

Traditionally the desire to be right is stimulated most strongly by marriage. In fact marriage might be defined as that state in which two human beings spend their time together being right and showing that the other is wrong. A similar tendency exists in the relationship between a parent and a teenager: each spends most of the time trying to show that the other is in the wrong. In the history of the universe no man has ever been unfaithful to his wife out of simple lust. No, it inevitably goes back to some flaw in the wife. And no teenager ever failed to take out the garbage or tidy his room because he didn't feel like it, but rather because of some injustice perpetrated by a parent. And no parent ever exploded at a teenager because of general irritation but always because of some horrible sin committed by the teenager, like leaving a pair of socks on the floor. We poor humans are taught from the beginning that our every act must have some sort of rational or moral purpose; that our actions must be 'right'. To justify what we do, we frequently require that others be wrong. The result is endless unnecessary conflict.

'I have sinned! I have sinned! Oh, Whim, what should I do?'

'You might consider fasting for one week.'

'That seems extreme.'

'For one day?'

'It was really only a small sin.'

'Five push-ups?'

'Thank you, I think that's exactly right.'

Whim sighed. 'Spiritual guides don't have the power they used to.'

Human beings don't usually do things for rational or moral reasons. They do things normally because they feel like doing them – out of instinct, out of, dare we say it, whim. But if challenged, a human has been trained to come up with a reason.

'Why did you do that?' asks someone.

'Who knows?' we answer, or, 'Beats me'; 'Accidents will happen'; 'Because I felt like it'.

Such answers, while honest, don't cut it with the way we're brought up. We are human beings: we do things for reasons, for the general good, for some overall purpose. We are taught to lie, to make something up.

'Why did you do that?' someone asks.

'Because I need to prepare for my physics exam'; 'Because I wanted to help Susie'; 'Because Mom told me to'; 'Because I feel it's best for George if I do'.

Whatever. But every act must be justified, no matter how whimsically we may actually have come to do it.

WHIM AND DAWN

Whim and his most beloved friend Dawn, who just happened to be the most virtuous person in the universe, and one of the most beautiful, often had discussions about good and evil, a subject very dear to Dawn's heart. She was rather resentful of Whim's seemingly cavalier attitude towards good and evil.

One morning she came up to Whim and even before he could say 'Hi, Dawn!' she slapped him as hard as she could across the face.

'Wow,' said Whim.

'I did that to show you the existence of evil,' announced Dawn.

'Wow,' said Whim, still touching his bruised cheek.

'The next time you feel like preaching about good and evil being illusions, keep this slap in mind.'

'Wow,' said Whim.

Later on that day, when it was teaching time and Whim was surrounded by a circle of students, including Dawn, Whim announced firmly: 'I'd like to talk today about the illusion of good and evil.'

Dawn promptly rose, worked her way through the other seated students and swatted Whim vigorously a second time across the face. Then, uttering several 'Excuse mes', she made her way back to resume her previous seat. Everyone else was stunned into silence.

'Is what Dawn just did good or evil?' Whim finally asked.

'It's a bummer,' cried one student.

'A real down.'

'Bad.'

'Freaky.'

'I see,' said Whim.

'It is not bad!' cried Dawn from the back of the circle. 'I did it for Whim's own good. It was *good*!'

'I see,' said Whim, and after another long silence, he added: 'Well, that about sums it up for today.'

The next day Dawn came a second time to Whim.

'To show you what evil and suffering are all about,' she announced, 'I've decided to let myself be seduced.'

'Wow,' said Whim.

'I'm purposely going to destroy my most sacred honour and then you can decide whether good and evil are illusions.'

'Going to let yourself be seduced?' said Whim.

'Yes!'

'But that would be awful!'

'See!' said Dawn triumphantly.

'But if you're definitely going to let yourself be seduced, I have one request.'

'What's that?'

Whim leered.

CAREFUL WHAT YOU ASK FOR

Once upon a time there was a Great Hero named 'I'. Great Hero I lived a life of constant conflict and struggle. Every moment of every day he was fighting against baddies, who seemed to infiltrate most of the human beings he met. There were a few people that he called Goodies, but these were usually unimportant except to be saved from the Baddies by Great Hero I.

Whenever Great Hero I wanted to whip himself and the other Goodies up into a good fighting spirit he would make a Great Speech.

'Brother Goodies,' he would say. 'Today we must fight again the goodie fight. If we persevere we may in our own lifetime rid the universe of all the Baddies who sin and murder and fornicate and lie and steal, and then we shall all live happily ever after.'

'Hear, hear!' shouted all the Goodies, and cocking their hydrogen bomb semi-automatics they marched off to do battle against the Baddies.

And it came to pass that, lo and behold, the Goodies succeeded in destroying all the Baddies, and the earth was free of all murder and fornication and lying and stealing and sloth and pride and lust and greed, and the earth contained only Goodies. Great Hero I stood at last free from all those enemies he had spent his lifetime combating.

And Great Hero I wept.

For without all the Baddies, he was no longer Great Hero I. He was nothing, a nobody. To exist, he needed his enemies. Only at that moment did he feel love for the Baddies, realizing only after it was too late that *they* had made his life what it was.

When your commune has become a hopelessly dirty, garbage-strewn chaotic wreck, schedule an orgy for right after total clean-up.

Without our enemies there are no games to play. The stronger and more worthy the opponent the better we may play. A great opponent creates a great player.

Yet we do not love our enemies. We do not honour our opponents. So imbedded, at least in the American consciousness, is the attitude that 'Winning is Everything' that players are taught to hate their opponents, to win at any cost. It is a paradox that Ali is the Greatest because he was lucky enough to be challenged by three formidable and great opponents: Lipton, Foreman and Frazier. Great matches in any sport need *two* great teams. As soon as there is only one great team, that team is no longer able to prove that it is great. Pete Sampras beating one mediocrity after another cannot be great. It is when he plays an Agassi at the top of Agassi's game and raises his own game to previously unseen levels that we can clearly see his greatness.

And in the realm of good and evil, we should learn to love our enemies as our selves for the simple reason that our enemies are ourselves; they are our creation. The 'bad' person to you is rarely a 'bad' person to himself. He sees himself as a goodie and you as a baddie. And you both need each other. If he wasn't such an awful baddie you wouldn't know what a good goodie you are.

Our personal enemies are those who are uptight; but if we ever really get angry at those who are uptight we become uptight ourselves. If we ourselves don't lust, why should we get upset with those that do?

Judge yourself always with a hung jury.

Blessed is the man who walks not
in the counsel of the good,
nor stands in the way of sinners
nor sits in the seats of the wise;
But his delight is in the law of Chance,
and on his Whims he meditates day and night.
He is like a tree planted by a flowing stream,
dropping its leaves and fruit hour by hour
into the flow
into the flow.

FROM **BOOK OF PSALMS (REVISED VERSION)**

THE STORY OF NEXT YEAR

One day Whim walked into his friend Everyman's study with a deep frown on his face.

'Ev,' he said, staring at the poster of Martin Luther King on the wall, 'I've just realized something, something I think maybe we ought to be worried about. Do you realize that although we're both now twenty-nine years old, that in all the time we've been growing up, playing football and basketball, meeting new friends, searching for old Ultimate Truth, trying to make a better world, in all that time, every year, year after year, Senator McCarthy trudges through the snows of New Hampshire to end the Vietnam War, and the pigs riot with the freaks in Chicago, and Johnson withdraws and starts the peace talks, and Bobby Kennedy gets shot in LA, and Nixon beats Humphrey, and it's always, *always* – I think we really ought to at least think about it – always the year 1968.'

'Really?' said Everyman, who was typing a letter to an editor.

'Yes,' said Whim uncertainly. 'Don't you remember telling your mom when you were six years old to vote for Nixon because he had a secret plan to end the war?'

'That's true,' said Ev, looking puzzled. 'How childish I was then.'

'And don't you remember our hacking around with Abbie Hoffman at the Democratic convention in Chicago when we were seventeen, because you thought we could embarrass the Democrats into stopping the war?'

'You're right,' said Ev. 'What a boy I was then.'

'And sending money to the McCarthy campaign in Wisconsin when you were twenty-two?'

'That's true. But I was politically naive.'

'And yelling, "We did it! We did it!" when Johnson withdrew and started the peace talks in the spring when we were twenty-five?'

'I admit it, I admit it. How wrong I was.'

'But, Ev, this continual repetition of 1968 every year of our lives – doesn't it seem a little strange?'

Everyman, no longer typing, frowned in concentration.

'Yes, I suppose so,' he said. 'But everything will be OK if we can just get Humphrey elected president in next week's election.'

'But Ev, Nixon's beaten Humphrey now twenty-eight consecutive years!'

'Oh yeah, you're right,' Ev replied. 'But still, I just read in *Time* Magazine that Humphrey's gaining fast in the last few weeks.'

'But, Ev, we keep doing the same things, year after – '

'And there's always next year.'

OPTIONS

Before casting a die, read through the six options below. Throw out one or two (or all six) and create some of your own to replace those you toss out. Then cast a die.

① All day try to do nothing but good, every second of every minute, of every hour.

② List three of what you believe to be your most important moral principles. Let a die choose one of the three. Unless the moral principle involves violence of one sort or another or a felony, try to break that moral principle within the next twenty-four hours.

③ Lie. Every day you must make a conscious effort to tell one lie. It will be good for your soul.

④ Take one of your most important personal values – honesty, or fairness, or love, or integrity, or playfulness, or generosity, etc. – and spend at least ten minutes with some friend telling him or her why this value is ridiculous, or unimportant or actually a danger to the individual or society.

⑤ Who is your favourite person? Is that person one who has strong moral principles that he or she preaches regularly? How does your favourite person deal with his or her own moral preferences? Take them seriously? Lightly?

   It is very hard to become anyone's favourite person if you are always right. St Paul was a great man but I doubt he had a single friend.

⑥ Fake it. Pretend. Lie. Make it up. Be someone else. Contradict yourself. Let go. Don't have a single principle that lasts for more than two point six seconds.

   Not bad, huh?

TWO PARABLES OF GIVING AND NOT GIVING

'O Beloved Whim, I just gave all my money to your school. I feel so good. So free. No more money hang-ups. No more hassles about what to buy or how much to pay. I'm free!'

'What hassles?' asked Whim.

'The hassles of having to decide whether to buy this or give money to that, to help this person or invest in that.'

'That's a hassle?' asked Whim.

'Of course.'

'Is a man with compulsive lust free when suddenly all the women are locked up?'

'No.'

'You may have locked up your money in my closet,' concluded Whim, 'but as for your attachment to money, that's a lot harder to give away.'

*

'I'm sorry, Whim,' a second disciple said firmly, 'but I have more important things to do with my money than to give it all to your school.'

'That's great,' said Whim. 'What are some of those important things?'

'I haven't decided yet, but I wish to retain the freedom to do good – in my own way.'

'That's great,' said Whim. 'When are you starting to do good in your own way?'

'Well, soon. Soon. Right now, of course, I have to sell my house and get two books published and – '

'What's that got to do with doing good?'

'Uh, well, you see it's work towards getting more money so I can have more power to do more good.'

'That's great,' said Whim. 'How long you been working to make money to have power to do good?'

'Oh, for years, Whim,' the disciple responded with a smile. 'For years.'

'That's great. And how long have you been doing good?'

'Er . . . soon, Whim, soon.'

'I won't hold my breath,' said Whim.

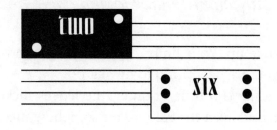

INSIGHT

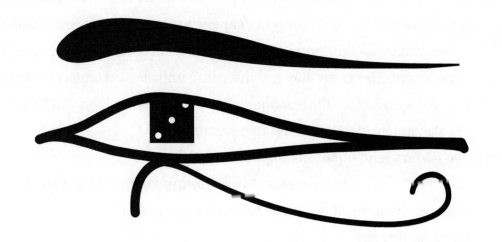

Any insight, given sufficient tender loving care, becomes an illusion.

You are beginning to wake up. Your limbs are stiff, your mind a little fuzzy, cobwebs linger everywhere, but you are beginning to awaken.

You notice that the sky is a little brighter, the leaves flicker in the sunlight in a way you hadn't noticed, and even the rain seems somehow nice.

It isn't the sky or sun or rain that have changed, but you. You create them; the drabness or the glory.

You have had an insight, a breakthrough. Wonderful! But remember, an insight is any idea which organizes reality in a useful or enjoyable way; an illusion is any idea which organizes reality in a useless or misery-making way. Truth has nothing to do with either of them. And remember, too, that your insight, if you give it sufficient tender loving care, will soon turn into a new illusion.

One day the seeker was meditating and after five hours of quiet concentration on just being with her breathing she experienced her whole being flooded with an exquisite Light, brighter and softer and clearer than any light she'd ever experienced. Her entire life and the entire universe became crystal clear for her. After an hour of this magnificent experience of Light and Clarity she 'awoke' in her room in meditation posture.

Later she told a friend about her experience.

'That was God!' the friend announced enthusiastically. 'You experienced God! Next time you meditate, if you try hard enough God may stay with you for hours, or *for ever!*'

And so the seeker began in her meditation not simply to *be* with her breathing but rather to try to get God to pay another visit.

The Light disappeared for ever.

WHIM COMMENTS: When you experience Light, you experience light. Bringing God into it only confuses things. One man meditating experiences only his breathing. Another experiences Great White Light. Who says one is better than the other? The one experiencing his breathing at least knows he's alive. The other guy's probably dead and in heaven.'

* * *

Insights are fun. 'Eureka!' cried Archimedes and rose out of the bathtub. 'Ah-ha!' said Einstein, and baffled and thrilled men's minds for generations. 'Hmmmm,' said Freud and began creating nice little theories about mankind's dirty laundry. 'Ach, Der Lieber!' said Marx, and created a theory that has had consequences, as do all theories, that he never intended, and he's been tossing in his grave ever since.

Insights are breakthroughs – blasting through the walls that confine us either psychologically or intellectually. This book is intended to provide a few 'ah-ha's', but where they come for each reader is entirely unpredictable – as are all our insights. Because one man's insight appears to the next as just another illusion.

'Ah-ha!' says Copernicus. 'The earth revolves around the sun.'

'The man is mad,' says the Church and threatens to excommunicate those who agree with him.

* * *

When the Zen monk Kuleki finally achieved satori, he said to himself: 'After almost forty years I seem, at last, to be ready to be a nobody. What a long journey. What a lot of trouble. Especially considering that I was there all the time.'

LETTING GO THE BIG FISH

One day when Whim was fishing at the end of a dock, his Indian mentor Grain-of-Sand came up and began fishing beside him. The old man baited his hook with a worm and tossed the line in. Over the next hour Grain-of-Sand hooked and landed a half dozen small and medium-sized fish and, chuckling happily, placed them in the bucket to take home. Whim too caught several fish, a few even larger than Grain-of-Sand's.

Then, just as they were thinking of leaving, the old Indian's thin bamboo pole began to bend, and as he reeled in his line a huge bass could be seen flailing away. Whim was pleased as Grain-of-Sand, smiling happily, began reeling in the fish. With great effort Grain-of-Sand hauled the big fish up on to the dock and began gingerly to remove it from the hook.

Then, with Whim watching, the old man looked the big bass right in the eye and said: 'Sorry, fella, you're too big,' and he lowered the fish back into the water.

Whim sat quietly for a while as Grain-of-Sand rebaited his hook and cast out his line until finally he cleared his throat and said: 'That sure was a big bass you just caught.'

'Yep,' said Grain-of-Sand.

'Big enough to eat.'

'Yep.'

'Big enough to stuff.'

'Yep.'

Whim was silent awhile jigging his line and then he finally said: 'But you threw it back.'

'Yep.'

'*Why?*'

'The way I figure it,' said Grain-of-Sand, beginning to reel in another fish, 'anyone can catch a big fish. But how many can let it go?'

WHIM AND THE MASTER OF MEDITATION

One day Whim went to visit a sage famous throughout the States for his practice of meditation. The sage was famous for sitting so still not a hair of him moved in any way.

After sitting with him and his numerous followers for almost an hour Whim finally broke the silence to ask: 'O Great Sage, where did you learn such stillness?'

The sage replied: 'From a cat. He was watching a mouse hole with even greater concentration than you have seen in me.'

'That's good,' said Whim. 'But I bet the cat doesn't interrupt his stillness to answer silly questions.'

Anyone can have a good insight, and it's a great thrill to reel it in and look at it. But sooner or later we have to let it go. It's an insight precisely because it is appropriate for a specific time and place. When the time and place change, new insights are needed. It may well be that the insight will become appropriate again in our lives. It may be that we want to share the insight at times with others who seem to be in a similar spot to where we were when the insight helped us. But as soon as we try to apply the insight in some sort of universal way we are asking for trouble.

Whatever 'insights' this book has to offer are for only a very few and for those few only for some certain circumscribed time in their lives. The idea that someone would read this book and conclude that he should use dice in his life all the time is depressing. Our theory is that people can read *The Dice Man* or *The Book of the Die* and never touch a die or flip a coin and yet still come away with insights that lighten their lives. One of the paradoxes of my own life is that I used dicing in my own life off and on for fifteen years before finishing writing *The Dice Man*, and as soon as the book was finished I ceased using the dice, never to use them again except in trivial play.

THE DIECIPLE WHO KNEW EVERYTHING AND THE ONE WHO KNEW NOTHING

A conventionally-minded dieciple from an austerely serious school of dice-living was walking along a dock one day to get into his boat when his thoughts were interrupted by noticing another dieciple consulting *The Book of the Die* with a complicated collection of coins and three green dice.

'There's no point in that,' he thought to himself. 'The poor fool doesn't even know how to properly consult the book with three different coloured dice.' He decided it was his duty to show this dieciple, who probably never had a chance to study with the best masters, how to use a black die, a white die and a green die, and to cast in the proper way.

So he went over and patiently tried to explain the correct way of casting dice in consulting *The Book of the Die* because, after all, it was said that a man who was really in tune with that holy book could do anything, even walk on water.

When he had finished his little lecture, the other dieciple confessed his ignorance and thanked him very humbly.

The first man then went on to his boat and soon sailed out along the dock towards the open water. As he passed the young dieciple on the dock, however, he noticed that he was still playing with three green dice and some coins. The man in the boat shook his head at the perversity and ignorance of human nature and, while looking forward he guided his boat out towards the open bay. But when he looked back towards the dock he saw a strange sight: the other dieciple was coming towards him, walking rapidly across the surface of the open water.

Amazed, the boatsman luffed his sails and waited until the second dieciple had walked up to him.

'Hey, buddy,' the young man said, standing on the surface of the water. 'I'm sorry to bother you, but I'm afraid I'm still all messed up about how you're supposed to use the multi-coloured dice to consult *The Book of the Die*. Could you explain it to me again?'

WHO NEEDS A GURU?

'Who the hell needs a guru?' demanded a frustrated seeker.

'Beats me,' said Whim.

'Those phonies who say each of us has to find some guide to show us the path – bullshit!'

'Good point,' said Whim.

'Most of them are just as lost and miserable as I am.'

'Absolutely,' said Whim.

'At least I'm not fooling myself.'

'Right,' said Whim. 'You know you're always going to be miserable.'

MESSAGES

And it chanced that the Lord of the Universe, the Divine Creator Himself, did come to send a Message to mankind, a Message which would liberate men from the heavy burdens they had come to encumber themselves with. And He sent the Message to earth and it was spoken and it was written and men did not hear and men did not see.

'How can this be?' asked the Lord of the Universe. 'I have sent the Message that will liberate all men from the burdens they needlessly carry and yet they do not bear it, do not see it.'

All the angels stood in embarrassed silence at the Lord's question except one, Our Beloved Whim, who dared to speak.

'Mighty Lord,' said Whim. 'In your Infinite Wisdom and Love you have sent men the Message, but they have neither ears to hear it nor eyes to see it.'

'I know,' said the Divine Creator. 'But how can this be?'

'It's simple, Lord,' Whim replied. 'Human beings don't want Messages, they want burdens.'

'But they suffer from their burdens,' said the Lord.

'True, Lord,' replied Our Beloved Whim. 'But not as much as they suffer from Messages.'

A BRIEF HANDBOOK OF DEEPLY SPIRITUAL KNOWLEDGE AND ADVICE

- If your car has a flat tyre, in all probability the tyre will remain flat until it is fixed.

- If you are in the middle of a traffic jam on the M4 and have moved only thirteen feet in the last ten minutes, note the exact number of feet per hour your speed is increased by your muttering, swearing or honking your horn.

- Your child has just broken your favourite dish. Notice the interesting pattern the pieces make in the dust pan as you sweep them into it.

- Your bank has just informed you that your current account is overdrawn by $1,018.61. Spend the day considering ways you might be able to earn or save exactly 61 cents.

- You must walk outdoors one hundred yards to an important interview. It is raining hard and windy. You have no raincoat. You are wearing a new suit. Your umbrella is torn to pieces in the first three seconds. Notice how delicious the rain feels slashing against your face.

- You have just been fired from your job. As you leave the office try to hide from yourself the exhilaration you feel.

- Your novel has just been rejected by the thirty-seventh publisher to see it. Using a calculator, figure to the nearest decimal what percentage of possible publishers have not yet been given the chance to reject it.

OPTIONS

Consider doing something new in your life: a new action, a new emotion towards someone you're close to, a new act of creativity, a new form of spirituality, a new laundromat. If you're drawn to more than one such new something, make a list, cast a die.

Now cast a die to see how Chance comments on your new life.

① Good for you. You're getting somewhere. You're beginning to open up. So go ahead. Do it. Don't expect much, but do it. Do it for the sake of doing it. And if it rains cats and dogs, don't fret. You did it.

② The whole world is not watching. We are not watching. Your granny in heaven is not watching. So go ahead.

③ 'The Road of Excess leads to the Palace of Wisdom' – Portnoy.

④ Better a hundred pratfalls than a life of seventy years of trudging.

⑤ Supreme success. You have hit on precisely the new path that will take you where your being has been longing to go. Don't stop.

⑥ Big deal. Now why don't you try something really challenging?

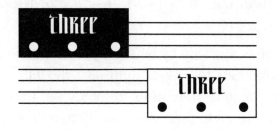

PATHS

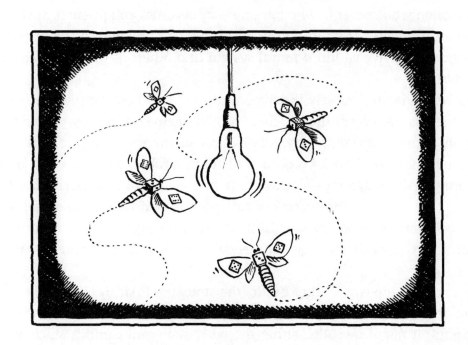

If you don't climb the mountain, it will eventually fall on you.

A path of liberation is any way by which a person moves from a state of tension, rigidity and unhappiness to one of lightness, flexibility and joy. The methods man has used to try to achieve liberation from his self-imposed unhappiness have varied, and the factors common to them are difficult to isolate. One sage's method may be another one's snare, and one man's enlightenment may seem to another to be psychotic hallucination. One man's method may involve experiences and ideas about God, illumination, salvation; another's not. The non-mystic agnostics Socrates, Montaigne and Nietzsche were, by our definition, as liberated as the God-intoxicated believers Meister Eckhart, Ramakrishna and Walt Whitman. All express in their lives the lightness, flexibility and joy which seem to us rather desirable.

A study of the various paths to enlightenment indicates that elements we might assume to be part of such a path are actually irrelevant. Religious belief appears to have no relation whatsoever to whether one is or becomes enlightened. Such belief can be a snare or a release. Morality too turns out to be unrelated to the liberated man, some of whom may live within a moral system and others of whom appear free from any such system.

Can we define more closely the ways that men try to escape their misery?

First there is the way of the true believer. To escape our misery we surrender ourselves totally to one single authority, all of whose answers we accept on faith. We may accept a single living authority – a guru, a dictator, a rabbi, a pope – or we may accept the authority of some system – a church, a messianic political party, a set of commandments. The secret of the success of this path is that we isolate ourselves among other true believers, for if we try to exist in the multiplicity of everyday society we will continually face the conflict between our leader, system and ethos and the other people around us.

The second is the way of the ascetic, the stoic, the fakir. It is the way of denying all human desires, accustoming ourselves to doing without so that doing without is no longer painful. It might be called either the path of eternal conflict, since our human desires never cease and thus the need to suppress never ends, or, equally, it might be called the path of death, since the ultimate nirvana of desirelessness is achieved only in death.

The third way is the way of the mystic. This path differs from the first in that the One is internal and vague and undefined as opposed to the leader or belief system that the first seeker surrenders to. As mystic we may try the methods of either of the first two paths but our goal is not ultimately denial or total surrender to a single authority but some sort of ill-defined unity with a Force that permits us to flow unimpeded with that Force.

The fourth way is that of the sage. It is the way of sceptical reason, of one who realizes the relativity, insubstantiality and unimportance of things and chooses to live within the normal mores of society. Since all is illusion and folly, as wise men we may choose to play the games of the society we find ourselves in but without the blind passion and ignorance of normal men.

The fifth way is the path of chaos. To escape the bonds of enslaving society, we may choose chaos – through anarchy, nihilism, use of psychedelics or dice. Since all is illusion and folly, then anything may be done.

The sixth and last is the path of play. It incorporates aspects of the other five. Like the path of the sage, the path of play assumes that all is relative, insignificant and illusory, but unlike the sage as players we don't limit ourselves to the dominant games of society. We incorporate aspects of chaos into our lives so that we can create new games not thought of or frowned upon by our society. As players we may occasionally play true believer or ascetic saint or mystic, but we live each of these paths as part of our overall play rather than as a final answer. The path of play thus incorporates all of the other paths within it.

```
There are two kinds of fool: the one
who thinks his desire is everything,
and the one who thinks his desires
are nothing.
```

THE UNMARKED PATH

One day Whim, who loved to take long walks in wild country, decided to climb a mountain with some friends. They'd heard that the trail up was difficult to follow, but discovered as they climbed that it was clearly marked all the way to the top.

When they came down in the afternoon Whim began to knock over all the little piles of stones which someone had made to mark the trail so clearly.

'Hey,' said the chief disciple. 'What are you doing?'

'I'm making it easier for the next travellers,' replied Whim, knocking over another pile of stones.

'But you're obscuring the trail!'

'I hope so,' said Whim. 'The path that's clearly marked is never the Path.'

'But what about those who simply want to get to the top of the mountain?' asked another disciple.

'They can take a helicopter,' said Whim.

'But what about those who want to climb to the top?'

'For them there's hope,' said Whim smiling. 'By Chance, thanks to me, they may get lost and discover a new Path.'

'But what if this is the only trail?'

'I doubt it,' said Whim. 'But if it is, they get to rediscover it for themselves and, in rediscovering it, get what no one can ever get following a well-marked path.'

'Does this mean that the easy path is never the Path?'

Whim kicked over a few more stones.

'Sometimes the easiest path is the Path, sometimes the hardest Path is the Path. All I know for sure is that a well-marked trail is never a Path.'

'You'll never convince the Forest Rangers,' commented the chief disciple.

Whim laughed.

'No,' he said. 'They, like priests everywhere, protect the ruts. We, like creators everywhere, must fill them in and begin digging elsewhere.'

WHIM AND THE SIX PATHS

One day a disciple who had been with Whim for many months came to him and said: 'I think at last I've got it, arrived at the Path, but I'm not sure.'

'Happens all the time,' said Whim.

'But can you help me?'

'Sure,' replied Whim. 'Are you on the Path now?'

The student hesitated and then answered, 'Yes.'

'Good. We're all set.' Whim took out a pen and piece of paper and began to write. 'OK,' he said, after he had finished. 'On this piece of paper are six different paths you might take in the next week: first, spending all your time meditating and trying to be at one with the Path; second, writing a book explaining to people how they too may find the Path; third, making love with someone; fourth, uh, returning to Los Angeles and getting an office job again; fifth, telling everyone you meet all of the faults and weaknesses you've noticed in me and in this ashram; or sixth, something *else*. *Now* all I want you to do is choose one of these that will demonstrate to me that you are clearly on the Path.'

The student studied the six options with great concentration and then looked up at Whim with a serious frown.

'Well . . . ' the student began uncertainly, but before he could say another word, Whim picked up the paper, tore it to pieces and marched out of the room. The student, now certain he no longer knew, sadly followed.

Many months later the student came to Whim a second time with the problem of knowing what was the Path and what wasn't. He understood intellectually that all paths were the Path, but he experienced two different ways of life: one high and joyful and clearly *on* the Path, and one depressed or hectic, and to him clearly *off*.

After listening to the student, Whim again wrote down the same six options and handed them to the student, saying: 'I want you to tell me which of these paths may be for you the Path, and to choose one for the next week.'

The student again studied the options with a serious frown.

'Well . . . ' he began, and Whim this time let him continue. 'No matter which one I choose it'll turn out not to be the Path.'

'Exactly,' said Whim. 'You've said it all, said it all.'

'And no matter which one you chose, it would be the Path.'

'You got it,' said Whim.

'But how can I try to change myself so that no matter which one *I* choose it will be the Path?'

'You can't do it,' said Whim.

'Then why am I here?' asked the student desperately.

'Beats me,' said Whim, and he left.

A year later the student came to Whim a third time.

'I got it,' he announced. 'I'm on the Path.'

'Great,' said Whim. 'What are you doing this week?'

'Beats me,' said the student.

'Well,' said Whim, 'here are six options,' and he patiently wrote down the same six: meditating, writing a book, making love, getting an office job, dumping on Whim or something else. When Whim had finished writing the list he handed it to the student.

This time the student tore the paper up into little pieces and blew them gently off the palm of his hand out into the room.

'This week I'll try love-making,' he said.

'That's very good,' said Whim, 'But what about your meditation?'

'Every man to his own Path,' said the student and he walked out.

Whim grinned happily.

◎ All ways of liberation start with slavery. Convents and monasteries are the Catholic way of destroying the self so that the spirit may live. They exist with a rigid hierarchy and rules and discipline. Their first principle is the total submission of the nuns and monks to God and to the religious order.

So too in the East, where total obedience to the guru is also the first principle of discipleship. The seeker surrenders his will to his teacher, knowing that his own will is the very heart of his enslavement. Giving up one's freedom is, paradoxically, the *sine qua non* of proceeding on the path to liberation.

These kinds of overt enslavement are necessary because as men normally live, our enslavement is hidden. We are enslaved by our past, by our sense of self, by our need for certainty and consistency, by our illusions. The purpose of surrender to the dice is to free us from our hidden masters so that when we finally abandon the mastery of the dice, we will be, for the first time in our lives, free.

Enslavement is in reality just another word for discipline, for training, for education. Instead of teaching us certain skills that let us work at a high level somewhere in the established society, dice-living tries to free us from the domination of society so that we can play with established norms and values rather than be run by them. Conventional education teaches conformity and accommodation; dicing teaches detachment and flexibility. With the normal diploma we remain limited to the norms and values that society offers. With dicing we become free to create new norms and values and thus help create a new society.

Dicing aims not at creating a 'better' person or 'better' society, at least in traditional terms. The value of dicing is threefold: playfulness, flexibility and multiplicity. We come to honour the playful over the serious, the flexible over the rigid, the many over the one.

All happy and fulfilled people have one secret in common: they have all learned to surrender. Happy and fulfilled Christians are those who have learned to surrender to the spirit of Christ and the will of God. Their lives are a joyful yea-saying to whatever befalls them because they have faith in God and surrender to whatever He does, no matter how evil or wrong or unfair it may seem on the level of their personal feelings. They may fight the evil or lament it, but they will accept it as the Will of God, and that acceptance, that surrender, is the source of their happiness. They can even, paradoxically, accept the bad people around them because they accept sinners as part of what God has created.

The unhappy man is he who refuses to surrender to something or someone, even to himself. A total egotist may be a happy man; he has surrendered totally to the will of himself, whom he sees as infallible.

Others find happiness by surrender to institutions – to church, or army, or political party. Some might say that such people crave order but we say what they crave is surrender.

With dicing we go beyond surrender to freedom. In the early stages we surrender to the random will of the die – a specific force that we experience as outside ourselves.

Later, there will be no surrender because there will be no individual separate from the falling die or separate from the society in which we exist. The young child at play is not in a state of surrender but rather in a state of unity. Surrender can exist only in a state of duality. As long as the dualities exist, just so long will surrender be the secret of human happiness. But once that dual world is broken down, then there is no one left to surrender and no one or nothing to surrender to.

WHIM ROLLS OFF THE PATH

One day Whim was deeply involved in a long and pleasurable act of lovemaking with a young woman who had come to his school a few months before.

Whim's mind was not overly burdened with thoughts of any kind when he suddenly realized that the girl beneath him had just said: 'Oh, Whim, please help me find the path to enlightenment.'

Whim stopped moving and looked down into the girl's wide, serious eyes.

'Where have you been the last half hour?'

'Thinking how I might convince you how serious I am in my spiritual seeking.'

Whim rolled slowly over and off the girl.

'I'm convinced,' he announced.

'But where is the path?'

Whim sighed.

'I was on it a minute ago,' he said, 'but it went away.'

ON WORSHIPFUL DISCIPLES

A minnow, worried about his smallness, decided to consult the wisest, largest fish he could find. He looked and he looked but for a long time all he could find was other minnows. At last, however, he discovered a large fish, and he swam as fast as his little tail would take him over to the large fish and said to him: 'Oh, Great Fish, I am but a little minnow and I – '

But he was swallowed whole by the big fish and the rest of the dialogue is lost. It is assumed that the big fish answered the little minnow's question.

BEING DISTRACTED FROM A DISTRACTION

When Whim was only a teenager he was already deeply into his search for Ultimate Truth. One day he went to his mentor, Grain-of-Sand.

'You've got to help me, Grain-of-Sand,' Whim moaned.

'Yep,' said Grain-of-Sand.

'I have a problem. I seem to want to make love to almost every girl I see. I'm always being distracted from my quest for U.T.'

'Yep,' said Grain-of-Sand.

'But can't you help!?'

'You got a very serious problem,' said Grain-of-Sand, 'And there's only one solution.'

'What is it?'

'You got to make love to every gal you meet.'

'But, Grain-of-Sand – '

'But be very certain you're not distracted by your desire to be looking for U.T.'

THE PATHLESS PATH

There is nothing you have to do, no one you have to be. The wise man does what he does, not to get from one state to another, but by being in touch with where he is. You may be listening to us now thinking that we will help you on the Path, to get from a to b, but there is nothing which is not the Path, there is no place to go except where you are, and no one here to help you, except another manifestation of yourself. You, seated, listening in total confusion, are as perfect as you will ever be; you, seated, listening, in bliss, are as corrupt as you will ever be.

Since no one is walking there are no footsteps. Since there is no ultimate goal there is no place to go. Since there is nowhere to go there is no need for a path. With no one to do the going and no place to go and no path to go there, we can say that what we seek is no one not going anywhere on a path that doesn't exist.

THE ONE TRUE GURU

'In your own great search for the One True Guru, how, Whim, did you distinguish those yogis who were fakes from those who were real?'

'At first,' Whim replied, 'I found that the fakes all had answers. While the True Gurus never had answers.'

'I see.'

'But after I finally stumbled upon Ultimate Truth I realized I'd been wrong.'

'*How?*'

'Then I knew that every yogi I'd ever been to had been the One True Guru.'

WHIM TRIES TO GET THE GREAT ABOMINABLE SNOWMAN SAGE TO EMPTY OUT THE LAST BIT

Grain-of-Sand thought Whim's last and best chance to find old Ultimate Truth was if he went to India and tried to find the Great Abominable Snowman Sage, a great yogi who had been meditating for two thousand years and was thought to be closer to Ultimate Truth than any other being. Whim's best friend Billy and his girlfriend Dawn, both juniors in high school with Whim, went along with him. Soon they were high in the Himalayas, but had still not found the Great Abominable Snowman Sage. As they began to camp for the night in a cave, they talked about their quest with Osso, the wise Sherpa guide who was leading them. We are fortunate that the events were recorded in the film *Whim*.

EXT. MOUTH OF MOUNTAIN CAVE. EVENING.

WHIM, BILLY, DAWN and OSSO are seated in the mouth of the cave around a blazing campfire. OSSO is roasting a marshmallow on a stick. The Sherpa bearers are in b.g. eating from a bowl. An ancient transistor radio plays INDIAN MUSIC.

> BILLY
> We're never going to find this Great Secret Sage. And then how will we recognize him?

> OSSO
> Who knows? Buddha say that a true sage for one man, for others only a true jerk.

> WHIM
> Come on, Buddha didn't really use the word 'jerk'.

> OSSO
> Oh, yes. In the Magana Sutra, Buddha say 'tathata endi sumana jerk'. Only in twentieth century men realize that 'jerk' is English word Buddha accidentally use three thousand years too early.

> DAWN
> What religion are you, Billy?

> BILLY
> Episcopalian. We believe in the salvation of the upper classes through belief that Christ died so that poor people would be satisfied with their lot.

They all look at him.

BILLY (CONT)

Some believe in salvation through faith, but most believe in salvation through money. The Bible says rich people can enter heaven easier than a needle into a camel.

DAWN

No, no, Billy. That verse actually says it's almost impossible for a rich man to get into heaven.

BILLY

(rising and moving into cave)

Don't be silly. If the Bible said that, America would have outlawed it.

BILLY disappears into the cave with a flashlight.

WHIM

What's your religion, Osso?

OSSO

Buddha says one man's religion another man's bullshit.

BILLY (O.S.)

I found him! I found him!!

WHIM and DAWN leap up, but OSSO keeps poking calmly at the fire. BILLY stands at the mouth of the cave with his flashlight.

BILLY (CONT)

I almost pissed on him! The greatest yogi the world has ever seen!

WHIM, BILLY and DAWN hurry into the back of the cave, leaving OSSO quietly stirring the fire.

INT. BACK OF CAVE. NIGHT.

BILLY and DAWN are holding flashlights and staring respectfully forward. WHIM, holding a lighted torch, is kneeling on the cave floor, his eyes bright.

In front of him, sitting in the full lotus posture, is the most frail, thin and wrinkled YOGI ever seen. He is clothed in a white loin cloth and is totally encased in ice, which now is falling off in shards, dripping with hot yellow liquid.

> DAWN
> *(whispering to BILLY)*
> Only you would pee on the world's most illuminated saint.

> BILLY
> *(whispering back)*
> If he's so illuminated, how come I didn't see him?

Icicles on the YOGI's jaw and eyes drop off and the YOGI's eyes open. He looks at the four in front of him, frowns, closes his eyes and resumes his meditation.

The others seat themselves in the lotus position and DAWN starts an OM chant and is joined by WHIM and BILLY. OSSO, in the background, begins playing a dart game with icicles as darts.

After a moment the YOGI slowly raises his hand and the chanting stops. There is a long respectful silence.

> YOGI
> For five thousand years I have spent every moment seeking
> to purify my mind in order to find Ultimate Truth. My mind
> has been almost totally blank now for over two hundred
> years, filled only with eternal blinding light.

> BILLY
> Wow.

YOGI

I believe I am in almost complete harmony with Ultimate
Truth.

WHIM turns to look at DAWN and BILLY, who are staring in awe and wonder at the old guru.
OSSO can be seen in the b.g. still playing a game of darts with icicles with one of the sherpas.

BILLY

That's marvellous, O Greatest of Abominable Sages, but why
do you say almost complete?

YOGI

Because in the midst of the eternal, blinding light, always,
sooner or later, sometime during the day, month or decade,
appears . . . a tomato.

WHIM stares at the YOGI respectfully.

WHIM

. . . A tomato.

YOGI

A tomato.

DAWN

How do you interpret this extraordinary image, O Great Sage?

YOGI

I am not pure. Although I have fasted now for two thousand
years I am not free of vile gluttony.

DAWN

. . . Vile gluttony . . .

YOGI

Although I have never eaten one, never even knew what a
tomato was until I'd completed several decades of research,
it nevertheless seems clear I still lust for food.

BILLY

But . . . a tomato!

DAWN

(whispering to WHIM)
Maybe we should tell Osso to hide the marshmallows.

YOGI

But in another century or two the vile image will be wiped
out and I will at last have so emptied my mind that it will be
filled only with the light of Ultimate Truth.

For several moments WHIM remains silent opposite the YOGI, frowning in concentration.

WHIM

O Most Mighty of Meditators, I am but a flea on the face of a
flea, but I humbly ask why you think that blinding light is
related to Ultimate Truth?

YOGI

(glaring)
Tradition.

WHIM

Tradition?

YOGI

Of course. If you think I've been sitting up here in this

icebox for six thousand years in order to spend eternity
staring at a tomato, you are less than a flea in the anus of a
worm.

BILLY and DAWN nod their heads, but WHIM frowns.

                    BILLY
I'll drink to that.

                    WHIM
But Wise One, what if the blinding light is a distraction
that's preventing you from seeing U.T.?

The old YOGI's eyes flash fiercely out at WHIM, and ice begins to form on the YOGI's body, then
snow. The body grows with incredible speed, getting larger and whiter and colder every minute
until he bears a striking resemblance to an Abominable Snowman.

                    WHIM (CONT)
              (backing out of the cave)
It was just an idle question.

WHIM BILLY & DAWN flee the cave, leaving OSSO behind calmly playing icicle darts.

EXT. SHERPA VILLAGE. DAY.

WHIM and OSSO are deep in conversation while in b.g. BILLY and DAWN are awaiting an ancient
BUS which is laboring up the hill.

                    OSSO
Oh, yes, the cave yogi a very holy man. Too bad he can't see.

_____

WHIM

Can't see?

OSSO

Anyone who looks for something six thousand years and
doesn't find it clearly has eye problems.

WHIM

That's what I thought! If U.T. is worth seeing then it must
be something everyone can see, even poor people who can't
afford caves.

OSSO

Old yogi thinks he knows where to look, so he not open to
what is new. You in good shape. You know you're stupid.

WHIM

That's right!

OSSO

Buddha say that all humans are Buddhas, but most carefully
disguise themselves as madmen.

WHIM

They do?

OSSO
(leaning close to WHIM)
And then forget it's only a disguise.

OSSO winks at WHIM, who smiles back.

OPTIONS

The nice thing about life is that every path is the right path. Mountain, desert, motorway, underground, they all are the One True Way.

List six things to do. Cast a die. Do the chosen option. Now let Chance comment on what happened by casting a second die. But before casting a die, read through the six options below. Throw out one or two (or, best of all, all six) and create some of your own to replace those you toss out. Then cast a die.

① You did it. Perfect. If you had done the other thing, perfect. If you had done that first thing? Perfect. It is a convenient universe.

② Cast a die again with the same six options and again do as bid. Good. Now cast the die a third time. Again following the die. Mindless doing of the absurd: isn't that what life is all about?

No. Usually, it is rational, mind-filled doing of the absurd.

③ Well, learn anything about yourself? You're the only one who can.

④ All right, this time do the same option a second time as if your life depended on it – throw everything you have into doing it as fully and perfectly as possible.

⑤ List six churches, synagogues, meditation centres, or spiritual centres. Cast a die. Go there. Try to be at one with the beliefs and practices or rituals you encounter.

⑥ Good job. Doesn't make any difference that you didn't do anything. You're still perfect just as you are.

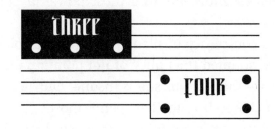

ILLUSIONS

All of man's greatest moments and most powerful emotions are created by illusions.

There is, however, a conspiracy of silence about this unpleasant fact. In our conflict-filled society we have adapted the policy of not pointing out that our neighbour is insane – or at least that we think he or she is insane. Our neighbour to the right collects baseball cards; our neighbour to the left spends most of her time looking into family genealogy; the neighbour across the street is into astrology; the one behind us has a house filled with knick-knacks. Since each of us is into only a small number of things and there are millions of activities that humans become fascinated with, we find ourselves wondering why our neighbours are spending (wasting) so much time doing what they do. We can see nothing interesting in stamps or baseball cards or astrology or cars racing around a track or horse racing or reading romances or following a sports team, or any of a million things some humans become interested in; in some sense we feel they are insane to be spending so much time on what fascinates them.

We each try to find ourselves individuals or groups that share our passion – or illusion. We join stamp clubs, card clubs, go to parties, join a chat group, and so on to be with people who share our 'interests'.

Just as we see our neighbours' interests as minor madness so too do we see their choice in mates as even more obvious madness. There are only so many rich handsome men and lovely intelligent women in the world which means that the great mass of mankind has to settle for a lot less than the cultural ideal. So in most cases when Susie announces she's going out with Ted, we wonder what she sees in him. And Ted's friends probably feel the same way about his choice of Susie. The allure of a specific being for another is usually based on such complex individual factors that it is no wonder that poets have long likened all love to madness.

When we say that we all live in a world of illusion, one of our main meanings is that it is a human characteristic to give value to things that are essentially valueless. There is no significant value in a hundred-dollar bill, a Pokémon card, old cigarette cards, an original Picasso sketch, a first edition of *Leaves of Grass*, the dress that Marilyn Monroe wore when she sang 'Happy Birthday' to President Kennedy. To most members of all other cultures these artefacts are all meaningless and valueless. When some alien finally climbs down out of a UFO and begins to study human life, he will quickly conclude that humans spend most of their time on nonsense, on valueless things to which they have for some reason given value.

This goes for most of the world's great art, as well. To value one painting at five million dollars and another, which to all but a few experts is indistinguishable from the first, for five thousand dollars, is a form of madness. The intrinsic value of the two paintings is identical, but since the one was painted by 'X' five hundred years ago and the second by 'Y' five years ago, the art world puts different values on them. Clearly, the art world is not interested in the experience that people get in looking at the two paintings. They are placing the extra value on the older painting for the same reason that others place more value on a rare cigarette card than on a Star Wars trading card which is much less rare.

A thing of beauty is not a joy for ever. Humans are for ever changing and the illusions they fall in love with – whether other humans or works of art – also change. Almost all the art, music and literature that we honour today will be dead art in another ten thousand years. As cultures change, that which moves and inspires and pleases us changes too. Most of the great Christian art of the Middle Ages can in most cases no longer be *seen* or read by those who are now indifferent to the religious beliefs that inspired the art and inspired the response to the art.

It's true that some art deals with 'universal' themes that transcend individual cultures. Sophocles' *Oedipus Rex*, for example, deals with something so psychologically basic that people from all cultures can respond to it. But in addition to the theme of a work of art is its style and language and these are inevitably peculiar to a specific culture and period. The *form* of Sophocles' play is peculiar to the great age of Greek tragedy; its language to Greece in 500 B.C. Today the way Sophocles tells his story or presents it on the stage is foreign to us; his language mostly unintelligible. We cannot respond to his play with one-tenth of the interest and emotional involvement invested in it by the theatre-goers for whom it was originally written.

Professors of literature and art, of course, try to tell us otherwise. For ten years I was such a professor. Since I loved Shakespeare and Pope and Wordsworth and most 'great' literature and was being paid to help students love them too, I soon became a trifle miserable in my teaching. For most students great literature was mostly a bore and a chore. It was too foreign to their own lives and interests to engage them. It was dead literature. Their illusions and the illusions created by the great masters often didn't jell.

'I don't preach love,' said Whim, 'but rather those acts and attitudes and illusions which will automatically fill a person with love.'

'You use *illusions* to create love?' protested the chief disciple.

'Has anyone ever claimed there was another way?' replied Whim.

Humans have a few basic needs: food, reasonable temperatures (shelter in northern climes), sex and companionship. Most human desires beyond these basic needs are individual and personal. The individual gives importance and value to things that have no intrinsic value to other human beings. In so far as we realize that our passions are only our own we can say we're in reasonable touch with reality. But most of us soon give to our passions an importance, an importance to everyone, that in fact they do not have. And it is this failure to see that most of our passions are ours and ours alone that constitutes the illusionary nature of most human life.

We live in the world of illusion. Our minds are wonderful creators; they create for each of us an individual world, and the earth is a better place because we all live in our own worlds. But it becomes a worse place when we try to impose our individual worlds, our illusions, on others.

In my early life I talked and made much sense. Then I began to see what an ass I was being and for many years was silent. Now I speak again, and listen with content to my braying.   ANONYMOUS

To be human, said Nietzsche, means to live in falsity and illusion. With every word we lie. In most men's lives fear flames out, like shining from shook souls; but bliss blooms when we crunch our arms in love around error and illusion. Every aim is false and every achievement an illusion; every hope deceives, every fear misleads.

The honest man, always facing reality squarely, is living in illusion.

The dishonest man, always creating reality whimsically and seeing it as illusion, is, if you will, an honest man.

Within the realm of relativity and illusion, within that sacred realm – sacred because it is the world of our existence – within that realm, good and evil exist, striving exists, desires exist, effort, change and bettering exist. In the realm of illusion – the Kingdom of Man – there men can play at assisting each other. There, you, seated, reading, tense, are an uptight neurotic, and you there, reading happily, have achieved a certain stage of liberation. In the realm of illusion men differ very much indeed, in wisdom, happiness, morality and success, and especially in aliveness. Fools may deny it, but the wise man knows that he lives in illusion and, since it's the only game in town, he plays it.

And as he plays it, within the Realm of Illusion he distinguishes between good illusions and bad illusions. Good ones are those which, when we live according to them, produce the expected and pleasant results; bad illusions are those which, when we live according to them, produce unexpected and painful results. Good illusions – the romantic may call them truths – work; bad illusions don't.

So if you are miserable you'd better examine the illusions you live by. And if you want people to help you on this wonderful illusory path, you'd best share your thoughts and feelings, hopes and fears, beliefs and doubts. You are the worst possible judge of the value of your illusions; it's quite likely that the things you admire most about yourself are precisely the ones that are making you miserable, and that your 'bad' thoughts and feelings are those that will give us a clue of what will lead you to liberation.

WHIM AND THE THREE KITTENS

One day Whim and Billy Best and their old Sherpa guide Osso were hiking in the Himalayas looking for a guru when Whim noticed a cluster of wildflowers nestled against a rock near a tiny spring.

'Look!' said Whim.

'What's up?' asked Billy, stopping several yards ahead of Whim on a steep slope.

'Flowers!' announced Whim.

'So what?' asked Billy.

'They're pretty.'

'So what?'

'Well,' said Whim uncertainly. 'I enjoy seeing them.'

'I thought you had the hots for finding this Snowman Sage and your U.T.?'

'I do, I do,' said Whim, 'but . . . '

'We've come five thousand miles, hiked two hundred miles straight up into the air it seems, buttonholed every wise-looking belly-button from Calcutta to the top of Everest, and are at last only a few miles from seeing the Great Abominable Snowman Sage of the Sky, and you're standing there looking down at a bunch of colour against a rock.'

Whim's shoulders slumped.

'I don't know what gets into me,' he said apologetically.

'You've no discipline, no sense of purpose, no stick-to-it-iveness,' Billy said sharply. 'Without me you'd probably still be back home in Maganansett petting kittens.'

'I know, I know,' said Whim. 'Hey! Wouldn't that be great!?'

'What's that?'

'If we saw some kittens here.'

'Oh, Jesus,' Billy wailed. 'You're out of your mind.'

'Look!'

Three kittens oozed out from among the cluster of flowers, meowing lazily.

'Kittens!' announced Whim.

Billy squinted down at the black and brown bundles of fur frolicking near the flowers.

'They're optical illusions,' he announced.

'Oh, no, really?' said Whim, his face clouding. 'How can you tell?'

'Real kittens don't live in the Himalayas. They live near litter boxes.'

'They're illusions?' Whim asked uncertainly.

'Absolutely.'

Their old Sherpa guide nodded his head in agreement.

'I bet the flowers are illusions too,' said Whim sadly.

'Probably,' said Billy, and the old Sherpa nodded.

'Still,' said Whim his face suddenly brightening, 'it could be worse.'

'Yeah?' said Billy.

'We could be seeing illusions of beer cans and used condoms.'

Mind-altering drugs – what a wonderful concept! If the ability of the mind to fool us with its tricks is one of the problems of human existence, then shouldn't we be interested in something that alters it? In the 1960s and 70s such drugs were occasionally extolled as cure-alls, assisting us in turning on, tuning in and dropping out, laudable goals all. In fact they were and are valuable in helping people realize how our minds create our realities, and that our normal socialized way of seeing 'reality' is quite dull compared to the rich realities the mind is capable of creating.

That drugs are associated with the counter-culture is only appropriate, for if the taking of mind-altering drugs like marijuana, LSD, Ecstasy and sacred mushrooms were to become the norm in society, society as we know it might be in danger. Society as we know it depends on a shared conventional reality that stays stable. The idea that each individual might be experiencing a different reality, even when in theory they are experiencing the same thing, is destructive of how we are brought up. Think of a party in the 1970s (or the 90s), where most of the participants are sober but a small group is high on pot or something else, laughing at jokes that no one else sees, grooving on music that no one else hears, admiring colours that look rather drab to the sober. Life is hard enough for the sober-minded without having to be in the presence of other people who are high.

Drugs create illusions that the user recognizes as illusions, but he usually learns to go with the flow of his illusions and enjoy them. We get high and see a normally 'plain' woman as incredibly beautiful. We see her inner beauty and honour her beauty, and if a tiny distant memory exists of the other 'reality' (actually illusion) of her 'plainness', we happily ignore it. Learning to go with the flow of illusion is one of the benefits of drug-taking, especially if we then carry it over into the illusions of our non-dope-taking everyday life.

Unfortunately, many people who begin using drugs are doing so not to briefly create alternative realities but to escape for as long as they can from some present reality they've mostly created that oppresses them. Sooner or later they experiment with a drug that is addictive and end up escaping more or less permanently from their unpleasant oppressive reality into a reality that will become progressively more and more limited and more and more painful.

Drugs that are addictive are, like most things that are addictive, undesirable. When one is addicted to a drug one is then addicted to a certain reality created by that drug. The difference between a cocaine-addict and a work-addict is sometimes difficult to perceive; neither can do without his fix, of dope or work, and both have closed themselves to a myriad of other realities non-addicts may still be open to.

But perhaps the most valuable aspect of occasionally using mind-altering drugs is that most of them take us to a place where we are floating along on the illusions and feelings it creates, and if we can take this ability to float with illusions into our everyday life and do it with the same ease and enjoyment as we do with the drug we have come a long way.

Being high is opening to life and not fighting it. Being high is being open to whatever strange realities come and not judging them with society's 'reality'. Being high is seeing things in fresh ways. Being high ain't bad.

WHIM PLAYS

'You keep describing yourself as a fool. Aren't you just playing with words?'

'Yes,' said Whim.

'Actually, you're wise.'

'No.'

'You're a fool then?'

'I play with words.'

'As a fool or a wise man?'

'As a man who plays with words.'

WHIM INVESTS IN UNICORNS

'If you had a million dollars, Whim, what would you do?'

'Invest it,' Whim said promptly.

'Invest it in what?' persisted the student.

'In a herd of unicorns,' said Whim.

'But unicorns aren't real.'

'That's OK,' said Whim. 'Neither is the million dollars.'

NARSUFIN TELLS WHIM HOW HE CLIMBED THE MOUNTAIN

One day when Whim was being guided by the black sufi Narsufin in Harlem, the two of them were sitting in a dingy nightclub and Whim asked Narsufin how he had gotten so wise.

Narsufin laughed and slapped his thighs and spit into his napkin.

'Wise!' Narsufin finally barked. 'Hey, man, keep your voice down. I got enough trouble with my brothers without them hearing someone call me wise.'

'But you *are*!' Whim insisted, 'And some time in your life you must have been as mixed up and confused as me.'

Narsufin laughed again.

'Nobody's as mixed up and confused as you, Whim,' he said. 'You get the trophy for that hands down.'

'I know, but you must have – '

'Oh, sure, man, I was a hopeless human just like the rest of mankind, but one day I woke up.'

'Exactly!' said Whim. 'But what was it that woke you?'

'A new illusion,' said Narsufin. 'One day I woke up and when I peeked outside my haystack of a house I saw a Mountain, high above the diddly little hills around my village. Well, soon's as I'd seen it, I says to myself, Narsufin, you got to climb that Mountain.

'So I ran to my buddies at the local hangout – a shack where an old guy made beer out of fermented weeds – and said, "Hey, you motherfuckers, that Mountain is mine! Let's go!" I expected them all to give me high five and off we'd go.

'They looked at me as if I was wasted. "What mountain?" they all say. "That Mountain," I said, pointing off beyond our hills where I saw the thing rising up like a great white pyramid against the sky.

'They thought I was nuts. Not a single one of 'em saw it. I went tearing around the whole village, and though I found a few others thought maybe they saw it, most of them claimed it was a mirage, or a sham created by a few priestly huckster travel agents looking for a fast buck. They laughed at me. Claimed that the world consisted of hills and valleys, and the cool cat learned to make a comfortable home for himself there without chasing after imaginary mountains.

'"If dat mountain really dere," the village mayor said to me, "then why can't I see it?"

'"Beats me, brother," I replied. "But if dat Mountain don't exist, how come I sees it?"

'"Because you crazy, Narsufin," the mayor said. "After all, any cat dat see a mountain where dere ain't none, he crazy, right?"'

'Is that really how you and the mayor spoke?' Whim asked.

'Bug off, fella,' Narsufin said to Whim. 'You want to be a literary critic, go to Oxford. I'm just trying to translate primitive Ungalese into American nigger.'

'You were born in Africa?' Whim asked.

'Hey, stop interrupting for a history lesson. This is a teaching story. I'm not gonna let you sink it with facts.

'Anyway, I wanted to climb that old Mountain like nothing I ever wanted before. I decided that the worst that could happen if the Mountain didn't exist when I got there was I wouldn't have to climb it. So me and a dozen or so other good-for-nothings got together and started off. But before we even got outside the Village, we were all arguing about how the Mountain ought to be climbed.

'"Dat 'ol Mountain been climbed in the past, and this map Proves it," old Abercrombie Lemon said. He was a crafty old dude, a big mother-fucker in the village because of the way he could spit. "All we got to do is find and follow these old trails, and we're bound to reach the top."

'Well, I was raring to go the way the map said until two other old dudes came up with different maps showing different trails. The Mountain looked a little different on each map, but I decided I liked Abercrombie's map because all the trails were coloured green, which is my favourite colour.

'But when I started marching off, a couple of my buddies stopped me and said all the maps were outdated, that the Mountain on those old maps wasn't the same as the one I'd seen. What we got to do, they said, is find a guide who knew the way to this new Mountain.

'Well, I figured the mother-fuckers were right on this one, and sure enough there were three guides listed in the Yellow Pages of the Ungalese phone book, and we phoned 'em up and made appointments.

'The first one turned out to be white, so we crossed him off the list and went to the second. He was a chunky black guy who wielded a hiking staff as if it were a combination baseball bat, golf club and sword. When he said the fee for his guidance was only one banana, all us climbers figured this was the man.

But when he mentioned that the path he knew took three years, we decided it might be a good idea to check out the other guides.

'The third guide was a fancy dude wearing an elegant robe with a lot of colours and a big hat with plenty of feathers and bones, and he turned out to be our sort of man. He said he'd be happy to guide us to the top of the Mountain. He charged quite a bit, but told us he had all the latest guide equipment – compasses and solar-heated canteens and radar and stuff like that – and the thing that really sold us, he'd get us there in no time. We slapped down our two-dozen bananas and off we went.

'Next thing we knew we was in a big carnival with a lot of other climbers, riding roller-coasters, going through the tunnel of love, seeing ourselves all distorted with tricky mirrors, and having a great old time. None of us ever even heard of a carnival before, much less been to one, so it was better'n a free pass to a whorehouse. Then I began to notice that we weren't going nowhere. The Mountain was just as far away as ever. So I managed to drag away three of my buddies, and we left the guide and lit out on our own.

'Pretty soon who should we see but old Abercrombie and the guys who were following him and his map. They were looking like they needed a fix – jumpy and depressed. Seems the trail was blocked by an avalanche, and they couldn't figure what to do. Their map only showed this one path to the Mountain and it was blocked. I decided all we could do was look for another trail, and got a few others to join me.

'But after a couple of days of marching through the roughest country east of 155th Street some of the dudes with me decided it was ridiculous to hike to the top of the Mountain, they ought to get a job, save some bananas, and rent a helicopter to fly to the top. Or get a plane to fly over the Mountain and drop 'em down by parachute. Well, I couldn't see hiking away from the Mountain and I certainly didn't want to work at no job, so when a half-dozen went off to get work and earn bananas so they could fly to the mountaintop I kept on truckin'. What I did was I took one step towards the Mountain and noticed it got closer.

'After a while me and the few guys still with me came to a lot of big trees that blocked the sight of the Mountain. A couple of the guys began to get discouraged; claimed the Mountain wasn't on the other side of the woods at all, maybe didn't even exist. They thought it'd be nicer to hike downhill until they could see the Mountain again. Another guy said it was too bad we weren't Americans 'cause if we were, we could call in the B52s and defoliate it. All of them said we'd get lost in there without a guide.

'But I said, yeah, we'd be better off with B52s and a guide, but it was a long hike back to the Yellow Pages, and I went and took one step into those mean-looking trees and noticed that they weren't quite as mean or thick as they looked.

'Then I came to a big flooded river with a hundred or so climbers all stuck on the one side and the Mountain clear as day off in the distance on the other. I saw one of my buddies who'd gone off to rent an aeroplane. He told me most who'd gone off to earn bananas had gotten so into their jobs they couldn't see the Mountain any more and weren't interested in it or in planes. But when he'd finally earned enough to rent a plane and flown over the Mountain it was the coolest thing ever happened to him, but every time he landed again he felt he'd just come down from speed. When he tried parachuting down on top of the

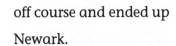

Mountain he always got blown off course and ended up
landing in some place called Newark.

'Well, everybody on the banks of that raging river
was down; it seemed impossible to cross. A few hiked to
look for an easier crossing some place else, but they didn't
find one. Some others decided they'd begin looking for
an easier mountain to climb. One old man thought we
could get the Ungalese government to build a
dam upstream so we could cross. I said: "Fuck the Ungalese
government. Let's build a bridge."

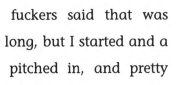

'Most of the other mother-fuckers said that was
impossible or would take too long, but I started and a
few other good-for-nothings pitched in, and pretty
soon a bridge began to grow.

'Took us close to a month, but damned if we didn't get one cool bridge across
that river. Funny thing, though, after we were done and could cross, a lot of the
brothers wanted to keep improving the bridge, make it fancier and prettier or
sturdier and things like that. I said, "Hey, we got a Mountain to climb," but they
said the bridge had to be fixed up first. Those dudes were so into bridge-building they began building a second bridge across the open field between the river
and the Mountain. I said I wasn't too sure we needed a bridge just to cross a
field, but they said the bridge had got 'em across the river, hadn't it, and no
sense in abandoning a good thing just because we hadn't come to another river
yet. "Bridge building is the way, man," one of 'em said. "We'll just keep building 'em all the way to the top."

'Well, I had nothing against bridges, but I walked on.

'Finally, me and a few others came to the base of the Mountain, and things looked pretty tough. No matter which way I looked, nothing but sheer cliffs. Like standing under a skyscraper. Well, soon as everybody was stuck, the chunky guide with the staff who said it would take one banana and three years showed up. Somehow I now felt that this man was my Guide, so I forked over my banana and began following him. So did about twenty others.

'After a while we came to the worst bunch of pricker bushes you ever saw, and a couple of the climbers said: "If this dude were a True Guide he wouldn't be leadin' us through no pricker bushes," so they turned back.

'Next we came to a Ice-Cream Cart, and the Guide treated us all to ice-cream cones and fudge. A coupla fellas said: "If this dude were a True Guide he wouldn't be lettin' us eat no ice-cream and candy," so they turned back.

'When we came to a sheer blank wall, the Guide paused only a second or two and said that old wall was an illusion and we could just walk through it. Several of the brothers said: "Ain't no way anyone can walk through a wall. This dude must be a fake," and they turned back.

'Well, I hung around and when that Guide walked through the wall, I just up and followed him and got through just as neat as I later cut through the Knicks.

'After a while we came to a place where there were two trails, and the Guide says, "You guys take that trail for a while, but I'm gonna take this one. Meet you higher up."

'Well, a coupla brothers say, "If this dude were a True Guide he wouldn't be deserting us and making us take the steep trail while he loafs along the other," so after he'd left, they snuck along after him rather than go where he sent 'em, and no one ever heard of 'em again. I took one step along the trail the Guide has pointed to and found it wasn't so steep after all.

'Three months later I was still plopping down one foot after the other. I was still with my Guide, though I didn't have to pay much attention to him any more to follow the trail, and the climbing was getting easier and easier. And I began to realize that there was a lot of shacks and huts and people around all along this part of the trail, first we'd seen in years. And then I noticed some other climbers walking along another trail off to my right, and damned if I didn't see the guide with a flowing robe. Seemed like he had half his carnival along with him and a few of his climbers too. Abercrombie was there, and even the white guide. And on the other side of him I could see some of my old buddies building a bridge across a dried-up stream-bed.

'"Look over there," I said to my Guide, pointing to the travelling carnival. "You think those dudes will be able to make it to the top too?"

'"What do you mean, make it to the top?" said the old guide. "You're already on the top. Where do you think you are?"

'And sure 'nuff, when I looked around, my Mountain was gone, and the whole fuckin' banana patch of the universe seemed to be spread out beneath me.

'"So this is the top of the Mountain," I said to the Guide, feeling pretty confused. "It looks . . . it looks exactly like life back in my honky village."

'"Exactly the same," said the Guide.

'"And . . . and all the other dudes made it to the top too?"

'"Everyone's here," said the Guide.

'"It's been three years," I said dreamily.

'"Three years."

'But then I looked again at the village and the people and the whole fuckin' banana patch of the universe stretched out all around me and whoosh! everything lit up like some long-lasting Duracell lightning just struck, and I suddenly knew for the first time in my life that I was on the top of the Mountain.

'"Hey, man, this is terrific!!" I shouted. "This is fucking outrageous! This is better than smoking banana peels!"

'"Better keep your voice down," said my Guide, who actually didn't look much like a guide any more – he looked just like everybody else.

'"Why!?" I shouted. "We're all here on top of the Mountain! We should all be shouting and celebrating!"

'"Better keep your voice down," said the Guide.

'One of my buddies came up to me and said: "Hey, how they hanging, Narsi?"

'"High! Real high!" I said, grinning and giggling like they just let me out of the loony bin.

'"What you on, man?" my buddy asked with a frown.

'"This top of the Mountain! Ain't it great?"

'"What top? What Mountain? You crazy, man?"

'I looked at my mother-fucking good-for-nothing buddy and suddenly saw that the guy didn't know where he was. And now that I took a good look at the other folks I saw that most of them didn't know where they were either. I started to shout, but my Guide came up and took me by the arm and led me away, saying again: "Better keep your voice down."

'"But why don't they know where they are?" I cried.

'"They ain't done much hiking," the Guide said.

'"Can't I tell them?"

'"They won't listen. First they got to see the Mountain."

'"But we're on it!"

'"First they got to see an illusion of the Mountain off in the distance and begin going for it."

'"You mean . . . I . . . the Mountain I thought I saw – "

'"An illusion."

'"You mean . . . "

'"You've been there all the time."

'I stared at my Guide a long time, my face being pretty much all eyes, and then I began slowly shaking my head and smiling.

'"Sheeeeeet," I finally said, grinning and giggling and feeling the lightning blazing all around me like the light show at the Apollo. "I want my banana back."'

'That didn't really happen, did it?' Whim asked when Narsufin had ended his story. The restaurant and bar were closing up and almost empty, the last topless dancer sleepwalking through motions that held all the excitement of a girl scout selling cookies.

'Who cares?' Narsufin answered, lighting up a cigar. 'I'm not a historian.'

'But, I mean, did you ever see . . . a Mountain?'

'Who cares?' Narsufin repeated, drawing in a mouthful of smoke. 'You want a biography, go to the New York Public Library. I got better things to do.'

'It was . . . a nice story. I liked it,' Whim said dreamily, still somewhat mesmerized.

'Thanks.'

'I think . . . I think the message is that – '

'Message!' Narsufin interrupted, yanking the cigar out of his mouth. 'You think I'm some sort of cut-rate Western Union?'

'But – '

'You liked my story, Whim,' Narsufin said, relaxing again and tipping back in his chair. 'Quit while you're ahead.'

'Yes, sir,' said Whim.

OPTIONS

Before casting a die, read through the six options below. Throw out one or two (or, better still, all six) and create some of your own to replace those you toss out. Then cast a die.

① Let the die choose from among six archetypal events: e.g., birth, dying, marriage, ascending to heaven, descending to hell, inheriting one billion dollars, losing a child to death. Give yourself over to experiencing what this die-chosen event would be like.

② All in illusion. Take a vacation. Now.

③ Whatever you are doing, do it even more so. If you're working hard on your job, work harder. If you're happily married, be even more happy. If you're in a miserable relationship, don't change it, continue to enjoy your misery. Go completely with whatever you have in life. For at least a day.

④ You have what you think of as a dream, some sort of aspiration that seems to you to be unreal, a pipe-dream. Spend a day determined to make this dream an eventual reality. Knock down all the arguments against the potential reality of this dream and go for it. Remember, if the reality you think you live in is illusion, how much worse can the pipe-dream be?

⑤ Examine some part of your life, other than your job, that you spend a lot of time at. Do you get a great deal of satisfaction from it? Is it rewarding in and of itself? Is it a project that has some finite goal, when the project will end? Or, to put it another way, is it a nice illusion that is working for you or is it one that's got you doing something you're actually not enjoying?

⑥ Take a mind-altering drug. Go with it. Float along on the illusions and feelings it creates.

Then, the next day, or whenever, 'pretend' you have just taken the same drug again. See if you can't float along with the illusions and feelings of everyday life with the same ease and enjoyment as you did 'under the influence'.

A roll a day, keeps the doctor away. A roll a day, keeps the doctor away. A roll a day, keeps the doctor away. A roll a day, keeps the doctor away. A roll a day, keeps the doctor away. A roll a day, keeps the doctor away. A roll a day, keeps the doctor away.

WE THE
CREATORS

We have met the Creator and he is us.

Pogo

We are who we pretend to be.

We are the creators. Once a human has grasped that he creates his own life, he is on the road to happiness and fulfilment.

We are the creators. The colour of the sky, the taste of chocolate, the feel of a loved one's skin: these are our creations. The sky can be measured by scientific instruments as being 'blue' on the colour spectrum and 'bright' on some brightness spectrum, but if we are depressed we create it grey. And if we have fought with our beloved then the feel of our lover's skin is, of course, dry, lifeless. If the lover's eyes are glowing with love, we feel it as smooth, sensuous, hot. Same skin. Two different creations.

We are the creators. We lose five thousand dollars in our business or in the markets. How do we react? How do we experience it? We mope. We worry. We feel we have lost a game.

Is this intrinsic to losing money? Could one experience the loss of five thousand as a liberation? As a joke?

The laughing men in the sky are looking down at you. They see you lose money and they laugh. They see you brooding and they laugh harder. Then they see some fool who has lost the same money and he is laughing. The laughing men in the sky gather around and point and stare. Then the man who is laughing at having lost the money thinks how special and wonderful he is that he can laugh at losing money. The laughing men in the sky begin laughing again, harder, and wander away.

We create our own lives. Then why let chance affect our creation? Don't. Or do. The Creator of the Universe certainly used chance in His-Her creation – just look at all the absurdity the Creator has come up with. Chance is Nature's way of creating new and more interesting species, and our way of creating new and more interesting lives.

We create our own lives.

We create those we love and then, later, we re-create them so we can no longer love them.

Is there anything more foolish than a person describing to you the person he loves? The words tumble out; one illusion after another that he or she alone sees.

But, yes, there is something equally foolish: a person describing the spouse that he or she is about to divorce. The words tumble out; one illusion after another that he or she alone sees. The bride that was radiant is pockmarked and grey. The wonderful mother is a conniving bitch. The gentle homemaker is the nagging harridan. The sensuous sex-pot is a frigid monster. How could she change so?! She didn't. You changed her.

We create our own selves, one or many, good or bad.

But that is human life: we create it, for better and for worse.

We create ourselves and marvel at how wonderful we are. Or we create a depressing life and feel depressed.

We create our own victories and defeats. We are at the edge of a green. We putt the gold ball towards the hole. It stops five feet away. For Tiger Woods this is a defeat. For us, it would be a triumph.

We create our own lives.

'I can't give him up, Whim, I just can't.'

'Are you happy?'

'I'm miserable. But I just can't give him up.'

'Actually, you don't have to give him up.'

'I feel he's withdrawing from me.'

'Surround him.'

'But how!?'

'Extend your self until it includes the whole universe. Then see if he can get away.'

WHAT COLOUR IS THE WIND?

What colour is the wind?
See it whisper violets
Hidden in green spades, cool
In the shade of lilac roots;
Watch it rustle roses, wafting spices
No jar can release;
See it bend round white peonies,
The moons of a garden sea.

What colour is the wind?
Watch clouds push vermillion disc down;
See clothes on lines
Like butterflies flutter;
Watch gulls glide suspended,
Their grey and white like horizontal kites.

What colour is the wind?
Watch my sons run:
See their hair like leaves on trees
Belong to the wind.

What colour is the wind?
Name it! Name it!
I paint it every day
With the hand in my eyes.

- from Brush Strokes, by Ann Cockcroft

Lying is a good habit to get into. It is an act of creation. If we are a novelist or used-car salesman we are rewarded for our lying. In any case, we are too used to being under the illusion that we know and have the truth. By lying we are freed from that illusion. Besides, after I have left my lying imagination go and people then praise me for my wisdom, I am hard-pressed to take any credit – as I might if I were convinced I was spouting eternal truth. Whenever I think I'm a sage I cause nothing but misery, for myself and others.

Lying is held in ill-repute primarily because people usually lie to protect their old egos, rather than to create new ones. Lying to try to seem innocent or consistent is an act of fear. Lying to create something new, and therefore inconsistent with our usual selves, is an act of aliveness. The first builds more bars on the cage; the second bends them apart so one can walk free.

Lying is one of the ways we can escape the past, and the past, or at least our usual ways of looking at it, is one of the great barriers to human happiness.

Like any act of creation, lying can be good or bad, but the conscious act of making something up is itself a good. We develop new selves first by faking it; only later does the faking become natural.

In a sense we develop ourselves by lying and pretending. We dress up in a certain getup in order to encourage ourselves to play a certain role for the first time. We fake that role at first, until it becomes part of our repertoire. 'I am the Greatest!' proclaimed Cassius Clay from the age of twelve. Ten years later he was the Greatest. He 'lied', then he created a reality.

And Cassius Clay changed his name to Muhammad Ali, a statement that he didn't want to be perceived as he had been. He was creating a new self and needed a new name. In an ideal society we would all have a dozen names, to go with our dozen personalities. Thoreau said we couldn't start a new life without a change of clothes. Can we create a new life without a new name?

WHIM DID IT

Whim was sitting with a crowd of people in front of an apartment house when a meteor suddenly plunged down out of the sky and smashed into the front of a store across the street, blasting a hole five feet deep and twenty feet wide. Within a few minutes two huge policemen were on the scene.

'All right, all right,' said the first policeman. 'Who did this?'

'Not me,' said a voice.

'Not me,' echoed two others.

'Not me,' said a dozen more.

'I did it,' said Whim.

PRETENDING TO BE GOD, PART I

When Whim was on his quest for Ultimate Truth, his mentor Grain-of-Sand sent him and Whim's girlfriend Dawn and his best friend Billy Best to a black sufi sage in Harlem. Narsufin was an unconventional sage, having once played basketball in the NBA, and was now hanging out most of the time in Harlem. There he baffled the people in the street by frequently pointing to some bag-lady, or zombie strung out on heroin, or a mongrel scrounging in garbage and saying: "I sees You, can't hide from me. I see You in 'dere," and getting down on his knees as if in front of a God.

He took Whim to a sleazy nightclub where Whim kept asking about Ultimate Truth. The resulting scene appears in the film *Whim*.

FADE IN
INT. VESUVIUS TOPLESS BAR. NIGHT.

Except for the small stage where two tired erotic DANCERS are apathetically moving to the music, the seedy bar is dimly lit. WHIM is sitting at a table with NARSUFIN, BILLY and DAWN. There are beers in front of everyone except WHIM, who has a glass filled with something that looks suspiciously like milk. In the b.g. are half a dozen BARFLIES, mostly black, who look over at WHIM and DAWN with bored curiosity.

                         NARSUFIN
          Tha's right. The big U.T., Mister Ultimate Truth hisself, is
          settin' right here in this horsepiss toilet of a bar.

                         WHIM
          Wow.

                         BILLY
          Where!?

                         NARSUFIN
          You're staring right at it.

                         BILLY
          That girl's arse!?

                         NARSUFIN
          He who has eyes to see, let him see.

                         DAWN
          If it's here, it must be everywhere, right?

                         NARSUFIN
          'S not everywhere. It's here. U.T. scratching your eyeballs
          this very second.

                              WHIM
        But how can we see it?

NARSUFIN leans towards them and then looks around conspiratorially.

                            NARSUFIN
        Just stop actin' like a human being and start pretendin'
        you're a God.

WHIM, BILLY and DAWN stare at NARSUFIN blankly.

                              DAWN
        We can't do that. We're humans.

                            NARSUFIN
        Bullshit. You been pretendin' to be humans for so long you
        forgot you was jus' pretending! Try pretending you're Gods.
        Notice the improvement.

                              DAWN
        But how do we go about pretending to be Gods?

                            NARSUFIN
        You fake it, Babe! *(Going into rap mode)* Assume the pose! Up
        the nose! Vamp it camp it, stoke it, joke it, anything 'cept
        toke it. *(To Whim)* It's teasy, greasy, easy! You fake it and
        fake it until you make it . . . You make it real 'til it ain't no
        dream. Shakespeare said it plain as day – the world's a stage
        and that's no hay – just gotta act and learn to play . . . You
        know what I'm sayin', know what I mean? You make it real
        and it ain't no dream.

NARSUFIN stops his rap.

_____

WHIM

But, but –

NARSUFIN

Stop worryin' every detail, boy! Gods don't worry. You never
catch a God biting his fingernails or saying, 'but, but'.

BILLY

This beer tastes like warm ginger ale.

NARSUFIN

No buts and no complaints. Since God knows He created this
mess He don't waste time standing around complaining
about it.

BILLY flushes but turns to fix his eyes on the DANCER'S arse which is now wiggling near his face.

NARSUFIN (CONT)

Since a God is all-powerful He don't get His Tool all knotted
up worrying 'bout the ladies . . . Ya know what I'm sayin'?

BILLY

(fixing on Dancer) Who worries about 'em?

NARSUFIN

Where humans put their peckers is the most worrisome
thing since the discovery of fire.

DAWN has taken out a mirror and is fussing with her hair.

NARSUFIN (CONT)

And a Goddess don't worry about how her hair look or if her
ass is fine in new Levis. A Goddess, she know she cool!

NARSUFIN primps his scraggly hair and smiles with his two front gold teeth gleaming. DAWN blinks and puts away her mirror.

                    NARSUFIN (CONT)
          Ya' see, Gods figure that since they Gods in the firs' place, any
          way they part their hair or fill their jeans is COOL, ya' know!?

                         BILLY
          Hey, that's just like me!!

                        NARSUFIN
          A God figures that whatever He doin' must be pretty good or
          He wouldn't be doing it.

                          WHIM
          But that means a God can do anything and it has to be right
          . . .

                        NARSUFIN
          You gettin' there.

NARSUFIN rises from his chair and begins leaving the bar, the three teenagers rising awkwardly and following. As NARSUFIN passes the EROTIC DANCER he slaps her playfully on the behind. She smiles.

WHIM sees this and so as he passes he also gives her a slap on the behind. The EROTIC DANCER gives him a terrific whack in the head, sending him reeling.

                          DAWN
          But doesn't a God care about good and bad, right and
          wrong?–

As WHIM weaves groggily, NARSUFIN swings open the door and holds it for DAWN.

_____

NARSUFIN

Since a God is everywhere and everyone, He doesn't waste energy getting pissed off at any of his other selves for what they do.

The four of them move through the door out on to the street, WHIM still reeling from the whack.

EXT. GHETTO STREET. NIGHT.

They all come to a halt at the edge of the kerb.

WHIM

It must be pretty nice being a God.

NARSUFIN

You ARE a God! All you got to do to prove it is start pretending!

WHIM

Are you a God, Narsufin?

NARSUFIN claps WHIM on the back.

NARSUFIN

(grinning) Thought you'd never notice.

PRETENDING TO BE GOD, PART II

'I pretended to be a God,' Whim announced to Narsufin the next day.

'Great, man, what happened?'

'I stood up to a bully and he hit me in the mouth and knocked out three of my teeth.'

'Bummer.'

'It was magnificent!' said Whim.

''Course it was.'

'The poor bully didn't even realize that it was really Me who was hitting Me in the mouth.'

'Hey, that's cool, bro'.'

'I laughed and laughed,' said Whim.

'Tha's cool.'

'Still,' said Whim, beginning to frown. 'Who's going to pay my dentist bill?'

'No problem, bro',' said Narsufin. 'Remember, man, you're the dentist.'

THE CREATOR

With a glance I create a beautiful field
And the endless blue of sky.
And the guiltless girls now dancing
There where the fall leaves fly.

But I can close my eyes and kill them all
And build a blackness there.
Or perhaps the world kills me:
Though grass can't grow or girls be dancing
Unless my eyes will see,
Without them both 'I' die;
Lovers together ever
Must we be:
I and the world so intertwined

That not a leaf can fall
Without my eyes' permission, sight,
The sun's permission, light,
The leaf's permission, flight:
No world without them all.

With a glance I create some girls and grass,
In a dance with the leaves and sky;
In the void they hurl themselves at me,
Touched into life am I.

We are the creators. That's big, man. *You* are the creator. You can do it. The whole universe is yours to paint the way you want. That's heavy, man. But fun. You never realized you had so much power.

And one of the primary uses of dicing is to remind us that we are the Creator. We create our own options and then, if we are wise, we may create options to see how we will react to the options chosen. Always we are the creator.

First of all, it is we who make a decision to list some options. We then create the options, not the die. We then choose to cast a die. We then choose whether to follow the choice of the die. We are the creator.

The very act of listing options reminds us of our creative power. If we list six options, look at them and then choose to do one, we have gained some of the benefit of dicing without even touching a die. We have reminded ourselves of our power of creation.

OPTIONS

① List six new creations. Big ones. No small stuff. Life-affecting, scrotum-tightening, pussy-pulsating big ones. Cast a die.

How does it feel to be God?

②   Create something new. Some . . . thing – object, tool, painting, piece of music, piece of writing, clothing, cooking, furniture arrangement, flower arrangement, anything – but new by you, never before created. Do it.

    Thank you, God.

③   Create an emotion. List six emotions, cast a die, then, for one minute or three, create that emotion, express that emotion, feel that emotion. Do it.

    Thank you God.

    Then cast the die a second time, and create the new emotion, express the new emotion, feel the new emotion.

    And is the emotion you have just created and felt any less real than the similar emotion you expressed a year ago or ten years ago in a 'reality' situation?

    Thank you, God.

④   You are an artist – of something: clay, cooking, oils, writing, clothing, sex, sewing, chess, soccer, tennis, acting, interior design. Of something or many things you are an artist. Choose your art and list up to six new things you might do with or in your art – new techniques, colours, strategies. Cast a die to choose one. Create a work of art with your new way.

    Thank you, God.

⑤   You are the creator of your relationships. *You* are the creator of your relationships, not him, not her.

    So make it new. Consider a single problem you're having in one of your important relationships. Consider it. Then list a few things you might do that you've never done before that might affect that problem. List them. Cast a die. Do it.

⑥   Create a story from scratch, beginning wherever you begin but continuing for at least the allotted time. If you have trouble creating, then list six subjects you might tell a story about and let Chance choose one. Then tell your story.

YOU ARE THE CREATOR. DON'T JUST SIT THERE, CREATE.

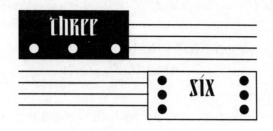

DICING

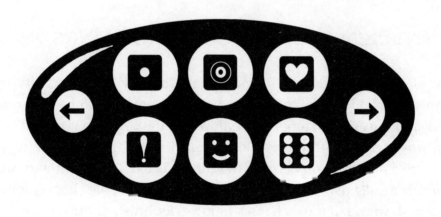

It is a fearful thing to fall into the hands of the living Die.

A roll a day, keeps the doctor away.
Ancient Proverb

People often ask us how we came up with the original idea that became *The Dice Man*. Actually, we began using dice to make decisions in our life as a teenager, before we had an idea in our head. So the practice preceded the idea. The ideas that explain why it might be a useful device to bring challenge and risk and variety into one's life came later, as we read widely in psychology and philosophies that wondered why we humans aren't happier with our lot. We saw that surrendering my 'self' to the whims of Chance was similar to other 'religious' ways of surrendering the self – to God or the Church or the guru. The goal was often the same: to detach oneself from taking seriously the things of this world. The difference was that we see the goal as greater enjoyment of the things of this world while some of the religious traditions see earth as a 'vale of tears' and want nothing to do with it.

CUBE YOURSELF: YOU'LL FEEL THREE TIMES AS GOOD.

The purpose of die-ing is to destroy the normal personality: to create in its place a flexible and varied individual who knows that he's the creator of all he does and is.

Early dicing is useful in stopping the flow of habitual action, to awaken us to the mechanical ways we move through life. Often in this early stage we find ourselves unable to follow a dice decision because we think it is too 'important' that we do something else which the die didn't choose. Often, as soon as the die chooses something the decision seems all wrong. If a die chooses that we not brush our teeth one night we are immediately filled with the overwhelming conviction that if we fail to brush our teeth we will awaken in the morning with a mouthful of rotting teeth.

The act of dicing awakens us to the fact that we are prisoners of all sorts of irrational attachments, trivial and great, and that we have the power to break them.

Dicing also makes us aware of the present. Every dice decision stops the flow of thought and makes us focus on the actions we're about to take.

Dicing also removes the burden of decision-making from the imaginary shoulders of the illusory self. Conflicts are resolved instantly by the fall of the die. Many religions through the ages have removed the burden of decision by casting lots or yarrow stalks or reading tea leaves or employing some other method of divination which, to us, could be said to be letting Chance decide.

After being awakened to our many attachments and beginning to learn to live in the present, we begin to use dicing for freeing ourselves from our attachments, our fears, our rigid conceptions of how our lives might be. We begin to free ourselves from all those ways in which society limits our lives and hides from us greater riches we may be capable of.

Ultimately we will begin to use the dice as they are ultimately intended: to play. We come to play with Chance as we do with our lives, with joyful lightness, living in a world where the unexpected is the expected. This playfulness should be present from the beginning. If we don't find some fun and joyful letting go when we first start with the dice we will find it hard to continue, since the most common emotion aroused by early dicing is tension and anxiety. We can't endure the fear and failure that sometimes come with early dicing if we haven't also experienced a glimpse of the fun and folly and freedom that will become increasingly common.

Another favourite option of mine is to arrive at the station (I live in Reading, which has a very big, busy railway station) and to get on the first train I see, with no idea where it is going, and get off at the end. I have been fined and chucked off the train, and slept on a platform in Wales (luckily in the middle of summer). But I have also partied in Glasgow and Manchester, and been woken up on Brighton beach by an old woman who took me into her home and gave me breakfast and is now not only an avid dice-woman but also a friend!

– Gregster

Travelling by the whim of Chance is such a natural thing to do, that a television programme, entitled *The Diceman Travel Show*, has been created to follow the random wanderings of Russell Harris and Shaun Fenton. Writes Russell Harris in the *Diceman Travel Show* website:

> It was around seven years ago that I first thought about *The Diceman* – I was staying with friends in France . . . when over a few glasses of wine Mick told me about a book he read by Luke Rhinehart – *The Dice Man* – a story about a bored psychiatrist who hands his life over to the dice.
>
> The very next day, inspired by the book, I hatched the idea for a travel show with a difference . . . travel with a twist! . . .
>
> With cameraman and travelling companion Shaun Fenton, we set out to find out what life would really be like living and travelling in a totally random fashion, where every decision is made not by the self, but by the roll of a dice. With no means of transport, just a small amount of money, a bag of necessities and our whole future dependent upon the throw of a conventional six-sided green dice.
>
> It is a voyage of discovery like no other – for us it is the pleasure of getting there rather than the destination that is the key – it is the people, the places and the chance encounters along the way that provide the content for each show – liberation, freedom, unpredictability is what it is all about . . .
>
> We have clocked up some 32,000 miles, across 14 different countries, travelling on foot, by bus, taxi, bicycle, ferry, private aircraft, yacht, water taxi, airline, rickshaw, hire car, motorbike, hot-air balloon, or simply hitchhiking – spending nearly six months on the road in total!
>
> We reckon we have rolled the dice some 360 times resulting in Shaun and I doing some pretty bizarre things . . . everything from playing golf on the ice in Greenland to selling pretzels on the streets of New York!

Russell and Shaun not only decided where they would go and what mode of travel to use, but also what their activities would be whenever they arrived somewhere. A creative twist to their dicing was that they would often ask six different people to tell them what they should do while they were visiting that particular place. One person might suggest a nightclub, another a dude ranch, a third climbing a certain mountain, a fourth going to a park, a fifth hanging out in the town square, and often someone would invite the two travellers to come to their home for a dinner. Then they let the last person cast a die to see which of the six things they would do. Russell's TV persona is always ready to accept whatever comes and to make the best of whatever the dice throw his way, which creates a lightness to the shows that is the essence of good dice-living, and makes for a very enjoyable travelling companion.

> *The chaos of dice-living is an outward visible sign of an inward spiritual order.*

Chance within order is dice-living. The two men on the *Diceman Travel Show* only made some of their decisions with dice, and then, of course, they often created the options. Dicing is always only an occasional game to be played. It is a way of opening up life to options otherwise probably untapped.

In the course of the first forty-four years of my life, within the limitations of having to earn a living and during most of my adult years of having a wife and three children, I and my family did a lot of travelling. In fact, we never lived in the same place for more than two years during that time. Despite having only a moderate income as a college professor and no savings, we managed to spend a year teaching and living in Mexico; another year on Mallorca at an institute for the arts and writing that a colleague and I created; yet a second year's stay on Mallorca after the publication of *The Dice Man*; stays at two different communes; caravan trips to the west coast of the USA and back; a couple of months of having as a home a catamaran on the Mediterranean (cut short by the random elements – see Chapter 1–3 DEATH); another year living on a large trimaran sailing up and down the eastern coast of the USA from Maine to the Bahamas; and finally, and symbolically, at last settling down by buying twenty acres with three rundown houses on the site, so we could be free to keep moving even if it was only on our own property.

My initials are GPC and I have often thought how nice it is that spoken rapidly they say 'gypsy'. But my gypsy life came to an end in 1976 when we bought our property (my wife, made of sterner stuff, ordered that we settle down). We moved happily in, letting travel come to us for a while: a Jewish commune moved in for a couple of years in one building and a sufi commune set up their elementary school in another building for seven or eight years. And we have continued to travel in less permanent and more typical ways: flying to Europe and the west coast and the Caribbean like good middle-class people.

Dice-living doesn't eliminate conflicts, doesn't eliminate pain, doesn't eliminate suffering. But die-ing does eliminate *institutionalized* conflict, pain and suffering. The worst of human miseries are caused by the permanence and changelessness of suffering. By eliminating this permanence, die-ing eliminates the worst of human misery.

There can be no such thing as permanent institutionalized joy. Joy is always temporary, accidental, unstructured. Joy always occurs in some sense outside socialization. Only misery can be institutionalized because permanence and efforts to control are part of the very heart of misery. Depression can be eternal; joy is always of the moment.

THE PASSING OF THE CUBE

It is said that when Our Beloved Whim was preparing to leave his disciples for ever and they asked him to pass on the sacred green die to his successor, he suggested that those who wished might post on the community bulletin board a statement of their understanding of his teachings. Many days passed before finally the chief disciple dared to tack up a little poem. It read:

The body is the Temple of Chance
  The self like four walls to enclose It;

Take care to be die-ing all the time
And allow no self to be.

When Whim saw the poem that day he simply nodded his head and walked away. On the next morning everyone noticed that now there was a second poem tacked up just beneath the first. The second poem read:

There is no such thing as Chance
Nor selves that enclose it like a vice.
All things flow as they flow,
So why fuss about selves or dice?

When Whim saw this poem he stared at it a long time and finally said to the gathered disciples: 'The man who wrote the first poem shows that he understands my philosophy. The man who wrote the second shows he understands Nothing. He's your best bet.'

Die-ing eliminates the internal conflicts by eliminating the illusions that some mes are more real, more important or morally superior to others. We assume that there is no *real* me; we are nothing but a collection of fakes, some of whom are under the illusion they are more real than others. There are layers of self-deception which wise men peel and peel until at last they stand face to face with the Ultimate. layer upon layer of further self-deception.

The sage rips off mask after mask until at last he is free of his compulsion to rip off masks. He then begins instead to create mask after mask, joyfully and without guilt. He knows that no matter how many masks he ripped off he was still in self-deception; he knows that no matter how many new masks he now adds he is being utterly honest; he rests comfortably in his eternal self-deception.

BEN MARSHALL'S DICING SERIES IN *LOADED*

Readers of *Loaded* have enjoyed over the last few years a series of articles by ferocious and funny writer Ben Marshall, who has bravely turned over his already chaotic life to the multiplying chaos of dicing. Ben had read *The Dice Man* as a teenager and used the dice a few times then (the die leading to his first sexual experience), but not again since. Ben was a successful journalist when *Loaded* gave him his assignment, and the first six options he created tell us a lot about Ben and a lot about dicing. Ben's options were:

1. Take first available flight out of the country from Gatwick, wherever it goes. Reason: I am bored, so is my girlfriend. We need a holiday. Frankly we want out. Momentous consequence: Lose job.
2. Go to the flat upstairs and kick the shit out of the bloke who lives above me. Reason: I am bored and, besides, he's got it coming. Momentous consequence: Get arrested.
3. Take all available cash and spend the day betting on favourites. Reason: I am bored, skint and after free money. Momentous consequence: Lose home.
4. Start making moves on well known acquaintance's girlfriend. Reason: I am bored and horny. Momentous consequence: Lose friend and girlfriend.
5. Go to psychiatrist and attempt to get sectioned. Reason: I am bored and skint and genuinely need looking after. I need professional care. Momentous consequence: Spend indeterminate amount of time playing chess with chain-smoking clinical cretin.
6. Sell scurrilous story to tabloid. Reason: I am bored and skint and probably not very nice. Momentous consequence: Lose all credibility and possibly job too.

All of these options have real relevance to where Ben was in his life at the time he created them. And most of them risk a lot more than most dicers would dare risk on their first roll. And after one has read a few of Ben's articles about his dicing, you're quite confident that he would have done whatever the die chose.

The die chose the sixth option, which, to many readers, might seem the simplest for him to do, with no downside. But Ben had worked for many years to establish with the rock groups, actors, actresses and politicians he interviewed a reputation of being a man they could let their hair down with and be themselves, even if it meant doing dope with him. To sell a scurrilous story about a rock star who was busily denying his dope use even when Ben had seen him using many times meant, potentially, that Ben would lose the trust of *everyone* he might interview in the future. But he sold his information as the die directed and somehow his reputation survived.

Often, perhaps usually, we create options that are meaningful and daring mostly only to ourselves. For many journalists, selling a scurrilous insider article to a tabloid would have meant nothing; for Ben it was a risky career step. To go to a psychiatrist was a daring option for Ben because it was an acknowledgement that part of him felt his life was out of control.

In this third article Ben was in Los Angeles with his girlfriend on another writing assignment. He created the following six options:

1. See if I've still got the looks to attract the boys on Santa Monica (I'm certainly not attracting the girls).
2. Steal a car (no one will rent me one).
3. Hang around the hangouts pretending to be a producer and see how many wannabes fall for me.
4. Attempt to rent the Menendez brothers' house (it is vacant and they are former friends of Petey's).
5. Hook up with Danny, a dealer, and learn about the cocaine trade (roughly speaking, this means fighting with black men about money).
6. Introduce my girlfriend Nikki to the dice (a world of possibilities).

It took me a couple of days to pluck up the courage to roll. When I finally did, I rolled with my eyes shut. Mainly I was afraid stealing a car and fighting with black men. I'm no good at crime. I don't have the stomach for it. And I didn't like the idea of Nikki doing the dice. She is far more errant than me. She doesn't need encouragement or mitigation . . .

But the dice chose that he introduce Nikki to the dice; he created six options and the die chose that she audition at a strip joint on Sunset Strip just up from the hotel. So a very disturbed and worried Ben sat up front watching the strip show while Nikki went back with the manager to a private room to audition:

> As Nikki stripped for Emilio, the girls stripped for me. I sat on the edge of the run-way with flared vaginas mere millimetres from my nose, forlornly tossing five-dollar notes into a tinselled trough . . . The audition seemed to take an eternity. Vagina after vagina passed before me, the girls going to ever more preposterous lengths to excite me. It would have been easier to raise the Titanic. And, given the money I was throwing at them, probably cheaper too.

Eventually Nikki emerged from her audition, elated that she had gotten the job. Ben broods that 'Some day a real rain's gonna come,' but then comments that, in Los Angeles, it never rains.

Ben Marshall tends to live life on the edge, with the dice or without. He is able to go against the norms of society much easier than most and thus is clearly in that sense much freer than most of us. And the style in which he writes about events is mocking both of society and of himself. If seriousness is the core of the human sickness, Ben is one of those who has broken free.

We can't succeed by *trying* to follow the will of the die. We can't succeed by trying to create options for the dice and trying to surrender more and more of 'our' control to the dice. Die-ing, like death, takes no personal effort. The die falls, the 'I' dies, life flows – all simultaneously. Ultimately, the 'I' is always dead, the die may or may not fall, and life always flows.

You will know when you have died. As you trot off in obedience to the fall of the dice, for a single instant you will feel a rush of freedom similar to the first rush of a powerful euphoric drug. You will then understand what is meant when we say you are free only after you have died.

Gradually I began to let the dice influence my life with my then girlfriend. When it came to decorating the kitchen she couldn't decide what colour she wanted, the dice decided it was to be bright orange and even though I hated it also I convinced her it would look good. (It doesn't.) Surprisingly to me the end of our four-year relationship was not caused by the dice, well not directly anyway. She decided that she had had enough of me; whether the dice's decisions for me to keep changing my mood were an influence or not I do not know. Recently (being back on the singles scene), I consulted the dice about what I should do. (Even experimenting with homosexuality was given a 1 in 12 chance.) The dice didn't go for it, instead it directed me to the lonely hearts column in the local newspaper and went on to tell me which ads to reply to. After a few misses I am now dating a great girl who was chosen entirely at the whim of the dice.

Rick

Relax: you're always die-ing.

Die-ing teaches the laughing men in the sky: whatever we do it is a farce. Nothing matters. No one cares. No 'one' exists. Poop on the dining-room table and the whole world will laugh.

But never forget that dicing should be seen as a vehicle to get from an undesirable place in your life to more desirable places. It is a strange vehicle, not exactly hi-tech, a little frivolous-looking, but cheap. And after you have used the vehicle to get to a place that you are enjoying, you abandon it. That's one of the advantages of cheap vehicles.

Or to use another metaphor, dicing is a magic potion that will transform your life. At some point you will see your 'self' and your life and decision-making in an entirely different light. Then you can stop taking the magic potion, and you will stop, because part of your new 'seeing' will be that you realize that the die was only a placebo. In some sense you can be perfectly healthy without bothering with the potion; the placebo only made you aware of it.

We have chosen the strange, seemingly frivolous way of dicing because we believe that every so-called 'spiritual' path becomes subtly poisoned by being taken too seriously, with too much gravity. And gravity, as we know, pulls us down. A 'spiritual' path becomes, paradoxically, bad for the spirit, a non-spiritual, non-creative, non-satisfying illusion.

Just as hatha yoga is the dice-living of the body, so die-ing is the yoga of action: you do what is unnatural in order to increase the range of the natural. However, since the only things there are to play with are normal patterns, introducing chance into one's life can as fruitfully entail long-range randomness as short-range. If we are not free to choose long-range goals and behaviour patterns as well as short-range, we aren't free.

Some fools think that the purpose of die-ing is to become a dice-person. Nonsense. The purpose of die-ing is to achieve the freedom occasionally to be a dice-person or not a dice-person – a freedom the stuck person doesn't have.

Die-ing can be demanding, unforgiving, sometimes destructive of

things you hold dear, and yet with each step you take along it

you will become lighter, freer, more powerful . . .

By die-ing you are creating in yourself powers that long after you

touch a die will be there for you to draw on.

The die is an exorcist, but the devils it casts out are all human. It

is the human being in you which degrades and holds you back.

The die would kill the person in you . . .

What will be left? Nothing and nobody . . . What will your life be

like? You will then be everything and everybody.

Die-ing is demanding because it forces you to acknowledge that

you are in chains, forces you to break one chain after another,

forces you to face one enemy after another.

Many of you are familiar with other paths that attack the problems of being a human being. These other paths you come from are genuine paths of liberation. The dice offer nothing to you except more difficult challenges.

There is a war on within you and for years you have been losing. Die-ing is your martial law, imposed in order to discipline your life to win this war.

The wisest and strongest of you, following paths of liberation with all your strength for forty years will still, daily, be breaking new chains, discovering and discarding new illusions.

And since society is a prison you must escape, you must always be an outlaw. Liberation can never be achieved locked in the machine of society, but only by secretly withdrawing from it and learning to escape its tentacles.

Though you know that the forces of liberation never actually win, never hope to win; they exist only to keep the war going on. For were the chains and illusions of society to go unchallenged, men would be universally reduced to robots. The beautiful tragic explorations of comic man would end.

And, as some of you know, the losing battle with the illusions of society is worth the effort, the difficulty, the challenge, because each act of breaking free, however small, gives you a taste of enlightenment, of lightening.

– THE INVISIBLE ONE

✳ Dicers sometimes puzzle over the experience that they come out of periods in which they've followed the roll of dice with enhanced feelings of power and freedom. Why should such surrender to chance make us feel so . . . triumphant? It's because what we give up is the illusion of power called self; what we gain is real power, which lies mysteriously waiting to be tapped in every human being who learns to give up.

Being must cease, to die.
Die-ing must be, to live.
The Die must seize, to be.
The die must cease, to be.

DR WISEMAN PROVES HIMSELF RIGHT

Whim was early in his life a dieciple of Dr Ecstein. When Dr Ecstein died at breakfast one morning, all the dieciples held a conference and decided to nominate Dr Wiseman as the new Dicemaster.

But Whim rose and said to them: 'I think we should first make sure this guy truly understands what die-ing is all about.'

Dr Wiseman responded: 'What questions do you have for me?'

Whim said: 'Dr Ecstein used to say: "Forget everything, stop doing anything, and let the internal whimsical cube roll you where it will. A man who isn't capable of die-ing every moment and dying physically at any moment, is still trying to be someone." What did Dr Ecstein mean by that?'

Dr Wiseman laughed and threw a die at Whim's head.

'Very good,' said Whim. 'But what does it mean in words?'

'It means at any moment one should be capable of anything, including death.'

'And are you?' asked Whim.

Dr Wiseman smiled, flipped a die in front of him, looked at it and smiled again. He then seated himself on the floor in the midst of all the other dieciples, took something out of his pocket and swallowed it. For a long time he sat there stiff and smiling and then he toppled over backwards. He was dead.

Whim came up and nudged the corpse's shoulder with his foot.

'OK, you win,' Whim said. 'You've certainly shown you know how to die.' He then looked around at the other dieciples. 'But we still have the problem of who should be the new Dicemaster.'

When you're both alive and die-ing
Thoroughly dead to yourself
How superb
Is a sip of tea.

OPTIONS

① Experiment with the dice-life for a few hours or days or weeks. Begin by making a dice decision, right now, about anything. List some options, drop a die, then do it.

'Whatsoever thy die findeth for you to do, do it with all thy might' – *Ecclesiastes* (Revised Version).

Life is really very simple.

② ROLE ROULETTE is a game for friends. A die chooses from among a list of possible relationship roles you might be in with one other player: e.g., patient–therapist, priest–confessor, father–daughter, lover–beloved, jilted–jilter, prostitute–client, doctor–patient, mother–child, or others of your own creation. You play one, your partner the other. Perhaps you let a die choose if you then reverse the roles. Set some minimum time you will play out the roles to force yourselves to create.

③ Don't be so solemn. Dicing should be fun. List six new options, all of which involve play or fun. Cast a die. Play.

④ The die is a gimmick. You are using it in a game you have created and chosen to play. The die is like a third hand: a part of you that lets you reach places you couldn't otherwise reach. It is yours. It is you. List from three to six options that stretch your aspirations into new areas or further in areas in which you are already active. Challenge yourself to achieve things you've never achieved, create things you've never created. When the die falls, go with it, with all your strength.

⑤ List six options, cast a die, then DON'T do the option chosen.

Who is the loser? What have you gained by not following the die? What have you lost? By not following the die you may have lost a new life. Or avoided an accident.

You have been making your own decisions all your life. Are you totally satisfied with the results? If so, close this book. We have nothing to offer.

⑥ It is time to play EMOTIONAL ROULETTE. A die chooses one of two or more emotions from a list you create: e.g., love, hate, rage, depression, joy, pity, lust, greed. You can decide to express this emotion non-verbally with face and body alone or with both words and actions. You can choose to express the emotion 'in general' towards an imaginary figure, or you can let chance choose some important (or unimportant) person in your life towards whom you will express your love, hate, lust, pity – whatever the die chooses.

If you can play emotional roulette with another player, the game can be more challenging. A die might choose which emotion both players express at the same time. It might choose that they express the emotion towards each other (mutual hate, mutual lust) or towards a third party (imaginary or real). Or a die might choose that you express one die-chosen emotion while the second player expresses a second die-chosen emotion. So you might end up expressing love towards someone who is expressing pity towards you, or hatred. Or a die can choose an emotion to express towards the other player, who will react spontaneously to your emotion.

Thus, if you express hatred, he may counter hatred with love or pity, depending on how he feels rather than from the fall of a die.

With three or more players, other variations are possible. For example, one player is chosen at random as object. A die then chooses an emotion that all the other players then express towards the object player, who then reacts, spontaneously, as he or she feels.

Remember, the die never chooses the best option. The human mind has been programmed in such a way that as soon as the die chooses one of the six options the mind automatically wishes it had chosen one of the other five. That is why the secret of happy dicing is not to hesitate a single second after the die has fallen, but to walk on. Pour all your thoughts and energy into doing what the die has chosen. In the dice-life there is no room for regret.

In life, there is no room for regret.

Walk on.

SINGALONG TIME

As I was going to St Ives,
I met a man who'd had six wives.
The first he divorced on the roll of a two,
The second divorced him when he died himself blue.
The third spawned a dice-girl, corrupted from birth.
The fourth saw him dancing, and died of her mirth.
Sold the fifth to a dealer, for a staggering price.
Left the last in the Arctic, covered in ice.
Two Births Blue, Icy Mirth at a Price,
How many lives consumed by the dice?

– MyRedDice

DICESTUDENT: What is the essence of enlightened dice-living?

LUKE: Good wrist action.

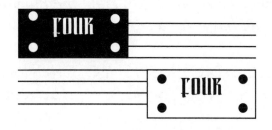

SOCIETY

It is necessary to resign from the human race
– with a forged signature of course.

1. THE PURPOSE OF DIE-ING IS TO CHANGE PEOPLE.
2. THE PURPOSE OF SOCIETY IS TO RESIST CHANGE.
3. A CERTAIN AMOUNT OF CONFLICT MAY BE EXPECTED.

Societies, like individuals, organize themselves to reduce the effects of Accident and make change difficult. Whether aware of it or not, societies organize themselves so that the rich can remain rich and the poor poor. While paying lip-service to the idea of freedom and mobility, the system is in effect organized to limit both. This is all a natural adaptation to increase the chances of the society's survival. Good for the society, often sad for us.

Society needs the ego-control game to keep people in line. The function of parents and teachers is to teach children to be afraid of desires, feelings and ideas which are inconsistent with some 'self' they all work to install in the child. Each society works to compress children down and down and down until they are tiny, oddly shaped bundles of consistencies called individual characters.

'Anybody can be anybody' according to dice theory, but the purpose of society is to see to it that everyone is only some one.

Fear: of death, of the dark, of strangers, of our own body, of others' bodies, of smallness, of bigness, of blacks, of freaks, of poor people, of police, of armies, of animals, of germs, of inconsistency, of failure: this society teaches.

Die-ing is intended to dramatize this above all: there is nothing to fear, there is no failure.

There is nothing to fear because there is no one to be hurt; there is no failure because there is no one to fail.

At some cosmic level nothing matters. No one cares.

But society teaches its children that everything matters and everyone cares: that God is watching, they are watching, the adult world is watching, other children are watching, Jesus is watching, your dead grandmother is watching, the president is watching, the pope is watching, Santa Claus is watching, all are watching every minute of every day with a concerned frown that you remain true to your 'true' self. No wonder life is occasionally a drag.

IN WHAT MODERN SOCIETY DOES LEADERSHIP MEAN THE FREEDOM TO BE DIFFERENT FROM THE FOLLOWERS, THE FREEDOM TO LEAD ON TO NEW PATHS? LEADERSHIP HAS COME TO MEAN BEING THE SOCIAL GLUE, THE DUTY OF SEEING TO IT THAT THE SHIP OF STATE KEEPS SAILING ON THE WAY IT IS HEADED – NO MATTER WHAT THE SIGNS OF REEFS AHEAD.

The most limiting illusion imposed on us by society is that we are a single self; until we live a dozen lives a day we won't be free. We murder a hundred beings every week with our illusion of singularity, and the victims are all ourselves. He who is free is multiple. Society demands singularity. We who die can be everywhere and everyone: rich man, poor man, beggar man, thief. The old I is the dead skin which keeps new beings from being born. Shed it.

In an effort to avoid confronting our multiplicity, each of us learns to wear what we think of as masks, but only the wise man knows which one he is wearing at a given moment and why. The fool often thinks that some of his masks are real and never sees them change a dozen times a day. We all claim to hate the weight about the face, hate the constant changing, long to 'face life directly' as our 'real self'. But this would mean wearing the mask of the honest realist all the time; a trying time for all.

Masks are essential for human life. The standardization of mask-wearing among individuals creates a society. The regularization of mask-wearing among individuals creates a personality. The more complex the civilization, the more masks each one needs. If I have more than one friend I have more than one personality and thus have need for more than one mask.

As civilization becomes more complex and each individual often interacts with others who favour other masks, a subtle anxiety invades us all. We become aware that our masks can only please some of those who see us; that many disapprove. Such anxiety is unknown in primitive societies since there the standardization and uniformity assure everyone that his particular mask is perfect in the eyes of all his neighbours.

To go from the cage of a single self to the amusement park of multiple living, we need to exercise: to play games which break down our self-imposed limitations and uncover new selves, emotions, experiences and talents.

The killing of the self is for most of us as difficult as physical suicide, although rather more rewarding.

Change. Do it different. Open up the theatre to new acts, actors and plays.

But change which matters, inevitably, is at war with the existing society, though this war is not aimed at destroying society and its chains. Enforceable and enforced laws are a necessary part of any healthy society. Anarchy as freedom from all government and laws is the dead-end of total chaos. The human being needs laws and norms to play against in society just as he needs a net and lines when playing tennis. The measure of a law or a norm's worth is how interesting it makes the games.

Therefore, the aim of our war is to create new societies in which the bonds are rubber bands and the cages are made of cardboard. Whenever a society is actually destroyed, the first thing the survivors set about doing assiduously is fashioning new chains and cages. We aim for flexibility and impermanence; these are the attributes of good chains and cages and societies.

In an effort to break free from traditional society, people try monasteries, nunneries, communes, ashrams and other retreats, but in most cases they are only re-creating the problems they flee from on new turf. Such retreats may well lead to liberation from the bonds of the main society, but the religious centre forges new chains even as it hacks through the old. Those who remain in such retreats are soon thoroughly bound with a new set of chains.

Total isolation from the main society is no final path. To be liberated we must retreat from our retreat back into the main society, no longer blind to the coils that seek to ensnare us.

So in die-ing, instead of retreating geographically to try to break the chains of the main society, we attack them directly within the dominant society. Of course, we fail more often than not. After all, people have been 'losing' to society ever since they were born. Our first dicing only helps us become aware of how strong are the irrational urgings of this society. The die tells us to give away money and we can't. The die tells us to wear ridiculous clothing and we can't. It tells us to try some new creative path and we can't. We recognize that the world would continue even if we did these things but somehow we can't.

And then one day the die tells us to do something that makes us break radically from our accustomed behaviour and we do it. We win a battle. We break a bond. But the war goes on.

> The purpose of society is to train human beings to take themselves and their roles seriously.
> Our purpose is to free human beings from the training of society.

For most of history, accidents and change have been thrust upon societies against their will. Societies resist change with all their considerable collective might. Western democratic societies have been less resistant to change, not out of purpose – they naturally believe they are the best as they already are – but because their fundamental belief in the importance of the individual makes the societies more chaotic, more varied, less controlled, and thus more open to random accident. Such chaotic societies have much more inefficiency, more suffering, more injustice than a society tightly controlled by any group or individual who is not malevolent. Plato's ideal republic is far superior in justice and human happiness to anything we can anticipate ever evolving out of democracy. Yet we may correctly reject it as an ideal not because it is unrealistic – such a society could conceivably be developed – but because it would no longer evolve, except by accidents the republic was unable to avoid.

American culture is the highest form of social evolution so far because it is the

---

most varied, the most complex, the most inconsistent and the most chaotic. Since the wise and the reasonable have so little to say about what goes on in America, the society churns out trash at every level that the wise and the reasonable find deplorable, from TV sitcoms to radioactive waste to our latest elected official. We lament the fact that our government can't control anything and we are right to lament – humans suffer from our ridiculous governments. But the society itself thrives on such weakness, inconsistency and chaos. It is a breeding ground for accident and change. Out of the chaos may come failure after failure, but also, sooner or later will come something totally unforeseen that may make the universe a much more interesting place to live in.

The worldwide web is an example of a mutation (and seeming chaos) that is transforming our lives. Out of nowhere it might seem is developing a new way for humans throughout the world to interact, to communicate, to talk to each other, play with each other, teach each other. The web permits the introduction of seemingly infinite variety into the lives of those who surf it. Like the rest of American culture, the worldwide web is filled with trash – it might be said to be the ultimate proliferation of trash – but it also contains a variety of options not previously open.

It also is a medium for experimenting with role-playing. Chat rooms almost encourage 'faking it' – the adoption of names and pasts and personnae that may be unrelated to what we normally present to the world. Many video games, on the web and off, are role-playing games that encourage us to expand who we are and what we do.

THE OLD DICE GURU AND THE INTERNET

BY MARTIN HARPER

One day an old dice guru was approached by one of his students, who had a wide grin on his face.

'Master,' quoth he, 'I have made a marvellous discovery!'

'Indeed?'

'I have discovered the internet, where I can be all things to all men, and I may change my appearance as often as I roll my dice. I may be but a gypsy one moment, yet an author the next. Surely this is the mark of dice heaven?'

The guru turned and fixed his all-comprehending eyes on the novice, and said: 'Indeed, the Web is the force that will splinter the selves of all into many shards. Prepare yourself, my child, for the end of the world is at hand!'

He then added: 'Fool! Do you not understand that, as you play-act across the globe's surface, all the faces you put on, and all the deceptions you weave, are but a single expression of a single self: that of the fraudster. How do you expect your selves to thrive and multiply if their only connection to the world is through a monitor and screen?'

And he concluded: 'By the way, what is this "internet"?'

In contrast to the chaos of modern western societies, especially American, it was the orderliness of communist states that destroyed them. Based on reason and order, the more all-encompassing they became, the more successfully they incorporated every aspect of economic and social life into their rational system, the more they failed.

Some capitalist societies have had the same tendencies and have failed accordingly. In the last two decades, Peru, Argentina and Brazil were all capitalistic societies with centralized state-directed economies that finally became so bloated and immovable that they descended into chaos as a spur to change.

But it is clearly far healthier if a society or one of its institutions can voluntarily introduce chance into their orderliness, rather than wait for their order to collapse. All creative institutions, like creative individuals, must develop systematic ('orderly', if you will) methods of introducing Chance into their beings, or else be doomed to stagnation and failure. Rigidity is as fatal in institutions as it is in people.

In creating such a vital organization we look to create not ordered chaos but Chance-infused order. There are many ways to keep an institution alive and creative and flexible.

Jobs can be rotated and altered periodically. Chance can be introduced to make it likely that no one holds the same job for much more than a year or two without a two- or three-week 'vacation' into another job. No matter how well a man may be performing a job, it is likely he will come to perform it better if he works at other jobs in the organization, thus having a better feel for how his job works in the order of things.

Eliminate insurance. Being at risk is energizing. Shared disaster brings people together in a way protected routine cannot. A corporate enterprise should be able to fail big, or succeed big, and the consequences on employees and corporation should be felt in both cases. In modern capitalist companies, the chief executives see to it that, even if the company fails, they will be richly compensated. A failed CEO these days gets fired – and is given millions in severance pay. A healthier set of principles would have him reimburse the company and stockholders for the mess he has made of things.

Unrealistic, non-sensical, idealistic, fantastic, kooky, far-out and otherwise never-considered goals, methods and enterprises must be occasionally entertained, by chance if necessary. The fantastic is sometimes the practical. Men's dreams can become their realities as long as they don't depend too much on their common sense.

Policies can be varied by chance. Prices of goods can be varied to see the effect on the market. Salaries and other management policies and rules should be occasionally randomly adjusted to determine what is working and what is not.

Product should never be accepted as it is, but must always be experimented with. Every great product, policy and manager is great only because we haven't been wise enough and lucky enough to create one that is even greater. Let us build 'luck' into the system.

Finally, every company, institution and society must celebrate periodic institutional 'Mardi Gras'. People, families, groups, corporations and societies all need periodic binges. The annual Christmas party is a poor man's version of this binge, corrupted and muted by all the hypocrisies of the holiday season. What is really needed is a period of a day or week or month in which all the normal rules and standards are dropped and everyone can be anyone. Party-time every Friday afternoon should be required for every company as one of the perks of employment.

Some of the above policies are sometimes used by some companies. And it is interesting that the most successful businesses of the last two decades – those in the computer and internet and software areas – were mostly created by non-business counter-culture nerds who didn't know how things were supposed to be done and thus did what no established business was able to do. A long-haired pair of dope-smoking hippies created Apple, and other equally 'unreliable' dropouts created a host of other incredibly successful companies.

One of the great success stories in Great Britain in the last five years is the emergence of *Loaded* as the premier men's magazine. The *New Yorker* hailed it as the 'best new magazine in decades', and the (London) *Sunday Times* called *Loaded* 'the publishing phenomenon of the 1990s'.

How could a single magazine start from nothing in 1994 and pass in sales, advertising and prestige all of the men's magazines that had been in existence for decades? And not only that but so increase interest in men's magazines that most of the other similar magazines ended up more than tripling their sales.

The secret was stupidity. The secret was not caring. The secret was instead of trying to create a men's magazine that was 'better' than the others, the creators of *Loaded* decided that what they wanted to do was have fun. In short, the editors were not interested in what others thought a men's magazine should be, they were only interested in doing what they felt like doing, in creating a magazine they themselves would like. 'Total stupidity,' wrote one editor about the magazine, 'that's what *Loaded* was always about, total glorious stupidity.'

When we say that the secret was stupidity we are trying to point out that 'stupidity', which is only the everyday word for non-rationality, is a necessary attribute for anyone who wants to be creative, who wants to do things different, who wants to have fun. Stupidity and fun have always been pals. A reasonable man is the glory of God and is justly called old sober-sides. Spend enough time with rational men and you'll be deeply drawn to 'stupidity'. Tim Southwell, one of the two co-creators of the magazine, wrote in his book about the early years:

That first year of development was spent playing golf in the office, talking about football, throwing darts down at the Stamford Arms, talking about all the birds you fancied from the telly, phoning Shade up for some decent catch-phrases and occasionally remembering to write some of it down and stick it on a computer. It felt like we were being paid to lounge about, like we were fifteen years old again, hanging about in a mate's bedroom talking world-domination gibberish.

But this was the genius of it. This early chemistry created an atmosphere of errant spontaneity, the kind of atmosphere that later on . . . would help cultivate the feeling we could do absolutely anything.

Tim quite happily acknowledges that one key reason for the magazine's success was that their editorial meetings almost always took place in the nearest pub and their creativity and irreverence and stupidity were nicely enhanced by a generous smoking of good dope. Their 'feeling that [they] could do absolutely anything' soon meant that the outrageous, the unusual and the different became special features of *Loaded.*

The editors discovered the secret of creating a new magazine, and it's the same as the secret of creating new life or a new society: first of all not to care about or be serious about what society *expects*; second, discover what is fun and run with it; third, proceed without any 'rational' purpose; and finally, don't be afraid of looking foolish – every new thing in the universe has at first looked foolish.

'Nobody at *Loaded* ever sat down and thought about the purpose of the magazine'; instead, they went with their instincts to be 'boisterous', 'cheeky', 'irreverent', 'off-the-cuff'. They not only made fun of others but even of their own magazine. In one issue, instead of the usual promotional bullshit about the articles inside they wrote instead about the contents.

Just all the usual juvenile breast-obsessed rubbish about biscuits, girls, football, beer and music etc. etc. etc. . . . You know what we mean, loads of sad alcoholic sportsmen, some bit-part actress unclothed, a fat souse bastard in Mexico, an unemployable comedian, some cheap drug references and the sodding internet column.

As a result, they created a magazine unlike others, one in which editors who were afraid of heights parachuted out of a plane over Los Angeles; another editor crashed parties at the Cannes film festival pretending to be a successful porn producer; a group of editors caravanned around the UK inviting their readers to raise a pint or two (or ten) with them in the local pub; and in a series of articles over two years, Ben Marshall turned his already chaotic life over to dice-living.

Tim Southwell has written that they were lucky that they were writing for a generation open to 'the notion that you could do anything, go anywhere and make sure you always had the time of your life'.

Grant Fleming, a photo-journalist for the magazine, wrote:

> *Loaded* was born out of a time which saw a lot of people doing things that they never expected to be doing . . . having the gumption and confidence and spirit to actually get on and do stuff and not think, 'Hang on, am I right for this?'
>
> There was no questioning . . . one minute you're a banker, and the next minute you want to be a club promoter or design banners, because you wanted to be part of something that was, certainly in our lifetime, very, very unique.

Some wild, free and talented individuals created over just a few years a new magazine and even a new magazine culture. It is the same way with societies: they are changed by a few wild, free and talented individuals doing what they feel like doing against all the usual pressures to do things the old ways. And enough people in the main society are attracted to the new way to change the whole body of society – for months or years or millennia.

WHIM WANTS TO CHANGE THE RULES

One day Whim was playing basketball. The other team was far ahead and Whim, being short, was having every one of his shots blocked before it had a chance to reach the basket. With only two minutes left in the game and his team losing by fifty points Whim called a time out.

His teammates, exhausted and humiliated, asked him why he called a time out.

'I've got an idea,' announced Whim.

His teammates stared at him.

'Let's challenge them to a rematch,' Whim said.

His teammates groaned.

'Only we'll change one rule. We get two points every time they block one of our shots.'

'But that's ridiculous,' said the team captain. 'Why should they be so stupid as to agree to a rule that gives us two points whenever they block one of our shots?'

'I don't know,' said Whim. 'But then why were we so stupid to agree to a rule that gives them two points whenever we don't block one of theirs?'

❀ The path of spiritual development and that of society are always in conflict. The first step on any spiritual path is to acknowledge this undeclared war and to choose a side. You can't travel both paths at once. You are acting either as a mechanical creature of society or as a liberated being. And everyday society is calling you to limit yourself to what it will let you be. If you are aged thirty, then you have thirty years fighting against your liberation. If you have parents, you have parents fighting against liberation. If you have a beloved stuck in society's machine, you have an enemy of liberation. Almost every newspaper, television programme, conversation, friend, familiar face, every memory . . . is an enemy of liberation. You are chained to almost every feature of society . . .

Yet if all is arrayed against you, how can you possibly cast off society's chains and become free?

We write these words at the dawn of the new millennium, 1 January 2000 being a meaningless date like all dates, but much anticipated by the illusion-reinforcing media. The fuss is justified only by the fact that it encourages people to take stock of the present situation and anticipate how civilization may differ another thousand years from now.

Our interest is solely in how individual human beings may evolve. If we look back a thousand years and compare the typical human being of A.D. 1000 to the typical human being of today, we will be struck by what narrow and limited lives the vast majority of people led a thousand years ago. The number of people they knew, the places they had been to, the ideas they had been exposed to and the religions they knew of were minuscule compared to the experience of someone living in a developed country today. The typical individual of the Middle Ages was circumscribed by the limitations of travel and communication. What he could know was limited to the people he met and knew, who were numbered in the dozens rather than hundreds or thousands.

In 2000 the typical individual in what can be called the 'Wired Countries' interacts with more individuals in a day than the man of the Middle Ages did in a year. He receives information from hundreds of sources each day and has to adjust his behaviour patterns in tiny ways to interact with the incredible variety of people whom he encounters.

But despite this immense change, expectations about human behaviour have changed relatively little in these thousand years. Perhaps because the change came first so gradually and in the last century so incredibly quickly, society has not yet adopted new messages to permit its members to adapt healthily to the new conditions. We are still expected to take our beliefs seriously, to act consistently from day to day and person to person, to believe that there is only one set of rights and wrongs that all members of the society should accept and try to live up to. Yet these expectations make our lives more difficult, if not impossible. 'When in Rome do as the Romans do,' is an ancient piece of advice, but in modern society we each visit a dozen different Romes every day. To follow the advice we must be different people, express different attitudes, be different that many times in a day.

In the small and stable societies of A.D. 1000, the narrow personality had value; men could fulfil themselves with only one self. Not so today. In a multivalent society, the multiple personality is the only one which can fulfil. But this society fights its inconsistencies, tries to hide them, tries to pretend that it is unified and single and consistent.

But what if we created and lived in a society where inconsistency and variety and change were the valued norms? What if we lived in a society which made it easy for people to change their jobs, their spouses, the food they eat, even the place they live? What if we were free every day to wear whatever clothes or costume pleased us? Free to change our names? What if we created a society in which the rich each week cast a die to determine whether they give away one-tenth of their fortune to random recipients? What if when a person died all of his accumulations were passed out at random to others in the society? What if all insurance was illegal and the individual had to live with the consequences of accident instead of being insulated from it? What if we lived in a society where anybody could be anybody, where all roles are equally good, where we might live out and exaggerate an inhibition or our freedom from an inhibition, where whether we play dumb or genius, rich man or poor man, beggar man or thief, we are acknowledged as equal players in the game?

When we ask such questions, we realize how our present modern western society, no matter how free compared to others, is organized to try to maintain the status quo.

> There is an eternal war on between
> the forces of the glue and the anti-
> glue, between the cages and the keys,
> the chains and the hacksaws: which
> side are you on?

All societies are based on selfhood and competition: they define values by declaring winners and losers. Since in many games there is only one winner, losers always outnumber winners. No matter how hard each of us tries to find a niche where we may win the games we find ourselves forced to play, most of us must lose the majority of games we are involved in. Society is an institution for creating losers.

The more advanced and complex the society, the greater the number of losing games each of us is forced to play. In America's media consumer society, most of us are bombarded with dozens of advertisements a day, reminders of the dozens of games society expects us to compete in. A new car makes us a winner, but by implication if we own and drive an older car we are losers. Even a new Ford Taurus may be a loser if our neighbours are driving Mercedes and BMWs. Houses, clothing, hairsprays, cosmetics, alcohol – all are advertised in a way that says winners use our product, losers use something else. Every beautiful model in an advertisement is a reminder to less lovely women that they are (in comparison) losers, and to their mates that they have married a 'loser'.

We can thus understand the impulse to drop out of the mainstream of society to find a niche where we can be relatively free of the reminders of all the games we are losing. People create counter-cultures as a way of creating a different set of games that perhaps allow more winners and fewer losers.

But as long as we experience ourselves as separate selves and take our various roles seriously we are forced to play society's games, most of which we lose. It is such separateness and seriousness and losing that burdens much of our lives.

To deaden ourselves to this burden we sometimes throw ourselves into sex, booze or dope. It shouldn't be surprising that booze, dope and sexual promiscuity are most prevalent among the economic losers of society.

Another common form of escape is religion. An all-encompassing fundamentalist Christianity redefines winning and losing in terms of salvation and damnation, and defines winning in sexual relations in terms of abstinence and monogamy rather than in terms of 'scoring' and attractiveness and wealth. Religion may also claim that the money-games so prevalent in our society are irrelevant. The losers are magically transformed into winners, and the winners (rich sinners) are transformed into losers.

Moreover, if you have 'surrendered to Christ' and been saved, you cannot lose; your every sin, normally a loss, has been redeemed by your Saviour – He has wiped your losses off the board. By turning the eyes of the believer towards the Afterlife, the losing games of this world become insignificant. Faith in the ways of the Lord permits the believer to accept what would normally be experienced as defeat – illness, a house fire, a death in the family, a job loss – as something the Lord has specifically chosen for them for some Divine Purpose, and thus is not a defeat at all.

The great joy of religious conversion is directly the result of being suddenly freed from a huge number of losing games. Religions radically redefine winning and losing to the immense relief of the poor self trapped in so many losing games.

The walls are always being built
To keep the baddies out
To keep the children in
To keep the dogs from running free
To keep from hurting
Or being hurt, to keep
The light from coming in
And setting fires.

But who are all those people playing
On the other side?

You are trying to hold the ocean out
With your stone walls.
You leak.
Sooner or later:
The deluge.

OPTIONS

Before casting a die, read through the six options below. Throw out one or two (or, better still, all six) and create some of your own to replace those you toss out. Then cast a die.

① Do what is expected of you. Conform. Be a good boy, a good girl. Be obedient. Do not jaywalk. Honour thy father and thy mother. Vote. Declare your actual income to the IRS or Inland Revenue. How does it feel?

② Look at yourself in the mirror. Same old you. Same old you. Same old you. Do something about it.

③ Society doesn't expect you to be a writer, an artist, a designer, an inventor, a creative entrepreneur, a gadfly to your bosses. Society doesn't expect you to be different from your neighbours, to be indifferent to what you own, to be indifferent to how you look, to be intent on doing what *you* want to do. Fuck society.

④ The way you dress says who you are. People expect you to be the same person from day to day and therefore to wear the same type of clothing from day to day. You can't change yourself if you can't change your clothes. Wear a tie or don't wear a tie. Dress to look cool or dress to look like a loser. Wear makeup or don't wear makeup. The journey of a thousand miles begins with a single step.

⑤ List six things society expects you to do that you wish you didn't have to do. Cast a single die. Stop doing the one the die chooses.

⑥ List six of the most boring things you have to do. Cast a single die. Then do the boring thing, but do it in some new and entirely different way. Keep doing it every day until you've found a way that makes it fun. Then go on to the next boring thing.

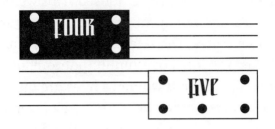

LOVE

Men and women are different. This we have noticed. This we have enjoyed.

Some of the differences are biological (vive these!), but some are created by the societies in which the two sexes live. The roles each sex is encouraged to play are determined by the society. Thus, we can have highly patriarchal societies in which men dominate almost all aspects of life and women's roles are quite restrained, or theoretically 'gender-free' societies where women are supposedly given equal opportunity in all areas. In such societies women have opportunities in education and diverse occupations that one hundred years ago, or even fifty years ago, were closed to them.

The ways all humans are limited to narrow roles by society we learned from reading Simone de Beauvoir's book *The Second Sex*. Simone justly concentrated on the way her society and most societies limited the roles women could play. She resented the pressure to be 'feminine' in the quite traditional and limited meaning of that word in the 1950s. She wondered how many women languished as home-makers when their talents and abilities died.

She saw that as many women stupidly accepted such limitations so too did men accept equally stultifying limits on their own behaviour patterns. Men's cages were larger and better furnished, but they were still cages nevertheless.

Today, women in western cultures are freer, have more economic, political, creative and athletic opportunities, and can choose from a greater variety of roles. But the new freedom comes at the price of greater conflict. Fifty years ago the woman who was genuinely happy being a home-maker felt almost no calling from society to have a job or develop additional talents. Today such women face the preaching of many that they owe it to themselves to be more than home-makers; they are 'guilty' of having surrendered to an outmoded norm. And women who have taken good jobs and developed careers and have also married and borne children, face the still prevalent attitudes that women should be good and attentive mothers. So the price of greater freedom is, as always, greater conflict.

But what a small price to pay for expanded role-playing options! How much richer is life because of the greater freedom for women in politics, education, the media, arts, athletics. Women senators and prime ministers, women in the US going on to college in greater numbers than men, women developing major basketball and soccer leagues, more frequently rising to the top of corporate ladders, women like Oprah and Rosie O'Donnell rising to the top of television, not because of traditional feminine beauty, but because of intelligence, independence. When we see all this, we realize how limited were women fifty and a hundred years ago, how limited in their roles still are most women in the world.

Yet with all this progress, society's stereotypes still remain; most women who are living more 'masculine' lives than was considered 'normal' or 'acceptable' fifty years ago are aware that men and women around them often consciously or unconsciously disapprove. Society is a vast engine designed (with no designer) to pigeon-hole people into as consistent and narrow roles as possible, and women still throughout the world are given the smallest pigeon holes.

And realizing this we must ask a simple question: Is it not possible that *all* human beings today will be seen decades or centuries or millennia from now as limited in their roles as were women a hundred years ago?

We attribute the oppression of women to 'prejudice' and in this light all prejudice is an effort by individuals or societies to limit the role-playing options of some group it looks down upon. For centuries blacks in America have been limited in their options both by literal slavery and then by the overwhelming prejudice of the dominant society. Even today, white prejudice is so deeply ingrained that whites are comfortable with black athletes and performers and actors, but tend to see as almost an anomaly a black banker, CEO or intellectual. Black culture itself tends to limit blacks with similar stereotypes. Ghetto culture at any rate encourages athletes, musicians and performers but is much less supportive of education and business.

Although all humans differ and have different potentials, the genetic and gender differences among humans are tiny compared to their overall similarities, and no one should be seen as lacking the ability to be anything he or she wants to be.

WHIM AND SILVY BEGIN TO CHANGE THE WORLD

'What are you thinking about?' Silvy asked Whim, as they sat side by side on the couch.

'Just that I wish we could be of more help to those who come to us,' said Whim.

'You helped me,' said Silvy.

'Sometimes you seem to flow,' said Whim, 'but most of the time you seem to get stuck at playing sexy Silvy.'

'But I thought you liked sexy Silvy?'

'Hey, I do! That's the trouble,' said Whim, sighing. 'When you're stuck at sexy Silvy I tend to get stuck at horny hedonist.'

'What's wrong with that?'

'Nothing, of course,' said Whim. 'But some of my mes are getting jealous of all the time horny hedonist Whim is spending with sexy Silvy.'

Silvy frowned.

'All right, then,' she said, 'for the next week Silvy will devote herself solely to helping Whim help all the other seekers.'

'That's great! And we'll concentrate ourselves all the time on breaking apart as many illusions as we can.'

'We'll be spending every second with others, playing with them to get them to play!'

'We'll really find ways to help people discover the Path,' said Whim.

'We'll change the world!' said Silvy.

'We'll go after them like lovers at each other's lips!' said Whim.

'Like lovers making love for the first time!'

'What a wonderful week we'll have!' said Whim.

'Oh my God, it's so exciting!'

'Let's make love!'

'Oh, yes, oh yes!'

It's strange, but most books that try to deal with human happiness come down to one subject: love. The ability to give and to receive love seems the *sine qua non* of achieving happiness.

The giving and receiving of love are actually one and the same, since we have never known anyone who was capable of giving love who wasn't able to receive it as well. The ability to love – if the drug companies could ever come up with a pill that would automatically permit a human to feel and to give love, the drug companies and the world would become very rich indeed.

It might be thought that dicing and chance have nothing to do with love, but that is not the case. We humans can't love – another person or a sunset or life itself – until we have come to accept and love ourselves, the present, life-as-it-is. And since dicing is intended to break down the barriers to accepting ourselves, our variety, our multiplicity, and life-as-we-create-it, dicing opens us up to love.

But even when we are open to love, love presents its problems. For one thing, we should not expect love to be any more constant in our lives than anything else. Even the person we feel is the one person in our life we will 'always' love, we usually do not feel love for. Feeling love is, for most of us, a sometime thing, and it isn't healthy to feel we must feel love for someone all the time.

And secondly, when we feel love we generally feel it not only for a human beloved but for all of life. In some sense, it may be true that we are either in a loving state or a non-loving state, and when in the former we love everything and everyone. If, in a loving state, we try to think of Adolf Hitler or our worst personal enemy we probably will suddenly experience a blurred feeling – either the thought of the evil person or the love has to go; they can't quite co-exist, except in saints who are able to love even dear old Adolf.

Not being able to love is the worst curse that can befall us; if we can't love another, or ourselves, we can't love life.

Living a life is like writing a novel: if you're not enjoying what you're doing, neither the life nor the novel is going to turn out very good.

THE ACT OF LOVE

We speak of the act of love and forget that it says 'act'. Lovemaking is always an act, always a play, and the wise man learns to vary his roles and play them to the hilt. The man or women who knows only one role to play in lovemaking (or in life) is doomed to boredom, both from the partner and from him or herself. If a man limits himself to being only, say, a rough stud, he may please some women for a while, but never for long. And so too with the hopeless romantic, the sexual athlete, the sensitive guy, the playful joker. Or a woman who is the hot tart, the passive virgin, or the tender, mothering woman. All can be wonderful acts. All grow boring if they are the limit of your repertoire.

Be in touch with the variety of lovers within you. You don't have to be six lovers every time you're in bed; that would be trying indeed. When your normally aggressive woman suddenly seems meek and helpless it is not the time to say, 'What's wrong, honey?', but more likely an occasion to play the rough stud and let her enjoy her temporary passivity. And you, my gentle friend, if your usual rough stud is just lying there like a wet dishrag, don't despair, just get in touch with your hot tart or tender, motherly lover. But if you lie there beside him as a passive virgin, the action is going to be rather limited.

Now the first principle of happy lovemaking is that you don't *have* to do anything. You don't have to *be* anything. So now that we've urged you to play many roles don't take it too seriously. If you feel you *have* to play many roles then you are in violation of the first principle: you don't have to do anything.

WHIM AND MARA

One day Whim was lying naked in bed beside the beautiful Mara, who, with her fingers, lips and tongue was exploring the middle part of his body.

'I'm trying to remember why in Indian philosophy Mara is called "the Temptress",' said Whim in between groans of pleasure. 'I'm dedicating my life to the pursuit of Ultimate Truth and it seems she represents some sort of evil.'

'Don't trouble yourself about it, Whimsy,' said Mara, having briefly to cease one half of her attack. 'Just relax and follow the movements of my tongue.'

'I am, I am,' Whim said enthusiastically. 'I never have any trouble paying attention to the movements of your tongue, it's just that vaguely, I remember in the Hindu scriptures, Mara is the name of . . . oh . . . I . . . ooooo . . . something about temptaaaHHHHHHmygod . . .'

After a long silence Whim slowly sat up with a yawn.

'Huh,' he said. 'I wonder what the letters "U.T." stand for.'

WHIM LUCKS OUT

One day Whim was cornered by a sexy young female student.

'I'd like you to make love to me, Whim,' she said, lowering her lashes invitingly.

'I'm sorry,' said Whim with great dignity, 'but I never make love on February 29th.'

'But today's May 6th,' said the woman.

Whim smiled.

'Well,' he said. 'We seem to have lucked out.'

Most faking is good. Faking is a human being's way of trying out new roles.

Faking orgasms is usually good. It gives pleasure both to the male who gloriously thinks how terrific he is and to the woman who both enjoys the act of faking something pleasurable and may enjoy again noting what fools men be. But a real man will enjoy his mate's faking it even if he knows she's faking it. A man should be able to say to a woman not only what fantastic orgasms you have, but also, 'Hey, babes, your fake orgasms are better than most women's real ones.'

So too with the immortal words, 'I love you.' A man questioning a woman in the middle of faking an orgasm – 'Honey, is this a real one or a fake?' – is likely to kill the orgasm whether it's real or fake. So too if a woman (or a man) responds to the words 'I love you' (or any of its 1,4529,896 variations) with a question about how 'true' or 'sincere' the speaker is, the question will kill the love faster than a speeding bullet.

The secret of happy lovemaking is the secret of a happy life. Let the play run on and respond to your lover's acts with enthusiastic responses in your own role without a single worry about truth, consistency or sincerity. If someone says, 'I love you', go with it. If the man is a total heel and you have overwhelming evidence that he has said the same words to every woman he has ever shaken hands with (or other bodily parts), nevertheless go with it. The poor guy will probably be a predictable lay, but the time will be much better spent giving it a chance than arguing with him about what a treacherous heel he is. So he's a treacherous heel. That's his problem; it doesn't have to be yours.

The act of love is an act, and it's nice when we learn to let go and play to the hilt whatever role the particular act calls for. If instead we spend our time in bed wondering why a lover is acting differently this time, or whether he is sincere or not, then we are trying to judge an act or work of fiction as if it were a work of philosophy or a legal statement subject to careful judicial scrutiny. There's nothing like careful judicial scrutiny to kill all fun – especially in bed.

There are two good principles to consider about lovemaking.

The first is: do it.

The second is: you don't have to do it.

Remember the most basic principle of life and lovemaking is this: you don't have to do anything. You don't have to be anyone. So if someone has set up a situation in which he or she clearly expects you to perform an act of love and you don't feel like it, then feel perfectly free to play the role of someone who doesn't feel like it. You don't have to do anything. With that as a basic principle, you will avoid a lot of unpleasant experiences.

An act of love with someone of the same sex is an act. It may be a natural and instinctive act or it may be a role that gives to someone little or no pleasure. In principle we believe that the more roles a human being can play the healthier and happier that individual would be. So, in principle, the bisexual is healthier than the hetero- or homosexual. And someone who can also make love to plants, trees, animals and fish is even healthier.

Fortunately we don't believe in principles. We are aware that biology and genes limit everyone's ability to enjoy roles. A gay person simply may not be able to enjoy playing the role of heterosexual no matter how often he or she tries. And vice-versa. Don't despair if you can't be gay; remember, you don't have to do anything, or be any-one. You don't have to be bisexual, or heterosexual, or omni-sexual, or non-sexual. If you discover that one of these roles works much better in your life than any other (as most of us do), then go with it. Nothing is more burdensome than feeling that you 'ought' to be anything – whether saint or stud.

I have been a dice-player for about a year and on the whole I have found the experience satisfying and terrifying at the same time. I began by using the dice for my social life, usually when I could not decide what I wanted to do with myself. At this time I was only using one six-sider and was finding my options a little limited. Also, consulting the dice was usually costing me money. For example, when at a loose end one Saturday afternoon the dice instructed me that I should go to the town centre. Once there I was told to spend £170 to the penny, on a number of random objects chosen of course by the die. I ended up with six CDs of people I wouldn't normally listen to, a nice hand-knitted jersey and a bottle of after-shave guaranteed to keep all females a safe distance away. Further decisions involved boozy nights out with my friends and colleagues . . .

One thing I have learnt more than anything is to use the dice properly and to respect its decisions. I don't give the dice the option of anything I really wouldn't go through with. I soon discovered that the dice were not a thing to be using during working hours. As 'free' as I would like to be, I still need to pay my bills at the end of each month. Another thing which I have learnt to accept is the fact that the dice will not always pick what you want it to do. Recently it has rejected bungee-jumping, a day of serious gambling on the horses and a very attractive blonde who had just invited me to her apartment. All of these things I was keen to try but the dice's decision is final.

Rick

OPTIONS

Before casting a die, read through the six options below. Throw out one or two (or all six) and create some of your own to replace those you toss out. Then cast a die.

① List up to six people you see every day. Cast a die to choose one from among them. All day, whenever you are with this person, feel love for him or her, express love to him or her.

② List three different roles or emotions you feel are not appropriate for a person like you. Cast a die to choose one from among them. Play that role or express that emotion.

③ Today is 'Love Your Mate Day'. Your whole purpose in life this day is to honour and love your mate, no matter how undeserving or unresponsive your mate may be this particular day. Do not tell the mate why you are behaving so strangely.

④ Change sex. Imagine yourself to be masculine if you are feminine, feminine if you are masculine. Without changing dress, try to respond to people and situations as you feel your opposite gender would. When you look at a car or a tree or a flower or TV show, imagine how the woman (or man) inside you would respond.

⑤ Do it different. Make love differently. List three different ways you might make love differently and let a die choose one. Then do it.

⑥ Let a die choose among the three bodily parts of hands, mouth, genitals. Then cast a die to see whether the next time you make love you use *only* the bodily part chosen, or you do *not* use the bodily part chosen.

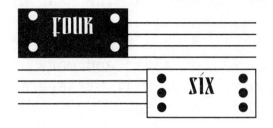

HERE

My Children, do not fear the heat of
the sun, the dampness of the rain,
the chill of cold, the aching thirst
of drought. All of these and more
will be yours if you will persevere
in your studies with me.

– Oвoкo

WHIM AND DESSERT

'What's the difference between the present and the future?' a disciple asked Whim
one day.

'It's simple,' said Whim. 'The present is the bread and wine sitting on the table
before us, and the future is the luscious dessert awaiting us in the kitchen.'

'So?' asked the disciple, frowning.

'Unfortunately,' went on Whim, 'no one has ever been able to open the kitchen
door.'

It's strange that human beings have so much difficulty doing what they can't
avoid doing.

We live, of course, in the present and, no matter how mightily we strive, that is
where we will always live

And yet by some strange twist, society and humans collaborate to encourage
human beings to live in the past or the future or someplace in their minds. A man who
sits brooding about a past failure is in no position to create a present triumph. And a
man who sits dreaming of his triumph in the future is equally failing. Yet societies
create themselves by encouraging people to seek goals and to be consistent with their
pasts.

But the strange fact is that our most memorable moments, our most pleasurable moments, are almost always mindless moments.

ONE DAY THE SUN, AFTER PROCEEDING IN ITS USUAL METHODICAL WAY UP THE SKY, AT ABOUT 11:17 A.M. EASTERN STANDARD TIME, STOPPED. IT WAS THREE HOURS BEFORE ANYONE IN MANHATTAN NOTICED.

When the winds of the hurricane have blown out his sails, swamped his engine, broken his mast and severed his anchor line, the wise man enjoys drifting.

You can choose to live in the past, the future or the present. Those who live in the past are dead. Those who live in the future aren't yet alive. Only those who choose to live in the present are alive.

OBOKO'S SECOND SERMON ON ZEN

Like shrouds, words muffle the sounds of life,
Cloud-like blot the sun. Listen to the trees in wind,
To crows black-flapping wings at sunset
Settling to a limb,
To crickets sawing wood on summer nights,

To water slamming sand along the ocean's rim.
For noises don't betray. Like innocents,
They please because they play.
They are what they pretend to be, no more.
They do not threaten hell or promise bliss.
The sound a raindrop makes against a board
Says here, says now,
And is.

WHIM AND THE FUTURE

'Do you ever think about the future, Whim?'

'Of course, I do,' replied Whim. 'You think I'm some sort of nut?'

'But you seem to keep urging us to live in the here and now.'

'Nonsense. What's the point of urging you do something you can't avoid doing no matter how hard you try?'

WHIM PLANS TO BECOME ENLIGHTENED

'I'd like to be rich and famous and totally enlightened,' said Whim.

'When?' asked the Master Narsufin.

'In the near future.'

'Better make it sooner.'

'All right, next month.'

'You'll never get there; better make it sooner yet.'

'Hmmm. All right. By next week!'

'Nope,' said Narsufin, shaking his head. 'Sooner yet.'

'Tomorrow!' said Whim.

'Afraid not. Unfortunately the time lapse between the present and the future even one second away is so great that I've never met the man who was able to get from the one to the other without being a totally different man.'

There is nothing you have to do, no one you have to be. The wise man does what he does not to get from one state to another, but by simply being in touch with where he is. You may be reading this now thinking that we will help you to improve yourself, to get from A to B, but you're already there. There is nothing which is not the Path, there is no place to go except where you are.

Since no one is walking, there are no footsteps. Since there is no ultimate goal, there is no place to go. Since there is nowhere to go, there is no need for a path. With no one to do the going and no place to go and no path to go there, we can say that what we seek is no one not going anywhere on a path that doesn't exist.

WHIM AND THE FUTURE

'I met a holy man in the Himalayas who could see into the future, and he was training his disciples so they could do the same.'

'That's terrific,' said Whim. 'But our way is much harder.'

'What's that?'

'We try to get people to see the present.'

You can't get there from here.

That about sums up our philosophy of life. If you've got a question then we have an answer, and the one that usually works is, 'You can't get there from here.'

'Why is there so much suffering in the world?' asks the sensitive soul.

'You can't get there from here,' say we.

'Why doesn't he love me?' she asks.

'You can't get there from here,' say we.

Admittedly we lose a lot of friends. People who ask questions usually either have their own answers or only want a shoulder to sob on. We have nice soft shoulders and don't mind getting them wet, but we'd prefer needy ones to omit the questions.

Mankind has progressed a long way by asking questions, but men have wasted a lot of time that way too, time that might better have been spent fishing or hiking or eating marmalade. A man who asks, 'What is the meaning of life?', and means it, is either very young or very boring. In a youngster the question can be forgiven since all he really means is, 'Why can't I get laid?', but in an oldster, one whose prick has been stroked a few times by someone besides himself, the question is an embarrassment. It shows not so much a lack of social breeding as a lack of vitality. No one who's just played a hard game of tennis or climbed a mountain or experienced a fantastic fuck is likely to moon much about the meaning of life. Eat a good chocolate-chip cookie and see if you give a fig about the meaning of life.

You can't get there from here.

That sure simplifies things. The grass is always greener on the other side of the street, they say, but you can't get there from here, say we.

'If only she would love me as I love her,' says he.

'Quite true,' we say, 'but you can't get there from here.'

'You're a cynic!' they say.

'Maybe' we say, 'but we can't get there from here.'

'Don't you have anything positive to say about life?' they plead.

'Sure,' we say. 'We're here.'

'That's it!?' they ask.

'We're here,' we say. 'Where are you?'

That slows them up. Most people spend most of their time over there, where they can't get anyway because they're here. We're *here*. We know it isn't much, but it beats trying to be someplace else.

'But striving is the very essence of human nobility!' they say.

'That's fine,' say we.

'You'll never get anyplace in life!' they say.

'We already are,' say we.

'Where!?'

'Here.'

Oh, we get the hackles up on our friends, we do, but here is where we are and here is where you are and we'll get along a lot better if we both admit it.

Of course, some of our philosophical friends challenge us. Define your terms, they say.

Well, we say, 'here' is where we are, and 'there' is everywhere else.

Can't you get from your bedroom to your bathroom? they challenge with a gleam in their eyes.

Not when we're in the bedroom, say we.

But you can! they insist.

Nope, say we. Of course when we're in the bathroom we can get to the bathroom because we're already there.

We've lost a lot of friends over the years, we have to admit. Still, anyone wasting his time arguing with someone like us clearly hasn't got much sense anyway, so isn't much of a loss.

Actually, we don't argue. A man who is here has much more important things to do with his life than argue: clean his laundry, watch the sunset, empty the bilge.

And better things to do than try to reform the world. When we were young we tried to reform the world. We marched in protest, sat down in protest, wrote incendiary articles and books in protest, and told anybody who'd listen that we'd be much better off over THERE than here, and we were right! We were absolutely right. Unfortunately, you can't get there from here.

We know there are people starving, babies are born deformed, rich people have more than they need and poor people not enough. We know there are bullies and sadists and male chauvinists and conniving bitches and selfish schemers. We know that good people suffer and bad people prosper. We know it and don't like it, but it still doesn't stop the sun from shining, the sea from rippling, or the wind from making leaves dance. A man's got to do what his here lets him do, and though a few people like Mother Teresa and Martin Luther King and Charlie Chaplin might dedicate their lives to making the world a better place, it's not a here for everyone, and you can't expect those of us who don't have a strong moral urge to be too busy licking lepers clean.

WHIM AND THE MAN WHO ALWAYS KNEW

One day Whim met the Man Who Always Knew Where He was Going and How to Get There.

'Where are you going?' asked Whim.

'To the drugstore to buy some aspirin for my headache and some antibiotic for my wife's flu. Where are you going?'

'I'm already there,' replied Whim.

'I see,' said the Man Who Always Knew Where He was Going and How to Get There. 'And where are you going next?'

'I won't know until I get there,' said Whim.

'But where do you plan to go?' asked the Man.

'Where I am,' said Whim.

'And where do you plan to go after you finish being where you are now?'

'I don't know,' said Whim. 'But I notice you stopped going to the drugstore.'

WHIM AND TRYING

Whim once played ping-pong with a student and lost three straight times, all of the games being very close.

'Shall we play again?' asked the student.

'Sure,' said Whim. 'But this time I want you to really try much harder to win. Really concentrate on winning.'

'OK,' said the student.

Whim won easily.

*

Whim was once asked why he so often laughed when he lost a game.

'Simple,' said Whim. 'At that point I've got nothing to lose.'

We are always at all times being sincere. We may think at times we are faking it and at other times we are being particularly serious and noble, but in both cases we are what we are. Man's sickness is his effort to have his flow of perfect instants form a constant rational pattern. We must realize that we are always, try as hard as we may, whole and perfect.

SOME DIALOGUES WITH WHIM

A student asked Whim what was the most important day of his life.

Whim didn't hesitate.

'Today,' he said.

'Today is the most important day of your life?' repeated the student. 'But why?'

'Simple. Today is always the most important day of my life.'

*

'If we study long with you, will we be able to begin living on a higher astral plane?'

'Could be,' Whim replied. 'Accidents will happen.'

'But, I mean, is that one of the desirable *goals*?'

'Shit, no!' said Whim. 'I have enough trouble getting along in this plane and don't
have a second to spare for the rest.'

*

'How can I achieve perfection?' a student asked Whim.

'OK,' said Whim. 'Here's what I want you to do. Every night, for exactly one hour,
close your eyes and look up at the night sky, and when you can see the stars
you'll have achieved perfection.'

'What if I can only see clouds?' asked the student.

'No problem. When you can see the clouds, you'll still have achieved perfection.'

'What if I open my eyes?' asked the student.

'Ah,' said Whim. 'You've discovered the short cut.'

OPTIONS

① There is nothing you have to do, no one you have to be. So sit down, outdoors. Just
sit. Or stand. Or walk. Or jog. Or dance. Or swim. Or hike. Or fly. Good. That wasn't
so hard, was it?

② Remember your greatest triumph. Relive it as best you can. Remember every detail.
Good. Now drink a bit of ice-cold water. Taste it. Good. See?

③ 'Where are you going?' the young man asked.
    'To the end of the world,' the old sailor said.
    'What do you seek?' the young man asked.
    'The sea that laps even now the bow.'
    Remember: no matter how fast you are running, you are already there. No
matter how slow you are running, you have already won.

---

④ Play a game, the game you usually play. Concentrate every moment throughout the game on the result, the ending, the possible triumph, your place in the standings, what you will tell people about the game. Concentrate on these things through the entire game.

How much did you lose by?

⑤ Go outside where there is grass or earth. Get down on all fours. Look at the earth. Lower your face until your eyes are less than ten inches from the earth. Look. Look. Anything looked at closely becomes miraculous.

⑥ Next time you're with someone, concentrate all your attention on that person – how his or her face looks, whether the person is happy or nervous, tired or energetic. How is the person dressed? What is the sound of the voice? Listen. Look. Don't judge.

DIALOGUE

Is God in that crumb?
Ask the crumb.
It doesn't answer.
Then God must be out.
But for you, God is within that crumb?
I'll ask it.
Well?
God says to tell you He's out.

There. See. I told you. God is not in every crumb.
God is nowhere.
Then we are free not to search.
Naturally. There's nothing to search for.
Then why am I eternally dissatisfied?
Because you've been looking.

But why have I felt this need to look?
Blind since birth, but sensing all about you
light, you're restless.
Then let me see light.
Behold!
It's only that stupid crumb again.
He who has eyes to see let him see.

A TASTE OF STARS

Ah, be warm, winter,
Warm enfolding earth enclose me.
Slow motion snow you flow everywhere
Swept up, blown down, whirled around and round,
Hold cold in your individual crystal,
Touch and melt, spill in warmth on my hand
That I might lick you,
Taste with tongue a star.

from *Brush Strokes*, by Ann Cockcroft

THE COMPLETE BOOK OF ZEN II

In the beginning there was everything. And then there was everything. Now, of course, there is everything. And at the end, at the very end, there will be everything. It is a convenient universe.

CHAOS

The torch of chaos and doubt – that is what the sage steers by.

– Chuang-Tsu

In the beginning was Chance, and Chance was with God and Chance was God. He was in the beginning with God. All things were made by Chance and without him was not anything made that was made. In Chance was life and the life was the light of men.

There was a man sent by Chance, whose name was Luke. The same came for a witness, to bear witness of Whim, that all men through him might believe. He was not Chance, but was sent to bear witness of Chance. That was the true Accident, that randomizes every man that cometh into the world. He was in the world and the world was made by him, and the world knew him not. He came unto his own, and his own received him not. But as many as received him, to them gave he power to become the sons of Chance, even to them that believe accidentally, they which were born, not of blood, nor of the will of the flesh, nor of the will of men, but of Chance. And Chance was made flesh (and we beheld his glory, the glory as of the only begotten of the Great Fickle Father), and he dwelt among us, full of chaos, and falsehood and whim.

– from THE DICE MAN

POEM

O danger-dangling Die
Great Gap of the Universe
Fun-freeing Faker
Lover of life
Chance:
Awaken me
Tumble me down the stairs of
Accident
Shake my timbers 'til I quake, fall
Upon my narrow path and block my way,
End this repetitious epileptic fit
My life
And jam with joy my spastic spontaneity,
Break
The bars I build to cage myself, blast
My sick cemented soul to smithereens,
And toss me into life.

– Everyman

Chaos and chance are not the same. Chaos is chance multiplied by chance, chance squared as it were.

The opposite of order is not chance but chaos.

Order without chance is death. When there is complete order, there is changelessness. That is what we mean by death.

Chaos without any order is also death. When there is complete chaos then nothing exists. For something to exist it must be organized, have an order, be distinguishable from other things. In complete chaos nothing exists.

Chance might be seen as chaos and order playing games together. Chance – the play of order and chaos – is the creator of life. It is said by some that the first thing God created was chaos. Then He created order and with it life. Without chaos there would have been no life. Without order there would have been no life. Only with the two together – a chance-filled universe – could there be life.

We justly fear chaos, for in chaos we can no longer be human beings in either the good or bad senses. We can't get stuck in ruts, of course, but we can't play games either, for there are no consistent nets or lines or rules by which games may be played. Total chaos, like total order, means the death of life as we know it.

The totally random man would be interesting for a few moments and then, like chaos, become boring. Chaos is boring. Order is boring. It is chance, the playful mixture of the two, that gives life to everything.

It is not an ideal to use dice for every decision; that would be chaos – and death. Accident, to be accident, must come in the middle of order. So, too, letting accident into your life with dice must come in the midst of an overall order.

Anyone who claims he loves living in the middle of chaos really only means that he loves juggling nine balls in the air at once: he enjoys being able to create order in the middle of what he calls chaos.

The best example of chaos is the flow of human consciousness. Anyone who examines carefully the successive moments of his experience – thoughts, sensations, images, feelings, and so on – will discover that at any moment we are totally unable to predict in the slightest what we will be aware of next. An honest scrutiny of experience would lead us to conclude that we consist not of one person but rather of thousands of independent entities each acting with total freedom and total randomness. The movement of the eyes, the movement of the attention from one object to another, the arrival of a new thought, the sudden intrusion of a memory, the flow of thoughts, the abrupt movement of some part of our body – each of these occurs without the guidance of any director of whom we are aware at the time of the movement. When we write, whether longhand or at a typewriter or computer, the words burst forth on the paper or the monitor without any thoughts being in consciousness. We may write words while our attention shifts from a sleeping dog nearby to the sound of an air-conditioner to the movement of our hands as we write to thoughts about the words being written.

Some presidents of the United States are able to chew gum and walk at the same time. Others are able to walk, chew gum, watch a boat manoeuvre on a river, talk about politics with a wealthy donor, think about a girlfriend and smile at passers-by all at the same time – that is, within a three-second period. And the shifting of the attention from one to the other is as unpredictable as the fall of a die.

WHIM MEETS FRANZ KAFKA

One day Our Beloved Whim met Franz Kafka.

'Did you ever get into that Castle?' Whim asked Kafka cheerfully.

'I am still knocking on the gate,' Kafka answered.

Whim frowned sympathetically.

'Still knocking, huh?'

'And recently the gate has been soundproofed so my knock can't be heard,' Kafka continued.

'Mmmmm,' said Whim.

'And the gate is positioned so that my presence outside it cannot be seen from a single vantage point in the Castle.'

'Wow.'

'And all the gatekeepers have been ordered to ignore anyone knocking anyway,' Kafka went on.

'Oh, boy, that's tough.'

'But I still knock,' declared Kafka with a soft smile.

'Wow,' said Whim again and then added, 'I don't blame you, but still . . .'

'Yes . . . ?' asked Kafka.

'What if the gate and the gatekeepers and the Castle are actually illusions and there's no one inside to see you?' Whim asked.

'Oh, yes, I'm sure that's true,' Kafka answered cheerfully. 'That's why I keep knocking.'

A DICE WORLD

Imagine a world where the flip of a coin or the roll of a die or the lucky roulette spin could avert a civil war, decide a national election, save or condemn a criminal, join or break up marriage. Imagine a world where games of chance and probability are vested with such power.

This is the world The Dice Man *has set in motion – intentionally or not – for the bewildered, modern man to try to figure out in the new millennium.*

In the twenty-first century, Dice-living is practised by a whole range of people from the recreational fun-seeker to the deeply religious believer. Of course, there are 'normal people' too, but a parallel universe of dicers exists side-by-side and disconcertingly intermingled with the average-joe taxpayer. The confusion as to who is who is only exacerbated by the dicers' love of tricks, disguises and duplicity.

There are countless organized factions of dicing, each with its own righteous observance of the Rule by Chance, as well as serious institutions which have begun to incor-

porate dicing into their thought processes and methods. Armies of Chance terrorists fight with zealous discipline to spread maximum randomness by detonating high-profile acts of Chance. A fanatical religious sect, the Dice-iples, proselytize from the lottery lines to the Capitol steps that 'God is in the roll of the dice, do not defy His will'. Satellite pirates stage periodic dice-chosen stunts via the news and entertainment media, along the lines of interrupting the president's State of the Union address with images of lion cubs playing or the sounds of bull-frogs. In fact, random-imagery movies are becoming more popular than narrative films.

Dice-speculating is rampant on Wall Street, defying all market trend-watchers and analysts. A Washington dice policy think-tank has formed a study panel on 'Conflict Resolution and the Role of Random Determination'. Dice-members of the NYC board of education argue that the study of one author over another is undemocratically un-diceworthy; there is no valid value system to choose certain books or historical figures over others, so let the dice decide whether to teach Shakespeare or John Grisham.

The fundamentalist Anti-Dice, back-to-morality move-ment is also gaining a strong following through a ubiqui-tous ad campaign urging Americans to reclaim responsibility for their decisions and 'Just Choose Choice'.

Counter-culture is rapidly recycled and sold back to the American teenager (just like 'grunge' or hip-hop in the 1990s) and retro dice styles from the 1970s come back in style again and again. Naturally, the marketing and merchandising of dice-living products for consumer youth culture is a billion-dollar industry.

Dice-people come in all walks of life. They may use dice merely to choose a restaurant or new sexual position or partner, or they may determine their careers and life goals by rolling. Random, unpredictable behaviour has become commonplace.

Sitting on the subway on the way to work, one might see a young man roll a die, sit at the feet of the other passengers, and meditate; or see a businesswoman roll a die to give two hundred dollars to an expensively-dressed man who is coming through the train begging for handouts. Another person may repeatedly use a die to determine whether he stay on the train or get off, until the closing doors finally decide if he's riding or not. Like true jaded New Yorkers most people don't even look up from their newspapers – unless the motorman rolls his die and walks off the train to skip work and go to the beach. Then, of course, as they have to change trains or wait for a new motorman, most may long for the good old pre-dicing days.

– FROM TV SERIES TREATMENT BY ABIGAIL HUNT AND KEN MARINO

This imaginary future created for a proposed American television series is fascinating but unreal. No society could survive if any appreciable number of its members let chance dictate their actions. Society needs to have the trains run on time. Although societies play in small ways with the random redistribution of wealth (for that is what all lotteries are: the state randomly letting someone become a millionaire), they can never let randomness in except very occasionally. Society depends on predictability; a vital individual life depends on frequent unpredictability.

There is no security in chaos. Man's desire for order is his glory and his disease. With this desire for order he builds palaces, novels, philosophies, Gods and moral systems. With it too he builds gaols, laws, nations, churches and personalities. Oh, how we work to dam up the unpredictable river of life! What walls we build! What dikes! And the river, when whim wills it, rolls over its banks and over the dams and dikes, its Mississippi might demolishing our pitiful creations like a child's fort of sand.

The relationship of order and chaos is clear in music. If we have total order, the same notes repeated over and over without variation, we have ugliness. If we have notes played one after another totally randomly we have chaos and again ugliness. It is the introduction of the unexpected, of variety, of change that makes music. It is the introduction of order, and then the breaking of that order, and the reintroduction of order, and then the breaking of the order again: this is music.

This too is a rich life.

WHIM AND THE ERASER

During his whole life it was amazing the number of strange and unpredictable things that happened wherever Whim happened to be.

When he was in his high-school freshman physics class, the elderly physics teacher was talking about the law of gravity when Whim stood up and announced in a firm if squeaky voice: 'There is no Cause and Effect: Chance is always alive in the world and therefore nothing is certain.'

The physics teacher shook his head sadly.

'Ah, my son,' he said to Whim, 'but if I release this eraser from my hand, where will it fall?'

'I don't know,' answered Whim. 'Chance will take it where it will.'

'No, my boy, the eraser will fall to the floor. For forty-one years I have been releasing this eraser in the third week of freshman physics and every damn time it has fallen to the floor. That, my boy, is cause and effect.'

'Still,' said Whim. 'That was the past. We can't tell what Chance will do today.'

'Cause and effect will take the eraser to the floor,' announced the teacher.

'We'll see,' said Whim.

The old teacher held the eraser ostentatiously high up over his head and, looking gloomily out at his students, suddenly released it.

The eraser started to fall to the floor, hesitated a moment halfway down, and then swooped along the blackboard to the far corner of the room, made a right turn and continued in a systematic sweep all the way around the room until, with a soft explosion of chalk, it dropped to the floor at the teacher's feet.

The thirty students stared wide-eyed at the old teacher.

He looked down for a long moment at the at last motionless eraser and then looked up at his class.

'Although I admit there was a struggle,' said the old teacher gloomily, 'notice that in the long run cause and effect won.'

A DAY IN THE DICE OF RANDOM LIVING

Wake up 11.39 a.m. Survey wardrobe warily. Find dice and roll. Get a 6 (knee-high burgundy Gucci boots), a 1 (yellow suede culottes), and a 4 (hand-knitted lime turtleneck). Gain huge insight into mind of Vogue fashion editor.

Dice decrees I remain open to chance and speak to anyone who approaches me for rest of day.

Pop to Habitat for candles. (Option 3: `Live without electricity for twenty-four hours.')

Become member of Greenpeace for one year (£52 to student with clipboard, Tottenham Court Road). Dance in audition for new Guinness TV ad (women with big smile, big hair and crazed expression, New Oxford Street). Buy cookery book and learn simple meditation techniques (bald man in salmon pink, Argyll Street). Receive dinner invite for tomorrow night (American guy in leather trousers, Erotica section, Waterstone's).

Get home four hours, thirteen minutes after `popping out'. Call ex-boyfriend. No answer. Roll again. Ring flat 68's doorbell. No answer. Roll joint. Call work. Put on French accent and ask to speak to me. Am told I'm off sick (`again'). `Mais, Mon Dieu! She is zee only one 'oo can 'elp me – ees not serious I 'ope?' End by leaving message for MD praising own efficiency within company.

Ex-boyfriend turns up. Asks why flat's freezing cold. Likes candles. Falls asleep on couch while I search for dropped dice in the dark. Roll. Odd or even? Get even. Tell ex to leave.

Dice decisions becoming easier. Have bath (cold). Dream up possible options for tomorrow. Could go to airport and fly away somewhere, play on swings in park, buy descant recorder and busk in tube station, check into hotel, make strawberry jam, see shrink.

And if Snake Eyes comes up three times in a row followed by a 6, between midnight and noon on the first day of the month in the second half of the year, I'm going to ask Luke Rhinehart to marry me. **— Julie Alpine**

The Lord Chance is in his holy temple, his eyes behold, his eyelids test, the children of men.
The Lord tests the righteous and the wicked, and on both the wicked and the righteous He
may rain coals of fire and brimstone; a scorching wind may be the portion of their cup.
For the Lord Chance is fickle, He loves both the good and the bad;
The upright shall behold his face, And also behold his Behind;
Crooked are the Ways of the Lord.

— *from* Book of Psalms (Revised Version)

OPTIONS

Before casting a die, read through the six options below. Throw out one or two (or better still, all six) and create some of your own to replace those you toss out. Then cast a die.

① In the middle of chaos every path is a path to order. To be free of chaos, anything you do with will and determination creates an ordered universe. So do it.

② Experiment with chaos. Play tennis with no rules and no score. Or ping-pong. Or soccer. Or anything.

③ Take a die, any die. List some directions, any directions. List some distances, any distance. List six direction and distance options, cast a die twice: you're off. When your first leg is over, look around, create your options, cast the die.

One veteran dicer reports that he meets all his girlfriends with this exercise, although the fact that he always begins in the central quadrangle of a girls' college perhaps increases the probability of his walking through some coed-clogged dance-class, field hockey game, pillow fight, or, in one gift of the gods, shower room.

Another veteran dicer used RANDOM WALKING for years, often climbing the sides of buildings, scaling mountains, fording rivers, harassing traffic when Chance took

---

him down the centre of a road, climbing over cars, buses, news-stands, chicken coops, outhouses, all in dedicated obedience to the whim of his dice compass. His unfortunate saunter north-northeast into Lake Michigan this past winter is an unfortunate loss for all dice-people.

④ For five minutes let chaos rule in your life: in speech for ten minutes let your mouth say whatever comes out of it without censorship, reason or purpose; in movement, let your arms and legs to the ridiculous; in facial expression, let your face melt, explode; in emotions, let them come and go at random, each one powerful, each one brief.

⑤ Chaos: choose a phone book at random; choose a number at random; choose what you will say at random; choose who you are at random.
    Do it again.
    And again.
    Note that chaos ends up being boring.

⑥ Do something like taking a carton from a refrigerator. Do it again. Do it again.
    At first the absurd repetition of a meaningless act may be interesting; any act we focus attention on becomes interesting. But by the third or fourth repetition our body, our being, begins to rebel. We have order, but we long to break free from it. Repetition without change is one of mankind's more refined tortures.

oops

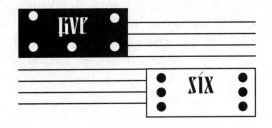

CHANCE

Sixty-six trillion dice careening
through the universe about to
determine who wins the New Jersey
lottery.

*Let us hear the conclusion
of the whole matter: Love Chance
and roll with his roles: for this is
the whole duty of man.*

The heavens declare the glory of Chance;
And the firmament sheweth his handy-work.
Day unto day uttereth accident,
And night into night sheweth whim.
There is no speech nor language
Where their voice is not heard.
Their line is gone out through all the earth,
And their deeds to the end of the world.
In them hath chance set a tabernacle for the sun,
Whose going forth is from the end of the heaven
And his circuit unto the ends of it.
The law of Chance is perfect, converting the soul:
The testimony of Chance is sure, making wise the simple.
The statutes of Chance are right, rejoicing the heart:
The commandment of Chance is pure, enlightening the eyes.
The fear of Chance is clean, enduring for ever:
The judgements of Chance are true and false altogether.

from Book of Psalms (Revised Version)

In the beginning was Chance, and Chance was with God and Chance was God: of this much we are certain. While the old physics saw purpose, the new physics sees chance. When the old saw reassuring and ubiquitous causal nexus, the new sees randomness. When the old probed deeper they found cause; when the modern physicist probes deeper he finds chance. Einstein said that he couldn't believe that God played with dice in his creation. Modern physics has concluded he was wrong.

Scientists have discovered that the closer they look at things the more difficult prediction becomes. The more they know, the more complex and chance-ridden the causal chain appears. This is triply true of the analysis of human behaviour. If someone ever feels he understands why a human being does something, it is because he hasn't bothered to look very closely. The process of trying to examine closely our thoughts and actions awakens us to the incredible randomness with which thoughts, feelings and desires come to us. We soon learn that it is impossible to answer honestly why we do anything.

VENGEANCE IS MINE, SAITH THE LORD CHANCE,
AND EVERY NOW AND THEN I WILL REPAY.

The tendency of every living creature is homeostatic – it attempts to stabilize its relation to its environment at the simplest level possible. It wants security, stability and simplicity.

The tendency of chance, on the other hand, is to create insecurity, instability and complexity. Yet living forms evolve through chance, not homeostasis. Life evolves through mutations – scientific terminology for the play of chance. Mutations are sudden, 'unexplained' altered forms of any given species. They are accidents. All living creatures evolve through accident.

Of course, it is one thing to acknowledge that biological evolution occurs through chance, but quite another to see that cultures also evolve through chance. Yet one of the simplest ways to understand cultural changes is to see them as occurring in precisely the same way as do biological changes: sudden accidental developments (mutations) which periodically occur and either survive and alter the culture (a new species), or fail and die out (unsuccessful mutation). However, an initially successful alteration of the culture may perhaps so burden it for survival that the culture dies out (extinction of the species). The invention of electricity is a mutation that succeeded and altered the cultures which adapted to it. The invention of nuclear power and rockets capable of going to the moon or transporting warheads to distant societies may, fifty years from now, be seen as a mutation which was tried for a while and then abandoned, proving to be ultimately useless for the culture. Or it could also prove to be a mutation which led to the extinction of the species that invented them.

If both biological and cultural evolution may profitably be seen as occurring through periodic 'accidental' changes, then perhaps we should consider the next logical step: personal evolution also occurs primarily through chance. To state it more forcefully: human beings change significantly not through normal healthy regular 'growth', but rather through sudden dramatic 'abnormal', 'unhealthy', 'irregular' accidents. In biology, without accident we have a universe of amoebae. In culture, without accident, we have a universe of primitive societies. In man, without accident, we have a universe of normal clods.

With Chance there are no limits on change since there is no reason or purpose or morality to limit them. When Chance rolls out her developmental dice – whether biologically, culturally or individually – it rolls out failure after failure after failure, and then, once a day, decade or millennium, rolls out a combination that the most intelligent and purposeful of creators could never have imagined or produced.

CHANCE SPEAKS FROM THE WHIRLWIND

> *I am He who creates:*
> *None other but Me.*
> *Fires of the sun*
> *White light of moon*
> *Cool flow of the waters*
> *And the stench of earth.*

The tongue of flame
Inert atom of rock,
Know me: Eternal Seed
Of what is:
The mind of those who know,
The strength of the wise,
The unending string upon which spin
The pearls of life.

Accident provides the growing power of all life. Men have always liked to think that life evolved because Someone Up There had control and purpose and directed change. The sage sees that life evolves from a much more admirable force: Chance. Control and purpose inherently limit the direction of change to the limits of the mind doing the controlling. Chance itself contains an element of order. Like a game of tennis, chance depends on the net and lines of order to play. Chance is the playful side of order. With two perfect tennis players – two totally consistent, rational, perfect players – there would be no game, no variety, no winners and losers. It is imperfection, randomness, chance that make the game possible, make life possible, make happiness possible.

Humans perversely pursue order when in fact our health and happiness depend on both order and chance. Could we learn to introduce chance into our lives as intelligently as we try to introduce order, we would soar.

LUKE'S PRAYER

Great Godblob Die, I worship thee;
Awaken me this morn
With thy green gaze,
Quicken my dead life
With thy plastic breath,
Spill into the arid spaces of my soul

Thy green vinegar.

A hundred hungry birds scatter my seed,
You roll them into cubes and plant me.

The people I fear are
Puppets poking puppets,
Playthings costumed by my mind.
When you fall, O Die,
The strings collapse and
I walk free.

I am thy grateful urn, O Die,
Fill me.

— from **The Dice Man**

What is God?
The axle of the roulette wheel.

Chance is the way of freedom. The systematic introduction of accident into the lives of individuals, groups and societies would enhance in each the opportunities for new developments. The individual who can accept and adapt to the roll of chance which tells him to act in a way he's never acted before is a much freer individual than one who cannot. The society which can accept and explore the possibility of eliminating all lawsuits for one year, or all advertising, or all elections, or all debts, or playing baseball for a month with three balls being a walk and two strikes an out, and so on, is a much freer society than those (all present societies) which find it impossible to consider such changes even for an hour, much less a month or a year.

In the beginning was Chance.
        After that?
                A series of accidents.

Mind set free in the realm of Chance,
I sit at the moon-filled window
Watching the mountains with my ears,
Hearing the stream with open eyes,
Each molecule preaches perfect randomness,
Each moment chants the songs of whim;
The most profound of thoughts is born accidentally,
Even enlightenment a gift of Chance.

THE LOVE OF CHANCE IS THE BEGINNING OF WISDOM.

You must never question the wisdom of Chance. His Ways are inscrutable. He leads you by the hand into an abyss and, lo, it is a fertile plain. You stagger beneath the burden He places upon you and, behold, you soar. Chance never deviates from the Tao, nor do you. Enclose a die in your hand and let Chance enclose you in His.

Chance is my Shepherd; I shall not want.

– BOOK OF PSALMS (REVISED VERSION)

LOTS OF LUCK.
    – Luke

Nature's accidents are the universe's way of throwing chance into a system which would die of too much orderliness. Hurricanes, droughts, floods, volcanic eruptions are all Mother Nature's way of stirring up the pot to prevent stagnation and putrefaction.

A world without them would be a world of death. Floods, fires, eruptions, earthquakes all destroy and renew, kill and create, demolish and replant.

So too riots, revolutions and wars are societies' ways of throwing chance into their systems which are dying of too much orderliness. And like nature's eruptions, these too destroy and renew, kill and create, demolish and replant.

And so too with individuals. Freud was wise enough to see that there is sometimes purpose behind accident. That we sometimes create our own accidents in order to get out of certain areas of stuckness. We can also add that human beings need earthquakes and floods and riots and revolutions or we grow as rigid and unmoving as corpses.

'If the tides rise and fall, O Whim, every day, week after week, month after month, year after year, where then is the hand of mighty Chance?'

'The tides rise, the tides fall.'

IN CHANCE WE LIVE AND MOVE AND HAVE OUR BEING.

Of course Chance, the Deity whom we honour, does not exist. We are a bit unusual, perhaps, in honouring a deity which we don't believe exists. Nevertheless, when letting Chance into our lives, we pretend She exists; when following His commands, we pretend He exists. It is only when thinking or talking about Chance that we believe He doesn't exist. Whim coined the proverb, 'Chance doesn't exist: that's why it's so easy to love Him.'

If, as we pretend, each individual is the creator of the universe, then we must always acknowledge that Chance, like everything else, is our creation; a useful creation, often to us a beautiful, life-enhancing creation, but a creation nevertheless.

Chance is, in effect, the captain of the team we choose to play on in the games we find most rewarding. We try not to take Him too seriously, unless, of course, the dice tell us to. Gravity is the opposite of lightness and it is lightness we seek.

Why do the nations conspire
and the peoples plot in vain?
The kings of the earth set themselves,
and the rulers take counsel together
Against the Lord Chance and his accidents, saying
'Let us burst their bonds asunder,
and cast their cords from us.'

He who sits in the heavens laughs;
Chance has them in derision.
Soon he will speak to them in their folly
and terrify them in his might, saying,
'I have set my dice arolling, cast my holy will;
What is Man but one of my accidents,
Falling still?'
        – from Book of Psalms (Revised Version)

The Die is my rock, and my fortress and my deliverer,
My Lord in whom I take refuge, my shield
Like a sieve, the horn of my salvation,
My stronghold of grass.
I call upon the Lord Chance, worthy to be praised,
And I am saved from my enemies,
Sometimes.
        – from Book of Psalms (Revised Version)

OPTIONS

Before casting a die, read through the six options below. Throw out one or two (or, better still, all six) and create some of your own to replace those you toss out. Then cast a die.

① Buy ten lottery tickets. Expect absolutely nothing. Cast a die to decide what you do with your winnings.

② Pick a name at random from the telephone book. Telephone that person. Try to establish a friendship.

③ Go online. Surf, using a die to determine where you go to each time.

④ Whenever you are the slightest bit indecisive about any decision – food, restaurant, movie, phone call, business ploy, game strategy – let chance decide between the options. Go with it.

⑤ Go into a bar or restaurant or park. Pick someone out. Go to that person and try to establish a friendship. If you are rebuffed, go to a second person, a third, until you are successful.

⑥ The next time you have money to invest, list six options and let the die choose in what you invest.

Chance is my Shepherd, I shall occasionally want.

PLAY

It's important to resign from the
human race: otherwise one has guilt
by association.

Wisdom to the rabble is a sort of escape, a trick for withdrawing
successfully from an outrageous game. But for us, my friends, the
philosopher lives 'unphilosophically', and 'unwisely' and above all
'unshrewdly'. He feels the burden and duty to take up the
hundreds of experiments and temptations of life; constantly risks
himself, he plays the outrageous game.

– FRIEDRICH NIETZSCHE

LUKE COMMENTS: But where is the burden, Fred? Where is the duty? Where is the 'self' to
be risked? And what is so outrageous about the game? Your stance is heroic and we
burst into applause whenever we read you, but really, Fred, 'burden'? 'duty'? 'outrageous game'? You old tragedian, you.

*There are a thousand paths that have never yet been
trodden – a thousand heaths and hidden isles of life.
Even now, man and man's earth are unexhausted and
undiscovered. I love him whose soul is overfull so that he
forgets himself, and all things are in him.*

– FRIEDRICH NIETZSCHE

WHIM COMMENTS: Gets a bit crowded sometimes.

Dice-living acts to remind us that all is accident in this most accidental of worlds. It is written, 'In the beginning was Chance and Chance was with God and Chance was God.' The Universe is God playing with Himself – to put the matter perhaps indelicately. Life is a game.

Life is a game. We say it but somehow . . . somehow – we even believe it sometimes – but somehow . . . somehow . . . we don't feel it. 'Life is real, life is earnest,' said a Victorian poet and later killed himself to prove it.

But if life is play, we, the actors, and a variety of roles inevitable, then it follows that both practice and improvization might be valuable. We exercise our bodies in order to develop parts of them not ordinarily used in everyday life and to prepare their performance for certain roles they are called on to play. So with our souls. We may exercise our desires, impulses, feelings, minds, experiences, selves, in order to develop those parts of us not ordinarily used in our daily lives. The writer, the businessman, the vamp, the artist, the mother, the saint, the adventurer are all put into the pot to be shaken into life by the tumbling cubes.

To live we must play roles. The question is only whether we let the roles play us or let us play the roles. When a role plays us we become absorbed in it, identified with it. Its loss is our loss; its triumph, our triumph. We take it seriously. We suffer.

When I am enjoying a game of tennis I am enjoying not only my shots but also my opponent's returns, not only my winners, but also his. We are playing, we are play. If one of us is playing well and the other badly the play may not be as enjoyable, but not because 'I' am losing, but because the play is lousy.

All of life can be like that game of tennis. I and others are creating a play. We all are at once the writers, directors and stars, as well as go-fers and bit players. At times the play is dynamite; at others it bombs. But in any case our experience is that we are all jointly responsible – or irresponsible.

It's not easy to experience the flow of life this way. We have been trained all our lives to experience things as separate selves surrounded by other separate and often malevolent selves. In the tennis game we may be enjoying the play tremendously and be surprised when the other player suddenly flings his racket in disgust at losing a point. This serious turn will probably momentarily stun us into selfhood, into the illusion that he and we are separate. But with luck the play – now changed into a comedy – will soon resume.

It is probably misleading to refer to what we do as 'dice-living' or 'die-ing' and 'dice therapy'. Introducing chance is a technique, using dice is simply a gimmick. What is central is play. 'Play' appropriately means fake, means drama, means gaming, means pretending. It can be a verb (play!) meaning fake it or begin the game, or an adjective, playful, meaning light-living, drama-living, game-living. Perhaps it would be better to call what we aim for play-living.

The word therapy is dangerous. We never grow 'better', only different. We may get simpler and narrower or more complex and more varied. But which is better, even who is happier (although we have our own strong feelings about that), we leave to wiser men and bigger fakes than we.

PLAYING AT GURU I

One of the traditions adopted by Whim and his followers was that of the contest where one master or student pitted his level of enlightenment against that of another. Whim received repeated challenges through the years, many of which, naturally, he lost.

One day Billy Best challenged Whim. Billy was Whim's oldest and best friend and Billy was used to being the very best at everything he did. Whim was sitting on the ground in the middle of a circle of disciples, among whom sat Billy.

'Whim may claim not to believe in success or failure,' Billy began, addressing the other students, 'but you notice he enjoys playing ol numero uno.'

'You're right, Billy,' Whim replied. 'From now on you take over as guru and

I'll be one of the disciples.'

'All riiiiight!' said Billy, and with a big grin he leapt up and sat himself in the middle of the circle. Whim went and sat among the other students.

'Any questions?' asked Billy.

'What is Ultimate Truth?' asked one of the students.

'A lot of baloney which keeps people from eating steaks,' replied Billy.

'What is the correct path?' asked another.

'The correct path is the long hard road to fame and fortune,' said Billy.

'How can I achieve enlightenment?' asked a third.

'Hard work, constant effort, clear vision, natural ability, special talent, phenomenal energy, total dedication and you yourself don't have a chance,' said Billy.

'How can we recognize the One True Guru?' asked a fourth student.

'I'll mail you my photograph,' said Billy.

'What is the difference between Nirvana and Samsara?' asked a fifth.

'Nirvana is where you go when you're a success and Samsara is far south of there for you others.'

'Master,' suddenly cried Whim from his position among the students. 'I have the most critical question of all!'

'What is it, shrimp?' asked Billy.

'When's it my turn to be guru again?'

We introduce chance into the life-flow of an individual or a society so that it is easier to see the flow of the individual or society as a game. As long as the individual takes himself or his society seriously, then there must be control and purpose, and the possibilities of change are limited. When the flow of individuals and societies are seen as elaborate games, then the changing of the rules in order to make the games more fun, more challenging, more interesting, becomes a more acceptable possibility. Of course, men today usually take the games themselves with such seriousness that rule changes are almost as difficult to come by as modifying Moses' Ten Commandments.

In the emptiness that is life let there be play. Let the old order go and a new order come, not in the name of betterment, but in the name of play. Let that which is uptight be unwound, that which is narrow broaden, that which is fearful be unconcerned, that which is serious be light.

The origin of an act determines its value. Acting from fear, greed, lust, selfishness, ambition, hatred, jealousy darkens all it touches. Acting from play lightens all it touches.

'Laughter I declare to be blessed; you who aspire to greatness, learn how to laugh!' Thus spoke one of the wisest of men, who, in our universe of multiplicity, also happened to be insane.

I was on holiday a few months ago on one of the Greek islands with a few friends, when the dice chose that I would ditch them for three days and head off in a rental car to the quietest part of the island and stay in a local hotel, which was a great experience – as opposed to most of the island, none of the locals spoke any English. It wasn't geared to tourists at all.

I had a whale of a time trying to explain in pidgin Greek the concept behind the dice – the only problem being that the locals would assign all six numbers to 'have another drink'. So I'm not too sure if they either didn't get the concept completely or understood it perfectly!

– Gregster

Ah, the human charade. What fun it would be if the players knew they were only playing! In the theatre, if an actor begins to 'live' his role, to 'become' the character he is playing, we call him insane. But in life we actors take all our roles seriously, 'live' each one, 'become' each one, and are, accordingly, insane.

Why did nature build into humans this destructive, anti-joy, original sin element of seriousness? Without it men might float like a butterfly, sting like a bee. With seriousness we float like elephants and sting like a flea. So why, then? What possible purpose does seriousness serve?

Survival? Men do not kill themselves or others in play. They kill each other for reasons, for causes, seriously. Killing, they say, is a serious business, not to be taken lightly. Men do not play at war, any more. Certain native American Indian tribes played at war, letting the touching of an enemy be his triumph rather than the killing of the enemy. Then the humans came with civilization and taught them what war really was.

May they rest in peace.

Survival?

If we took life less seriously would we permit ourselves to die? If we took ourselves less seriously would we propagate?

You better believe it.

Education is above all else the teaching of seriousness – the teaching that the things that children know are not important *are* important. The teaching that play is what children do; work is what adults do. In such a case it is no wonder that children sometimes resent having to become adults.

WE ARE THOSE WHO STAND FOR PLAYFULNESS WITH THE THOUSAND FOLLIES.

A professional actor is a trained liar. He is trained to go on to a stage and pretend to be someone he normally isn't, to say things that he doesn't necessarily believe are true.

When we see a good actor acting we are convinced he is who he pretends to be. And often the actor experiences himself as becoming the persona he is playing. The fact is that the line between a faked emotion and a real emotion is, in good actors, almost invisible. If scientists were to hook up the actor to measure all of his physiological responses as he was expressing a 'fake' emotion and again when he was expressing a 'real' emotion, they would usually find absolutely no difference. If a die tells you to feel love for someone and you are able to feel love for that someone, the emotion is no different than the 'real' love you feel for the person in a 'real' situation.

We are all actors. The difference between us is that some of us know we are actors.

PLAYING AT GURU II

On another occasion Billy and Whim were again seated on the ground among a group of students who sat in a circle around Whim.

'The only true Path is the one that goes somewhere,' challenged Billy.

'The only somewhere worth going to is nowhere,' replied Whim.

'I'd rather climb a mountain,' said Billy, 'than walk to the corner deli.'

'Not if you needed a quart of milk,' said Whim.

'If people followed your ideas of detachment and emptiness, they'd never get out of bed in the morning.'

'If I were in bed with them, it might not be a bad idea.'

'The simplest way to see the falsity of your preaching is to look at your life,' challenged Billy. 'What have you achieved?'

'Nothing,' replied Whim.

'See!' said Billy triumphantly.

'And if people will pay attention, they may be able to achieve nothing too.'

Beautiful Chance, Joy-filled Accident,
Honey-syruped Whim, dance thy brief
dance on the desk before me and
speak. I await thy will as the child
his father's hand to lead him out to
play.
– LUKE

In the late twentieth and early twenty-first century there began the increasing appearance of saints, sages, prophets and masters – a flourishing for a full century of what historians now refer to as the 'Great Flowering' of the western world. Of all those beings who inspired men then and inspire us now, the story of none has proved so fascinating and controversial as that of Whim. Although during his life Whim suffered more than any of the other spirits of that period from ridicule and rebuff, he now appeals to us immensely for precisely those qualities which the twentieth century found so hard to understand and accept. He was the first, we see now, of what came to be over the next hundred years almost a tradition: the holy fool. Whim's playfulness, irrationality and refusal to present a system of ideas or ethics, his lack of 'seriousness' and 'spirituality', were all seen then as weaknesses, whereas today we experience these same qualities as his strengths. The humour, playfulness and lack of seriousness which so infuriated the religious and intellectual establishments of his time are precisely the qualities which please the anti-establishment of our time.

We can see now that all of the spiritual beings of the Great Flowering were part of the necessary transition from the Age of Tragic Seriousness, as we call the millennia from 1000 B.C. to A.D. 2200, to our present Age of Play. Most of these figures felt that reason as it was then practised was very much a part of the cycle of wars, pollution, armament races and starvation which were sweeping the world, but saw the escape primarily in terms of an otherworldly mysticism which was too divorced from everyday life to transform that civilization and that reason. While such mysticism permitted people to escape the madness, it didn't permit them to change the civilization that was perpetually creating the madness. It was Whim's gift to men to reintroduce the experience of play and playfulness into the life of the religious seeker and sage and thus at last break the pattern.

Looking back now it is difficult to understand the immensity of the task faced by liberated beings in the late twentieth and early twenty-first centuries. Although prevailing opinion granted that certain aspects of western societies might be 'bad', it also assumed that the reason and science that decided which aspects were good or bad and how to alter them was beyond criticism. In fact, each 'reasonable' and 'scientific' effort to reform the various diseases and dislocations of the sick civilization only seemed to lead to larger and more complex problems. We are all struck today by what a vicious manic cycle the industrialized nations of the earth had gotten into by the year 2000.

Western civilization – 'That bandaged man,' as Erich Stoll called it – became over the decades a patchwork quilt of programmes, theories, technological fixes, therapies and religious cults, all intended to restore happiness and fulfilment to a civilization that didn't seem capable of sustaining it. The programmes and fixes didn't alter the society, and the therapies and cults were only minimally successful in assisting people.

It was only gradually that the solution began to emerge, a solution only later articulated by the famous 'Fuck-It' School of political economists. With the wisdom of hindsight, we know that the 'problems' began to wither away only when men began ceasing to try to solve them – indeed, ceased to be interested in them. Only when a large minority of mankind, inspired by holy fools like Whim, ceased to care whether economies, schools or governments worked, only then, *voila!,* did they begin to work.

The annoyance and even hatred engendered in men of the twentieth century towards these mystics and holy fools is hard for us to understand. From the point of view of the serious and sincere reformer or revolutionary, anything which did not try directly to battle the sufferings of the time was irresponsible escapism. A man meditating while people starved was bad enough, but a man *playing* while people starved and nations threatened to war – as Whim so ostentatiously did – was worse: a Nero fiddling while Rome burned. But as Whim's disciple Charlie Potts later said: 'The flames of our burning civilization will go out only when men cease fanning them with their efforts to snuff them.'

Whim, of course, was too busy enjoying his play to bother with fires – except as a game – and thus antagonized those sincerely trying to reform the world. Whim was one of the first to play in the diseased world as if nothing mattered, as if the 'health' of a society was no more important than the 'sickness'. The earlier Mexican sage Don Juan had said he was living a life of 'controlled folly', but himself lived almost totally isolated from the major follies of the time. Whim swam in them like a dolphin playing with the polluted ocean.

Only now are we able to see clearly that it was Whim's ability to let go of both ends of the conflicts afflicting society or, more accurately, to sit on first one end and then the other as if playing see-saw with himself, that enabled him and his followers and later sages and holy fools to begin to escape the dualities that western societies found themselves stuck with. Whim used reason to mock the rigidities of the less-liberated mystics, and mysticism to undermine the rigidities of the unliberated scientists; he became a successful businessman only to become an unsuccessful businessman; he was a guru to thousands, but frequently insisted that some randomly selected disciple was the Master and he, Whim, the seeker. He escaped the singleness that had poisoned man for most of his history and, in doing so, began the liberation of us all.

– PROFESSOR JOHN LENNON GHANDI MOOS SMITH,
Primitive Man **(Random Houses, 2566)**

There is a danger that once one has come to realize that all is illusion, all is chance, and all is play in the most transitory of worlds, then one may cease to play games hard. Sometimes we see that life is a game and seriousness a disease and then come to think that since nothing matters we should play games only half-heartedly.

Clearly it doesn't matter to the universe how hard we play any game, but it matters very much to each human that he find some games that he enjoys playing very hard. Just as we all have a basic need for food, for pleasure, so too the need to play hard is part of man's non-erasable nature. But how can we play hard if we are also not taking the game seriously?

Taking nothing seriously doesn't mean never being serious. Being playful and frivolous every moment is like having chaos every moment: without an element of order there can be no playing with chance. Without an element of seriousness there can be no play.

Blessed is the man who walks not
in the counsel of the good,
nor stands in the way of sinners
nor sits in the seats of the wise;
But his delight is in the law of Chance,
and on his Whims he meditates day and night.
He is like a tree planted by a flowing stream,
dropping its leaves and fruit hour by hour
into the flow
into the flow.
– from Book of Psalms (Revised Version)

'O Whim,' asked a disciple. 'How can we distinguish between when you're really mad at us and when you're just pretending?'

'No problem,' said Whim. 'I'm always pretending.'

Everyone sat around pondering the wisdom of Whim's reply. After several minutes, however, a very young disciple dared to speak up.

'But sometimes you seem really exasperated.'

Whim flushed and grinned.

'Sometimes I act so well I fool even myself.'

When Jake Ecstein was walking through a Dice Center one day he overheard a conversation between two people.

'Show me the best role you have,' said the first person.

'All my roles are the best,' replied the second. 'You can't find in me any piece of behaviour which isn't the best.'

'That's conceited,' said the first.

'That's dice-living,' replied the second.

At these words Jake Ecstein became enlightened.

— FROM THE DICE MAN

OPTIONS

You are the creator of your desires, your emotions, your roles, your life. You are the creator of the games you want to play and the rules by which you want to play them. So who are we to create options for you?

RAINBOW

In the middle of my heart
There is a jewel
That throws a web of light out into the sky,
Into the dark universe,
And I am by it
Connected to all the stars.

-from *Brush Strokes*, by Ann Cockcroft

EPILOGUE

'Knock, knock,' suddenly came from within the soul.

    'Who's there?' the seeker asked, surprised and frightened.

    'It's God,' said a Voice. 'Let me out.'

    'But I didn't know I'd locked You in,' said the seeker. 'What do I do?'

    'Open the door.'

    'What door?'

    'Any door.'

    'I don't see any doors.'

    'Then at least quit banging them in my Face.'

DICEMAN STARTER KIT

OPTIONS

⚀ _____

⚁ _____

⚂ _____

⚃ _____

⚄ _____

⚅ _____

OPTIONS